The Revolt from the Village
1915-1930

The Revolt from the Village 1915-1930

by Anthony Channell Hilfer

The University of North Carolina Press
Chapel Hill

To My Mother and Father

Acknowledgments

I owe an incalculable debt to C. Hugh Holman without whose inspiration and aid this book could never have been written although, needless to say, any errors and oversights in it are entirely my own. I should also like to thank Sheldon Grebstein for his generously full and incisively critical reading of the manuscript.

The University Research Institute of the University of Texas gave me a semester grant that I spent in a converted tenant cabin outside Chapel Hill, North Carolina, doing most of the writing of this book.

The Georgia Review has graciously granted me permission to quote earlier published material that forms a portion of my chapter on Thomas Wolfe.

Contents

The Revolt from the Village
1915-1930

1. The Revolt: What It Was About

Carl Van Doren identified "The Revolt from the Village" in 1921 in one of a series of articles on contemporary American fiction which he wrote for the *Nation*. Certain American novelists, Van Doren announced, were attacking one of the most cherished American beliefs: the belief that the American small town is a place characterized by sweet innocence, an environment in which the best in human nature could flower serenely, a rural paradise exempt from the vices, complexities, and irremediable tragedies of the city. These American writers were presenting a quite different and more realistic interpretation of the town, emphasizing its moral repressiveness and stultifying conformity, and protesting its standardized dullness. The protest began with *Spoon River Anthology* in 1915 and continued in *Winesburg, Ohio* (1919) but its *annus mirabilis* was 1920 with the publication of *Main Street,* which led what had become a full-scale assault.[1]

Since Van Doren's article, the term "Revolt from the Village" has become an accepted rubric of historical criticism. On the other hand, the term has for many critics unpleasant connotations; for every writer in this study, a critic can be found who admits that there may have been a "revolt from the village" movement but denies that any writer *he* likes belonged to it. A satisfactory definition of the

3

revolt will show how a writer could belong to it and not lose his respectability. The terms "revolt" and "village" have caused most of the confusion by being taken in too simplistic a manner.

Some critics presume that to show a writer's having ambivalent attitudes toward the village is to prove that he was not a part of the revolt. In fact *all* of the writers in this study had ambivalent attitudes. Since their fictive small towns were based on the real small towns of their childhood, an ambivalence between nostalgia and revolt was natural. Between 1915 and 1930, however, the revolt was more emphatic than the nostalgia. After 1930, as I shall show in my last chapter, the pendulum swang back, and the village was idealized by some of the same spirits who had led the twenties' attack—a switch that did not so much result from new attitudes as from a reordering and change in emphasis of the old. The revolt, even at its most extreme, was never total, for, bad as the village was, no alternative way of life did much more to satisfy the heart's desire.

The revolt, after all, should not be conceived too literally. It did not consist in a rabble of writers in red caps and sans-culottes charging up Main Street and flinging torches into the sheriff's office. The authors drew on the real towns of their childhood, but their creations are fictions, simpler and more patterned than any reality. What they opposed was not an actual village existing in time and space but a mental conception of the village existing in the mind of a great number of Americans.

The village was synechdoche and metaphor. The village represented what Americans thought they were, what they sometimes pretended (to themselves as well as others) they wanted to be, and if the small town was typically American, the Midwestern small town was doubly typical. The basic civilization of America was middle class, a fact somewhat obscured in city novels that tended to treat the extremes of the very rich and the very poor to the exclusion of the middle. Even the East, dominated by its cities, usually granted the superior "Americanism" of the Middle West. Thus the Midwestern novelists of the teens and twenties could see their locale as a microcosm of the nation and, provincial bourgeoises that they were, of the world. But their view was critical. The town was the focus of what was in actuality an over-all attack on middle-class American civilization.[2]

The town was especially vulnerable because it had been mythicized out of all reality. The myth of the small town was based on a set of ideal antitheses to the city. The cold impersonality of the city contrasted with the "togetherness" of the town; the vice of the city with the innocence of the town; the complexity of the city with the simplicity of the town. The sociological cause of the myth is evident enough: the myth of the small town served as a mental escape from the complexities, insecurities, and continual changes of a society in rapid transition from a dominantly rural to a dominantly urban and industrial civilization. The myth was a symptom of immaturity; it was sentimental, escapist, and simple-minded.

To understand the myth, it is necessary to clearly demarcate the small town from the city, on the one hand, and the farm, on the other. The U.S. Bureau of Census defines a place as rural if 2,499 people live there; with a single addition, the town is magically urbanized. The census definition may be operationally useful for the purpose of governmental statistics, but it does not accord with the commonly accepted meaning of "small town" and "city." As Max Lerner points out, the small town is "an entity hard to define, especially in drawing a line between the small town and the city." Even the more realistic figure of ten thousand to fifteen thousand would be arbitrary.[3] Fortunately, Mr. Lerner proposes a definition that perfectly correlates with the emotional meaning of "small town" which I am investigating in this chapter:

"The test is at what point the town grows too big to make life compassable. The value of small-town living lies in the face-to-face relations that it makes possible throughout the community. One might say that a small town ceases to be one as soon as someone who has lived in it a number of years finds unfamiliar faces as he walks down the street and is not moved to discover who they are and how they got there." [4]

Thus, the small town is difficult to distinguish from the city (the small city, at least) in hard and fast physical and statistical terms, but in emotional and attitudinal terms the difference is clear: the small town is where people know each other as opposed to the faceless metropolis. The farm, on the other hand, is easily distinguishable from the small town in objective terms. Physically, the American farm, particularly in the Midwest, has always been more isolated from the village than farms in England and on the Continent. Whereas the European farmer sometimes even lived in a village, the American farmer lived on his farm, the village serving him primarily as a supply base. Before the coming of the automobile, the farmer's trips to town were relatively infrequent, something of an undertaking and an adventure, particularly from the children's point of view when they were allowed to go along. Indeed, for a young boy on an isolated farm, a trip to town had some of the glamor that the trip to the city had for the town boy.

But if the town and farm are easily distinguishable in objective terms, they are far less so in emotional and attitudinal terms. To the nostalgic mind, the two often melt together as the serene and tranquil country opposed to the strident and vicious city. The scornful urbanite also identified the farm and town as the common home of the rube and the hayseed. Farm and small town often did agree in their common adherence to a narrow religious fundamentalism and a simplistic and puritanical social code. The escapist notion of a simple and innocent way of life was even more associated with the farm than with the small town. The agrarian myth of the virtuous farmer is in some of its aspects indistinguishable from the myth of the small town. Lewis Atherton points out that in McGuffey's readers, "Children learned that village and country life surpassed that in cities. As a rule, McGuffey simply ignored urban ways or used them as examples of corruption." [5]

Townsmen and farmer might temporarily ally themselves against the supposed corruption of the cities, but their more usual relation was one of mutual hostility. Thorstein Veblen saw the small town as an economic parasite, living off the farmer.[6] Indeed, the small town merchants were the groups that most bitterly fought against rural free delivery (and its consequent expansion of the mail-order trade), thereby further exacerbating the already unfriendly feelings of the farmers.[7] Moreover, the townspeople envied the city as much as they distrusted it. Looking to the city for his social values, the townsman was scornful of his country cousin, all the more so because of his lurking knowledge of their kinship.[8]

Of course, these actual differences between town and farm were often blurred or ignored in the myth of country virtue. But there was one important aspect in which the town myth thoroughly differed from the agrarian myth and this was in its emphasis on community. American farm life might be extolled for its home and family life, but it put somewhat too much of a strain on credulity to idealize the community life of the relatively isolated American farmer. The small town myth, by contrast, is primarily a myth of community. If some of the classic American writers such as Hawthorne, Melville, Twain, and James tried to create through the verbal structures of their fiction an ideal community, "a world elsewhere," [9] those who glorified the American village complacently assured their readers that the ideal community really existed: it was the American small town. Because the town myth appeals so strongly to the American desire for community, it has been much more important to American literature than the agrarian myth. As Meredith Nicholson notes: "Imaginative literature has done little to invest the farm with glamour. The sailor and the warrior, the fisherman and the hunter are celebrated in song and story, but the farmer has inspired no ringing saga or iliad, and the lyric muse has only added to the general joyless impression of the farmer's life." [10]

The small town, it is true, equally lacks glamour, but its very freedom from glamour and excitement was one of its endearing qualities to the American consciousness, and it has never lacked a literature of glorification. We shall now examine some varying examples of this literature, concentrating on the major motifs in the myth of the village: the vision of stasis, and the folks and their folksiness.

The classic celebration of the village is Oliver Goldsmith's poem, *The Deserted Village* (1770). As Ima Honaker Herron shows, the first American praises of village innocence, Philip Freneau's *The American Village* (1772) and Timothy Dwight's *Greenfield Hill* (1794), were mere mediocre imitative transplantations of the Goldsmithian village tradition to America.[11] Americans read Goldsmith far more than they read his imitators, and it is to Goldsmith himself that we must look for one of the most revealing avatars of the myth of the small town.

Of course, Goldsmith's poem is about the English village, a community that, as we have seen, differed from the small town as English and Continental farmers sometimes lived in the villages rather than on isolated farms. In Goldsmith's poem then, the agrarian and town myth are one and the same. "Sweet Auburn, loveliest village of the plain" is characterized by "innocence and ease," by "humble happiness." Most revealing of the emotions evoked by the village is that the poet thinks of it as a place to retire to, an escape from strife to the original refuge:

> And as an hare whom hounds and horns pursue,
> Pants to the place from whence at first she flew,
> I still had hopes, my long vexations past,
> Here to return—and die at home at last.

The symbolic identity of home and womb hardly needs stressing. Although Goldsmith's poem was intended as a protest against the enclosure movement that was forcing the English farmer off his traditionally held lands, the mood evoked is escapist rather than critical. In keeping with the masterfully maintained womb-like quietude and serenity of the poem is Goldsmith's avoidance of sharp-edged particularities; everything is seen from a softening and tranquilizing distance:

> Sweet was the sound when oft at evening's close,
> Up yonder hill the village murmur rose;
> There as I past with careless steps and slow,
> The mingling notes came softened from below.

Neither ambition nor pride exists to jar this atmosphere. One of the chief men of the village is the preacher, but he has no pride of place:

> A man he was, to all the country dear,
> And passing rich with forty pounds a year
> Remote from towns he ran his goodly race;
> Nor e'er had changed, nor wished to change his
>   place;
> Unpractised he to fawn, or seek for power,
> By doctrines fashioned to the varying hour;
> Far other aims his heart had learned to prize,
> More skilled to raise the wretched than to rise.

To the urbanite, Goldsmith's village may sound sweet but rather lifeless. His defense is that the village offers natural and spontaneous joys as opposed to the artificial pleasures of the city which can lead only to ennui:

> Yes! let the rich deride, the proud disdain
> These simple blessings of the lowly train;
> To me more dear, congenial to my heart,
> One native charm, than all the gloss of art;
> Spontaneous joys, where Nature has its play,
> The soul adopts, and owns their first born sway;
> Lightly they frolic o'er the vacant mind,
> Unenvied, unmolested, unconfined,
> But the long pomp, the midnight masquerade,
> With all the freaks of wanton wealth amazed,
> In these, ere triflers half their wish obtain,
> The toiling pleasure sickens into pain;
> And even while fashion's brightest arts decoy,
> The heart distrusting asks, if this be joy.

The suggestion of regression in the spontaneous joys in which "the vacant mind" delights needs no elaboration, but as a pre-Freudian poet, Goldsmith identifies natural "first-born" joys with innocence and peace rather than with aggression and greed. The village is a natural world and nature is innocent, akin to heaven; even the villager's transition from life to death is natural and peaceful. One hardly knows he has left the village:

> But on he moves to meet his latter end
> Angels around befriending virtue's friend;
> Bends to the grave with unperceived decay,
> While resignation gently slopes the way;
> And all his prospects brightening to the last
> His heaven commences ere the world be past!

In summary, the village world of Goldsmith's poem is evoked as a womb-like refuge, closer to death than life in its complete absence of competition and conflict. Being a completely natural world, it offers an escape from metaphysical as well as social conflicts. There is no need to question what is only "natural"; the villagers go gently into their good nights.

Goldsmith's imaginary refuge has little relation to any real village, this being its charm. The real English village is more to be found in George Crabbe's *The Village* (1783). Emphasizing the poverty and disease of rural life, Crabbe issues a challenge to his readers:

> No longer truth, though shown in verse, disdain,
> But own the Village Life a life of pain.

The English village life was in reality a "life of pain," and Crabbe's picture of it was far truer than Goldsmith's. Yet it is not hard to understand why Goldsmith's poem had a far more lasting and pervasive influence as it only purports to be about a real English village. Its setting is a mythological retreat, the great good place, a Heaven-haven. The poem's power derives from its assurance that the great good place really did exist, that it was, in fact, "Home," and that one could return there—were it not for the accidental and remediable moral evil of the enclosure movement. If the English simply reform their vices, then they *can* go home again. But the greatest appeal of the deserted village is its lostness.

The moving element in the poem is its elegiac nostalgia. In contrast, Crabbe's poem offers nothing but the truth. There is no informing or impassioning theme to his poem beyond the mere desire to set the record straight.

Goldsmith's village was not entirely transferable to American terms, but the general theme of a "natural" place free from vice and conflict does carry over to the American myth of the small town—and without the tension of a threatening enclosure movement. The glorification of stasis is as important an element in the American myth as in Goldsmith's.

Despite such imitators of Goldsmith as Frenau and Dwight, the glorification of the American village has been in the medium of the short story or sketch rather than in poetry. The real equivalent to Goldsmith's *Deserted Village* as a classic celebration of the American village is Sarah Orne Jewett's collection of stories, *The Country of the Pointed Firs* (1896). Miss Jewett's account of Dunnet Landing, a seacoast village in Maine, is neither sentimental nor unrealistic. The stories are accurate, sometimes brilliant vignettes of a New England town that is well past its economic and social prime. In one of Miss Jewett's stories, a character comments on the growing provincialism and narrowness of the community since the decline of shipping; in another story, Miss Jewett notes a country graveyard in which most of the home graves are those of women—the men having died in the war or at sea or gone west. The decline of New England into an increasingly marginal area is acknowledged if not emphasized in these stories.

But this is not only New England as it was but as Miss Jewett would have it be. Miss Jewett's imagination responds to adventure and vitality only in their subdued and sublimated forms: an old man's memories or an old maid's relics of her seafaring ancestors. Dunnet Landing is valuable to the first person narrator of Miss Jewett's stories, the author-surrogate, precisely because of its isolation from the center; for the narrator, it is a secure retreat from the forces of life. The few houses in the village are "securely wedged," [12] and the house the narrator shares with her landlady is a protective shell: "I had been living in the quaint little house with as much comfort and unconsciousness as if it were a larger body, or a double shell, in whose simple convolutions Mrs. Todd and I had secreted ourselves" (53). The narrator comes to Dunnet

Landing as an escape from the city that threatens her sense of identity and coherence:

> The hurry of life in a large town, the constant putting aside of preference to yield to a most unsatisfactory activity, began to vex me, and one day I took the train, and only left it for the eastward bound boat. Carlyle says somewhere that the only happiness a man ought to ask for is happiness enough to get his work done; and against this the complexity and futile ingenuity of social life seems a conspiracy. But the first salt wind from the east, the first sight of a lighthouse set boldly on its outer rock, the flash of a gull, the waiting procession of seaward-bound firs on an island made me feel solid and definite again, instead of a poor incoherent being (147).

This quotation illustrates the positive values of the isolated village as an escape from the futile dissipation of self that seems a condition of urban living. But only a few sentences later the narrator describes the coast as "cold and sterile"; the escape has its costs.

One of Miss Jewett's strengths as a writer is that she never denies the cost of escape; nevertheless, the values of retreat and isolation are her real subject. The retreat is from all forms of conflict and emotional intensity, especially sexual passion. There is, to be sure, one love affair within the book, but its protagonists are middle aged and their relation is tender rather than passionate. Otherwise sexual love is represented in the book simply as one more relic of the past. The country of pointed firs is a country of widows and widowers, not of young men.

Another story, one which is not part of *The Country of the Pointed Firs,* casts some light on Miss Jewett's need to escape. "A White Heron" (originally published in *A White Heron and Other Stories* in 1886) is a seemingly insignificant story about a shy eight-year-old girl, Sylvia, who has moved from town to live on an isolated inland farm with her grandmother. Driving her cow home in the late afternoon, Sylvia has unpleasant memories of "the noisy town"; "the thought of the great red-faced boy who used to chase and frighten her made her hurry along the path to escape from the shadow of the trees" (163). Suddenly she hears a whistle, "not a bird's whistle, which would have a sort of friendliness, but a boy's whistle, determined and somewhat aggressive" (163). "The enemy" (163) turns out to be a young man with a game bag and a gun who is hunting birds for ornithological specimens. Once over her initial fear, Sylvia is stirred by the man: "the woman's heart, asleep in the child, was vaguely thrilled by a dream of love" (166), but she "would have liked him vastly better without his gun" (166). The young man is in search of a white heron, and Sylvia discovers its hiding place. Ultimately, despite her attraction for the hunter, Sylvia decides not to betray the heron to his gun. The rejection of masculine aggression could hardly be more clearly symbolized.

In Dunnet Landing, fortunately, no such choices are necessary for there are no challenges or conflicts. Miss Jewett once apologetically commented, "It seems to me I can furnish the theatre, and show you the actors, and the scenery, and the audience, but there never is any play." [13] Miss Jewett's best fiction is precisely an escape from drama into the shell of self. Some of the characters in her best book need even a greater refuge than Dunnet Landing affords, the most extreme being Joanna who lives entirely alone on "Shell-heap Island." Indeed, one of the things the narrator particularly admires about Dunnet Landing is its toleration of such voluntary hermitages. The narrator responds to such as the widower, Elijah Tilley, who would "rather tough it out alone" (106). For the narrator, as for Elijah, Dunnet Landing is a sufficient refuge, one in which they can be in a society yet preserve their most essential selves free from entangling alliances. The small town, as Miss Jewett sees it, is closer to the private island than to the city. The town is an escape from the complications and emotional demands of the city, its distractions and artifices into a place of peace where private memories whether of joy or more often of grief can be clearly and simply defined and then hung onto as a basis for life as Elijah Tilley hangs onto his memories of his wife. Things *have* happened in Dunnet Landing, but it is the past happenings and relationships that sustain the characters. Nothing *does* happen in Miss Jewett's stories because the stories and their setting are an escape, not only from the distraction and confusion of life, but also from its immediacy and intensity. The escape from complication is, in truth, an escape from the less manageable forms of life itself.

Thornton Wilder's *Our Town* (1938) resembles Miss Jewett's work in its image of a New England town as a pastoral retreat. Wilder's town, however, is more mythological and far less tied to reality than is Miss Jewett's. Grover's Corners, population 2,640, is described as a "very ordinary town." A bit dull, the audience is told, but the young people seem to like it since 90 per cent of those graduating from high school settle down there.[14] These mythical statistics are attributed to a New England town of the 1900–10 period, a time of actual widespread exodus from New England farms and small towns to larger towns and cities.[15] Another strange thing about Grover's Corners is the Spartan quality of its middle-class wives, such as those the Stage Manager euologizes. "I don't have to point out to the women in my audience that those ladies they see before them, both these ladies cooked three meals a day,—one of 'em for twenty years, the other for forty,—and no summer vacation. They brought up two children a piece; washed; cleaned the house—and never a nervous breakdown. Never thought themselves hard used either" (58). Earlier in the play the Stage Manager has told us of "Polish town" across the tracks. These New England ladies, unlike those in the rest of the country, take no advantage of this abundant supply of cheap maid service. Moreover, they suffer none of the breakdowns and show none of the queerness that native New England authors like Mary Wilkins described at about the same period in which Wilder's play is set.

Wilder's play could hardly afford to be realistic on these points. To have indicated the actual exodus from the New England small town would have subverted the smug complacency of the play's presentation of Grover's Corners as the great good place. Similarly out of place would have been a depiction of the actual queerness and meanness of small-town New England. For Grover's Corners does not represent an actual New Hampshire village but yet another version of the earthly paradise where life is simple, "natural," and "real." To emphasize their reality, Wilder has his characters speak entirely in clichés. The use of cliché is not, of course, the result of lack of sophistication or skill on Wilder's part. The clichés are deliberately calculated, and we are meant to see eternal truths behind them, truths all the more valid and universal because of their unpretentiously hackneyed form of expression. The action of the play is also a series of clichés, again quite calculated. As the Stage Manager sums it up: "The First Act was called the Daily Life. This Act is called Love and Marriage. There's another act coming after this: I reckon you can guess what that's about" (57).

Life seen from this perspective is itself a mellow cliché, holding no surprises, no terrors. Wilder uses the Stage Manager to enforce this perspective. From the Stage Manager's point of view, everything has already happened; events are robbed of their shock power and reduced to illustrations of the typical, the typical itself being defined in comfortably conventional middle-class terms. The knowledge that everything that happens is *natural* and therefore good is soothing. Even death has no sting in *Our Town* since, as the Stage

Manager assures us, "There's something way down deep that's eternal about every human being" (101).

Despite Wilder's knowing way with clichés, his play is, in fact, genuinely banal in its conception, and its language is smugly unpretentious and non-intellectual. Miss Jewett created a personal refuge out of real materials; Wilder merely mirrors the refuge of the collective American psyche: a simplified and idealized small town, a not too spacious womb in which the realities of time, history, and death can be evaded.

In the works of Goldsmith, Jewett, and Wilder, the first and last being written 158 years apart, we can see the persistence of the myth of the small town as a refuge from the complications and intensities of life. Civilized life in these works is divorced from tension and history and dissolved into nature. In the next group of works we shall consider, the emphasis is different, but the ultimate aim of escape is the same. The escape in this second group of books is into the perfect community, the ideal *Gemeinschaft* in which the class barriers and economic conflicts that jar actual human society are dissolved into a primal universal togetherness.

Where one finds this perfect community is in the Midwest, "The Valley of Democracy," as Meredith Nicholson termed it in his fulsome eulogy. What accounts for the superiority of the Midwest is expressed in the title of Nicholson's first chapter: "The Folks and Their Folksiness." The term "folks," Nicholson explains, is used by Midwesterners "in a sense that excluded the hurrying midday Broadway [New York City] throng and restricted its application to an infinitely superior breed of humanity, to be found on farms, in villages and cities remote from tidewater." [16] Though Nicholson deprecates the provincialism of this Midwestern self-acclaim, he falls into it himself when, quite without irony, he refers to "the real 'folksy' bread-and-butter people who are, after all, the mainstay of our democracy." [17] The folks, to Nicholson as to other Midwesterners, are a white Anglo-Saxon Protestant stock who live mainly in the Midwest and South, are solidly bourgeois but never snobbish, and work at varied occupations including farming (but not including factory labor). While emphasizing the importance and value of the farmers, it is this class of the "folks" that Nicholson feels least certain about. For the Midwestern farmer has a "class sense," and a class sense is the greatest danger to a democracy. Although Nicholson indiscriminately eulogizes the whole area of the Midwest—its farms, towns, and cities —the small town seems to represent folksy values at their purest, for it is in the small towns that the lines of class demarcation almost disappear. It is impossible for the woman who keeps help, for instance, "to ignore the fact that the 'girl' in her kitchen has, very likely, gone to school with her children or has been a member of her Sunday-school class." [18] Admitting that the Midwest has shown no aptitude for literature or the fine arts (1919), Nicholson offers the hope that Western culture will find its true expression in the achievement of justice and the establishment of a perfect system of government. In other words, the real strength of the Midwest is its sense of community.

This opinion Nicholson shared with several decades of Midwestern writers, though these writers had limited folksiness more exclusively to the small town. Some of the more extreme examples follow.

Hamlin Garland belongs to the revolt from the village much more than to the idealization of it. Nevertheless, as an instance of the ambivalence of many of our writers, it is difficult to find a more supremely saccharine apotheosis of Midwestern folksiness than that in "God's Ravens" (1894). The story is about a newspaper reporter, Robert Bloom, who tires of the rat race in the "great grimy terrible city" [19] of Chicago and decides to return to his Wisconsin home town where a year among the "kind, unhurried people" (307) will give him material for a book "telling about the people I meet and their queer ways, so quaint and good" (308). However, Bloom carries over his urban superciliousness to the small town and soon finds himself a social outcaste. Reacting to the petty gossip and dullness of the town, he and his wife decide that the townspeople are living caricatures and "their squat little town is a caricature like themselves" (318). So far, the story seems an anticipation of Sinclair Lewis' *Main Street* far more than the sort of idealization of the town that Lewis mocked. The twist comes in the denouement when Bloom, who is suffering from a debilitating illness, faints in the street. Immediately the entire town comes to his aid, showering him and his family with help and kindness. In his final vision of the townspeople, Bloom can only agree with his wife's affirmation, "They will never be caricatures again—to me" (323).

A more complete apotheosis of the folks appears in Booth Tarkington's *The Gentleman from Indiana* (1900). The people of Plattville, Indiana, are described as "one big, jolly family." [20] Tarkington's hero, John Harkless, who has been educated in the East and is thus presumably qualified to make comparisons, observes: "I always had a dim sort of feeling that the people out in these parts know more—had more *sense* and were less artificial, I mean—and were kinder, and tried less to be somebody else, than almost any other people anywhere" (139). Harkless later observes that "this is the place for a man who likes to live where people are kind to each other, and where they have the old-fashioned way of saying 'Home'" (369). Everybody belongs. Everybody in the middle classes, that is, for Tarkington's accolade extends only to the lowest level of the lower middle classes and not a millimeter further.

Luckily Plattville has no lower classes, this group having segregated itself in a sordid hamlet, Six-Cross-Roads, some miles away from the town. Harkless, editor of the local newspaper, has won the enmity of the Six-Cross-Roads people with an editorial crusade against their quasi-vigilante "White-Cap" organization. Knowing that White-Caps were often a middle-class form of violence and therefore respectable, Tarkington carefully differentiates the Six-Cross-Roads group: "Usually White-Caps are a vigilance committee going out after rascalities the law doesn't reach or won't reach, but these fellows are not that kind" (45). They get together to whip people over personal grudges or just for deviltry. Thus, the only element of evil in the novel is one outside of the community and, indeed, opposed to it. The Six-Cross-Roads people are a separate breed, completely outside the middle-class scale of values. After the Six-Cross-Roads people have nearly killed Harkless, the town expels them and destroys their hamlet. So at the end we see a community completely unified and unthreatened in its middle-class values. The "beautiful people," [21] as Tarkington calls the folks, have triumphed.

To Zona Gale, no less than Tarkington, the Midwestern village was the ideal community. In two books of stories, *Friendship Village* (1908) and *Friendship Village Love Stories* (1909), Miss Gale celebrated what she termed the "togetherness" [22] of the small town. In some of the stories, however, it would seem that Friendship Village is not so perfect a place as Tarkington's Plattville. The stories in *Friendship Village* show a number of apparent cracks in the town's togetherness. In one story, Mis' Postmaster Sykes, the social leader of Friendship, is offended at the effrontery of a one-time maid who has come into some money and invites the town to a reception. Mis' Postmaster Sykes gives a party the same day, knowing the town will come to her party rather than the other. In another story, a girl who ran away from Friendship with her sister's fiancé and was then abandoned covertly returns, believing herself a social outcaste and knowing she will be scorned by the town if they know of her presence. In *Friendship Village Love Stories,* there is a bossy newcomer whom the town ladies cannot bring themselves to tolerate, much less like. Moreover, there are at least two lonely people in the village, though the myth of the village held loneliness to be an exclusively urban phenomenon.

Naturally everything works out in the long run, for these apparent dissonances are merely part of what might be called the Scrooge strategy: setting up an apparent flaw in the social structure only for the sake of dissolving it in a resolution in which all villains repent, all lonely people find love, and no one is left out of "the universal togetherness." [23] The pattern operates so consistently, even relentlessly, in Miss Gale's fiction that only the dullest reader could feel surprised that Mis' Postmaster Sykes is eventually induced to appear with her whole entourage at the former maid's reception, that the runaway girl is discovered and embraced by the community, that the bossy newcomer is taken into Friendship's heart when she produces a baby, and that the only two altogether lonely people in Friendship eventually find *each other* and are presumably destined to live happily ever after. "How pleasant," says one of Miss Gale's characters, "it would be to make folk love folk." [24] Miss Gale enjoys exactly this pleasant relation with her puppets. No unhappiness is suffered to exist in Friendship: "If you want to love folks, just you get in some kind o' respectable trouble in Friendship, an' you'll see so much loveableness that the trouble'll kind o' spindle out an' leave nothin' but the love doin' business." [25] The town assimilates outsiders like a greedy amoeba. Zona Gale's is the warm dream of a world in which all conflict is resolved and everyone drinks from the cup of instant communion.

The village, in order to be appreciated, had to be seen from the outside. After all, one of its virtues was its supposed lack of self-consciousness. Therefore, it is not surprising that each piece of fiction we have examined, Thornton Wilder's excepted, has a narrator or spokesman who speaks from outside the village perspective. Even the apparent exception, Wilder's Stage Manager, proves the rule. Though he speaks in an imitation of the folksy accents of the small town, the narrator is not only cultivated but superhuman, able to suspend time and place and manipulate the other characters like puppets. Occasionally Wilder's attempts to have it both ways get him into embarrassing fakeries as in the line, "It's like one of those Middle West poets said: You've got to love life to have life, and you've got to have life to love life." [26] Wilder, the Stage Manager, and the audience know equally well that "one of those Middle West poets" is Edgar Lee Masters, and the Stage Manager's coyness has only the function of trying to keep up the pretense of his unpretentiousness.

Goldsmith and Garland were both refugees from small villages who, in the traditional manner, came to the city to win fame and fortune. If both show a nostalgia in the works just considered, any real return to the economically and intellectually depressed small towns of, respectively, Ireland and the Middle West was out of the question. The fact that there were reasons other than the enclosure movement that kept Goldsmith, as opposed to his narrator, from returning to the village can hardly be doubted.

Miss Jewett, of course, really was from a Maine town and made her permanent home there, but she was also in close touch with the cultivated world of Boston by virtue of both frequent visits and close contacts with the Boston intellectual community. Whereas the Maine townspeople of her stories have had their horizons narrowed since the decline of shipping, Miss Jewett herself had made the European trip expected of the genteel. Therefore, it is not an anomaly that she represents her narrator as an outsider, appreciating the village not patronizingly, to be sure, but somewhat in the fashion of a connoisseur who can escape personal involvement.

Similarly, Zona Gale was from Portage, Wisconsin, the source of Friendship Village, and lived there much of her life, including the time during which she was writing her glorifications, but her experiences also included an education at the University of Wisconsin and several years of newspaper reporting in Milwaukee and New York. She returned to Portage as a shelter from her frustrating romance with the poet, Ridgely Torrence. Her two village glorifications were written shortly after this romance was broken off, and it is no accident that part of the charm the word "Portage" held for her was its resemblance in sound to "hermitage." [27] Miss Gale's narrator becomes more directly involved in other characters' plots than Miss Jewett's, but she is essentially aloof and outside, not a native of the town like Miss Gale but a long-time and unusually appreciative visitor. *Friendship Village Love Stories* concludes with the narrator's deciding to live in the village forever, but the earlier collection has an ending more revealing of the actual function of the village myth. In it, the narrator comes to the village temporarily as a refuge and returns to the wider horizons of the city at the end of the story. The village myth itself served readers of such fiction as a temporary refuge from the supposedly peculiarly urban complications and tragedies of life. The reader of *Friendship Village* had a double advantage: he could imagine Friendship Village carrying on, becoming friendlier all the time, but he was in effect a temporary visitor who could make his own imaginary escape in the end. Villages are wonderful, except to live in.

Such might have been the viewpoint of Booth Tarkington who was from the small city of Indianapolis. Tarkington's Plattville is based on the town of Marshall, Illinois, which Tarkington visited shortly after having recovered from a severe psychosomatic illness brought on by a submerged personality conflict with one of his teachers.[28] Doubtless the peace and quiet of the small town helped Tarkington re-establish his emotional stability, a debt amply repaid in *The Gentleman From Indiana*. But even in that novel, the foreground is occupied by the cultivated, Eastern-educated hero and the equally Eastern-oriented heroine. The folks figure in the book only as a collective backdrop, a uniform blob of rural virtue. It would seem that Tarkington finds "the beautiful people" too *dull* to occupy the center of a novel. Moreover, after the expulsion of the White-Caps, what was there left to write about? The expelled White-Caps carried with them the only element of conflict and opposition in the novel. Thereafter, Tarkington's best fiction was centered on his more complicated home city of Indianapolis.

The village did (and does) often have a certain peacefulness and serenity. Some fascinating documents by Theodore Dreiser illustrate both the genuine appeal of the village myth and why a revolt against it was essential. These documents are *A Hoosier Holiday* (1916), Dreiser's account of a sentimental automobile journey through his home state of Indiana, and an illuminating passage from his autobiographical volume, *Newspaper Days* (1922).

Though Indiana was a relatively prosperous state, Dreiser's own family had been poor and disreputable. Nevertheless, Dreiser experiences a strong nostalgia as he returns to the state. The scenery "was so simple and yet so beautiful that it was like a dream—such a land as Goldsmith and Grey had in mind when they wrote." [29] This is true not only of the scenery but the human atmosphere: "The centre of Indiana is a region of calm and simplicity, untroubled to a large extent, as I have often felt, by the stormy emotions and distresses which so often affect other parts of America and the world." [30] Indiana is "a happy land of farms and simple industries which can scarcely be said to have worked harm to any man." [31] Warsaw, a small town in which the Dreiser family had lived some years, was "an idyllic town." [32]

Ironically, Dreiser had first read Goldsmith's *Deserted*

Village while living in a house in Evansville, Indiana, which was being paid for by his brother's mistress, the madame of a whorehouse.[33] Dreiser's unusual background quite naturally gave him a broad perspective of Indiana. In *A Hoosier Holiday* he candidly notes that "every one of those simple American towns through which we had been passing has its red light district."[34] Even Warsaw was not exempt from the universal human desire: "Aphrodite had many devotees in this simple christian village."[35] Moreover, small towns are intellectually confining.[36] Finally, these small towns have a certain obsolete, archaic quality. They represent the dead ideals of a home and family centered life: "Have we made the ten commandments work? Do not these small towns with their faded ideal homes stand almost as Karnack and Memphis—in their frail way pointing up the vanity of religious and moral ideals in the world?"[37] The "Home" used to be sacrosanct, but "It seems to me as if I myself have witnessed a great revolt against all the binding perfection which these lovely homes represented."[38] Dreiser, let us recall, was writing in 1916, at the beginning of the revolt from the village. In the remarks above, we can see some of the mood behind the revolt, but we can also see how strong an appeal the half-real, half-mythical peace and innocence of the village had to Dreiser—even to the point of his explicitly invoking Goldsmith.

To Dreiser, the town and farm emotionally represented the charm and appeal of childhood, but it was an appeal the adult had to resist. The city, by contrast, represented the appalling but *vital* present. The polarization is especially clear in an illuminating passage from *Newspaper Days* in which Dreiser recounts his visit to the Missouri farm of his fiancée's parents:

To me it seemed that all the spirit of rural America, its idealism, its dreams, the passions of a Brown, the courage and patience and sadness of a Lincoln, the dreams and courage of a

Lee or Jackson, all were here. The very soil smacked of American idealism and faith, a fixedness in sentimental and purely imaginative American tradition, in which I, alas! could not share. I was enraptured. Out of its charms and sentiments I might have composed an elegy or an epic, but I could not believe that it was more than a frail flower of romance. I had seen Pittsburgh. . . . I had seen Lithuanians and Hungarians in their "courts and hovels," I had seen the girls of that city walking the streets at night. This profound faith in God, in goodness, in virtue and duty that I saw here in no wise squared with the craft, the cruelty, the brutality and envy that I saw everywhere else. These parents were gracious and God-fearing, but to me they seemed asleep. They did not know life—could not. These boys and girls, as I soon found, respected love and marriage and duty and other things which the idealistic American still clings to.

Outside was all this other life that I had seen of which apparently these people knew nothing. They were as if suspended in dreams, lotus eaters.[39]

Dreiser's own writings show his freedom from the obsolete dreams of the farm and village. Indeed, the condition of a healthy American literature was to reject and destroy the myth of the village, for the whole myth was based on conceptions profoundly hostile to the imagination. The myth denied satire, tragedy, even comedy. Many small-town novels operating within the myth do attempt comedy but it is ersatz comedy, the kind that is supposed to prompt a gentle chuckle at the lovable foolishness of various good-hearted eccentrics. The archetypal subject of most genuine comedy—sex—is conspicuous by its absence. Satire would, of course, have spilled the beans, exposing all the illusions and lies that the myth was meant to promote—especially the illusion of middle-class virtue. Finally, the mythical village was anti-tragic. People could die there but never alone, never meaninglessly. Moreover, fiction written within the myth accepted a prescribed bourgeois morality. This does not mean that it was self-righteously puritanical. A "ruined" girl might be a sympathetic character, for instance, *but* only if she were properly repentant and properly unhappy about it. Dreiser's own *Sister Carrie* upset people because, although its heroine was unhappy at the end of the novel, it was not because she had "sinned"; *that* did not bother her or Dreiser either.

Dreiser was a central influence in the revolt from the village though he himself found his themes in the city or the industrial town. Dreiser's main contributions were two: first, he began the breakthrough to an honest treatment of sex; second, he developed the emotional mode of naturalistic pathos, a mode that defined his world in tragic rather than ethical terms, the tragic *emotion* of pity being substituted for an ethical *judgment*.[40] Dreiser freed writers to treat American life with honest and genuine, rather than faked, pathos. Dreiser's naturalism has been often maligned for supposedly reducing human dignity. In theory, this is true. In practice, the small-town myth that never questioned genteel ideals denied the dignity of suffering by false optimistic assurances or sentimentalized pieties. Pathos never really *counted;* it was used sentimentally, purely for the momentary sensation. Naturalistic pathos, by contrast, is final; there is no happy end.

Naturalistic pathos is mostly to be found in Masters, Anderson, and Wolfe, all of whom gave new dimensions to the theme of "the buried life." The subtitle of *Look Homeward, Angel: A Story of the Buried Life,* is an allusion to the poem of Matthew Arnold's that states the theme precisely:

> Alas! is even Love too weak
> To unlock the heart, and let it speak?
> Are even lovers powerless to reveal
> To one another what indeed they feel?
> I knew the mass of men conceal'd
> Their thoughts, for fear that if reveal'd
> They would by other men be met

> With blank indifference, or with blame reprov'd:
> I knew they liv'd and mov'd
> Trick'd in disguises, alien to the rest
> Of men, and alien to themselves—and yet
> The same heart beats in every human breast! [41]

The poem expresses a universal sense of alienation; part of the human condition is the near-inexpressibility of universal subjective emotions. But a culture worthy of the name does provide forms enabling just such expression. To American writers, it seemed as though their civilization—puritanical and materialistic—stultified life by denying, suppressing, and repressing the buried life, particularly in its most charged and painful burden of sexual feeling. To blame the puritans was, of course, too simple. Introspection was really part of, rather than opposed to, the puritan tradition. The enemy was a decayed form of puritanism, more aptly termed Victorianism or the genteel tradition. This puritanism (for convenience I shall follow the historically oversimplified usage of the teens and twenties in referring to all phenomena of sexual prudery and repression as puritanism) shrank from the inner life, burying it under the restraints of shame and ignorance. Despite his historical errors, the most interesting analysis of the buried life is that of Van Wyck Brooks, who put in abstract terms the ideas that Masters and Anderson embodied in literary forms.

But Brooks is important not so much because of his considerable influence but because he was the popularizer, summarizer, and symbolic representative of the theme of the buried life. Other writers may have had earlier and perhaps even more intelligent insights into the buried life than did Brooks, but no one so completely and consistently pursued and identified himself with the theme. In just such a way is H. L. Mencken the representative of the attack on conformity, on the stereotyped thoughts and values of the herd mind.

Writing in the Menckenian tradition, Sinclair Lewis and T. S. Stribling tended toward sociological fiction that assaulted the values and standards of the dominant middle class. A rough distinction between these two groups of writers is that the delineators of the buried life were concerned with hidden, misunderstood, inarticulate *feelings,* whereas the anticonformists were bothered by failures and suppressions of *thought.* Most Americans, the anticonformists believed, were incapable of genuine thought and distrusted and punished the few genuine thinkers in their midst. Placing themselves apart from the culture as though they were anthropologists observing some primitive tribe, Mencken, Lewis, and Stribling analyzed the strange mores and rituals of the *homo Americanus.* The result, however, was not sociological observation but a satire that used sociology as a convenient weapon.

The two themes of the buried life and the attack on conformity *are* the revolt from the village. H. L. Mencken was quite correct in his belief that the creative outburst of the teens and twenties was not a concerted movement but a case of each writer's responding individually.[42] What gave the revolt unity was that a number of writers, drawing from quite varied sources and influences, arrived at common themes. Even the difference between the two major groups is a matter of emphasis. Mencken and Lewis wrote (badly) about the buried life; Brooks and Anderson attacked American conformity. Although both themes go well beyond the small town in scope, both focus on the town. The town was, of course, what many of these writers knew, what came to hand, and even for such Eastern urbanites as Brooks and Mencken, the town was nicely adaptable to serving as an image for their major themes. To show the buried life of a town was, implicitly, to deny that a refuge could be found from the fear, loneliness, and insecurity of an urbanizing society. These alien and disorienting emotions had to be recognized and faced; American literature offered a mirror image of them, no longer an escape from them. The necessary refuge had to be found in creative acts of the spirit rather than in sentimental falsifications of reality. One of these creative acts was to honor and celebrate rather than evade the pathos of a lonely society.

The anticonformists had equal reason to concentrate on the town. Most Americans recognized a certain lack of depth, originality, and variety in the small-town intellect, but most Americans demonstrated a definite fear of intellect as well. Glorification of the small town was one of the many proofs of how unnecessary intellect was as opposed to "horse sense," simple honesty, etc. This function of the small-town myth shows most clearly in its use by business and the Republican party even though, ironically, it was the dynamics of business that was turning America into an urban and industrial nation. But whenever the immense problems, the needs for centralized control and increased governmental responsibility that these new conditions created were cited, the business propaganda mill would respond with question-begging evocations of a vanished (indeed, never-existent), idyllic, individualistic, small-town civilization wherein such controls were entirely unnecessary. To problems of urban crime and chaos, the propaganda responded by a self-righteous recommendation of small-town virtues, virtues that the small town doubtfully possessed and that were thoroughly inappropriate to national problems. Praise of the small town was a covert way of denying the need to think, a method of evading the admission that old formulas no longer served the new conditions.

The small towns of the myth were more virtuous and less complicated than any real small town, but the small towns of the new fiction were not entirely real either. In opposition to the idealized village of the myth, the rebels opposed an equally partial image made up of all the things that had been left out—the conformity, stupidity, loneliness, meanness, and physical ugliness of the village. They attacked an abstraction with a counter-abstraction. Yet of the two pictures, that of the rebels is far truer, for their abstractions were employed as a method rather than an evasion of thought and feeling. The harshness of their picture seems extreme only when we forget the ever-present tendency in American civilization to deny the bleaker realities.

There is, it must be admitted, a certain thinness in the revolt from the village. The rebels knew what they disliked but were somewhat vague concerning the alternatives. They shared in the general twenties' ignorance of the American historical tradition, a tradition that many supposed to be so much bunk. They saw themselves as rebels against the Protestant religion but, like the Transcendentalist rebels before them, they actually reaffirmed the Protestant tradition of attack on materialism and spiritual torpor.[43] They were *Protestant* atheists, pouring old wine into new bottles. Lewis, for one, was quite consciously indebted to Thoreau. There is not a great deal in the twenties' rebels that was not to some degree anticipated by the Transcendentalist movement.

For that matter, the interpretations of American society by Alexis de Tocqueville and James Fenimore Cooper question or attack much the same social evils as did Mencken and Lewis. Tocqueville is particularly acute in his analysis of the tyranny of public opinion:

When the inhabitant of a democratic country compares himself individually with all those about him, he feels with pride that he is the equal of any one of them; but when he comes to survey the totality of his fellows and to place himself in contrast with so huge a body, he is instantly overwhelmed by the sense of his own insignificance and weakness. The same equality that renders him independent of each of his fellow citizens, taken severally, exposes him alone and unprotected to the influence of the greater number. The public, therefore, among a democratic people, has a singular power, which aristocratic nations cannot conceive; for it does not persuade others to its beliefs, but it imposes them and makes them permeate the thinking of everyone by a sort of enormous pressure of the mind of all upon the individual intelligence.[44]

All of the writers in this study show an American world characterized by a startling and oppressive lack of emotional or mental freedom.

These writers partially belie another of Tocqueville's *aperçus*, the often-cited prediction that American literature would not be about man in society but "man himself taken aloof from his country and his age and standing in the presence of Nature and of God." [45] Some of the greatest American novels and poems almost exactly fit Tocqueville's prescription,[46] but not the revolt from the village, whose main topic was the effect—always malign—of society on man. The names of some of the important texts show their social leaning, their intention to make the locale a determinant rather than a mere backdrop: *Winesburg, Ohio, Spoon River Anthology, Main Street, Look Homeward, Angel*. Central characters in Lewis' novels are meant to caricature social types: Babbitt, Elmer Gantry. The values of the community are the actual and titular subject of "The Man That Corrupted Hadleyburg." Part of the definition of the revolt from the village is this emphasis on the effect of environment. Yet it may be that Tocqueville's prediction is partially borne out in a close look at the very writers to whom it would least seem to apply. Lewis sometimes attempts close distinctions between classes and class types, but they generally are clumsy and obvious. In Lewis as well as the others, society appears not in the sharp definition of a Balzac or even a Stendhal but as a vague, though all-pervasive, hostile force. Thus, even in the writings about communities, what comes through is not at all a defined society but a unified atmosphere. Tone in most of these writers is far more important than plot or character.

Winesburg and Spoon River are defined by an atmosphere of limitation, leanness, sterility, smother, and naturalistic pathos. *Spoon River Anthology* does give a vivid effect of village political conflict but *Winesburg* does not even provide this much information concerning the social structure of actual villages.

Cooper, who had suffered from it, was as hostile as Tocqueville to the tyranny of mass opinion. In *The American Democrat* (H. L. Mencken liked this well enough to write an introduction for the 1931 edition), Cooper shows much the same attitude toward democracy and the rule of the masses as Mencken himself and the other twenties' writers. Like them, no radical, Cooper thought democracy the best form of government, not because it was perfect, but because it was relatively less stupid and vicious than any other that had been tried. The rule of the "best," Cooper realized, was a fine ideal but unfortunately in practice the favored few proved to be no wiser, no less exempt from ignorance and prejudice, than the vulgar many. And the most corrupt government of all was oligarchy, the control of the government by business. So far, Cooper in no way differs from the sentiment of the twenties, and he is equally in accord with the anger at the illegitimate powers of public opinion:

It is putting the prejudices, provincialisms, ignorance and passions of a neighborhood in the place of statutes; or, it is establishing a power equally without general principles, and without responsibility.

Although the political liberty of this country is greater than that of nearly every other civilized nation, its personal liberty is said to be less. In other words, men are thought to be more under the control of extra-legal authority, and to defer more to those around them, in pursuing even their most lawful and innocent occupations, than in almost any other country.[47]

The rebels, with all of their kinship to nineteenth-century American ideas were more consciously influenced by English and continental writers. Much of the confusion in Van Wyck Brooks's work arises from his attempts to directly apply the theories of Ruskin and Morris to American culture. H. G. Wells was a central influence on both Brooks and Lewis. Mencken saw himself as a charter member of Nietzsche's elite, yet Mencken was more influenced by Mark Twain than by Nietzsche and indirectly passed this influence on to Lewis. In fact, the entire revolt of the teens and twenties had been acted out on a miniature scale in the eighties and nineties. The first revolt from the village even produced some authentic masterpieces: *Huckleberry Finn,* "The Man That Corrupted Hadleyburg," *The Damnation of Theron Ware.* E. W. Howe's *The Story of a Country Town* anticipated the theme of the buried life; nothing the anticonformists wrote went beyond Crane and Twain. It is one of the many ironies of American literary history that the second revolt was so little aware of the first.[48]

2. Eggleston to Frederic

The first revolt from the village may be dated by the books comprising it as extending from 1871 (*The Hoosier School-Master*) to 1899 ("The Man That Corrupted Hadleyburg"). Though beginning as a mere offshoot of the local color movement, the first revolt very early shows some remarkable anticipations of our two central themes of the buried life and the attack on conformity. In a few great stories of the nineties—stories by Twain, Frederic, and Crane—the best achievements of the later revolt are equalled if not bettered.

Edward Eggleston's *The Hoosier School-Master* (1871), generally considered to be the first realistic novel about the Middle West, grows out of little more than a desire to celebrate Midwestern local color. Eggleston himself notes in his preface that "It used to be a matter of no little jealousy with us . . . that the manners, customs, the thoughts, and feeling of the New England country people filled so large a place in books, while our life, no less interesting, not less romantic, and certainly not less filled with humourous or grotesque material, had no place in literature. It was as though we were shut out of good society. . . ."[1] In a second preface, written long after the original publication, Eggleston stressed dialect and local color as the most interesting aspects of the novel. His model was James Russell Lowell's

Biglow Papers. The main interest of the *Biglow Papers,* however, was not merely in the recording of rural New England dialect and manners, but in the aggressive political criticism conveyed through the vernacular mask. The political themes and the local color interact, each pointing up the other. The political critiques are energized by the bite and color of the New England vernacular, and the depiction of the New England countryman is given point by his ethical involvement in great national issues. Dialect and local color have a *function* in Lowell.

By contrast, Eggleston's interest in Hoosier dialect and manners is little more than mere antiquarianism. Although Eggleston asserts the literary interest of Midwestern life, his novel fails to bear him out. First, he has to go back to a somewhat earlier, less-civilized period of Indiana life to find literary material; the placid bourgeois state that Indiana had become by 1871 failed to excite his imagination. Then, even in this earlier state, the Midwestern country people he depicts occupy only the periphery of the novel whereas the center is held by his schoolmaster hero, a thoroughly conventional and genteel character whose manners and values in no way differ from those of any cultivated Easterner. There are a few depictions of genuine back-country Hoosiers such as Mrs. Means with her yellow face, corncob pipe, and straggly discolored teeth, and there are accurate renderings of Hoosier dialect, but to what purpose? Lowell establishes the ethical superiority of his Yankee character, but the nearest thing to a theme in *The Hoosier School-Master* is the easternization of Indiana and its gradual assimilation of the genteel tradition. Worst of all, even this pallid source of interest is overshadowed by a ridiculous, superimposed mystery-story plot.

Even the most promising theme in Eggleston's novel, his attack on the hard-shell Baptist religion, is not sufficiently developed, though he does anticipate a motif in antivillage literature that eventually culminated in Sinclair Lewis' *Elmer*

Gantry. But Eggleston's presentation of a modern liberal Protestant belief in good works in opposition to the hardshell Baptist's belief in predestination too often breaks down into sentimentality, as in the following dialogue between his schoolmaster hero and a backwoods pupil, Bud Means, who is trying to discover how to be a good Christian:

> "Do you think I could begin without being baptized?" Bud asked presently.
> "Why not? Let's begin now to do the best we can, by his help."
> "You mean, then that I'm to begin now to put in my best licks for Jesus Christ, and that he'll help me?" (160–161)

Eggleston's later novels provide a fuller picture of the surface of Midwestern life than does *A Hoosier School-Master,* but they share the common failure to pierce beneath the surface to explore the essential realities of Midwestern life. Such a complaint cannot be made about E. W. Howe's strange and brilliant novel, *The Story of a Country Town* (1884). For one thing, Howe is much closer to the life he writes of. Eggleston tells his stories from the outside, the point of view being centered on his conventional genteel heroes who share neither dialect nor manners with the backcountry types around them. The locale of *The Hoosier School-Master* is not Eggleston's civilized home town of Vevay but back-woods Indiana, country Eggleston knew only from a visitor's viewpoint. Howe's novel, however, grows out of his childhood in Bethany, Missouri, the Twin Mounds of *Story.* The narrator, Ned Westlock, as provincial as anyone in the novel, is a mask for Howe himself, and much of *Story* is directly autobiographical.

As Howe's title indicates, the subject of the novel is the town itself. Howe has only scorn for romantic notions of Midwestern life. Twin Mounds is a backwater, out of the main current of westward expansion. It is settled by natural losers since, as one of Howe's characters sardonically notes, successful people had no need to go west. The bored towns-people invent scandals in order to give some color to their dreary lives but are too afraid of each other to commit any major sins. In an early version of the anticonformity theme, Howe shows his townspeople as futile, smug, conceited con-formists, living their lives by some second-hand formula—as does the man who "carried on a bank in awful silence be-cause he had heard that still water runs deep." [2]

This mordant commentary, as Claude M. Simpson points out, comes in the form of editorial comment through the narrator, Ned Westlock, rather than through the action of the novel.[3] Brom Weber further shows that Howe's melodra-matic central plots gradually overshadow the social commen-tary as the novel proceeds. The two main plots have to do with: (1) Ned Westlock's childhood and adolescence in the shadow of his father, John Westlock, a narrow, unloving, moralistic fundamentalist minister, who eventually reveals a new facet by running off with a grotesquely ugly member of his flock; (2) Jo Erring's pathological jealousy, leading to the murder of a one-time suitor of his wife. Both plots are semi-autobiographical. John Westlock is a direct portrait of Howe's father and Jo Erring's jealousy reflects Howe's; in Howe's autobiography, he tells of reading *The Kreutzer Son-ata* with an intense shock of recognition.[4]

The stories of Ned Westlock and Jo Erring may lead away from an explicit commentary on Twin Mounds, but they lead toward an even more interesting implicit commentary. Jo Erring's jealousy stems from an impossibly perfectionist and puritanical temperament and an absurdly idealized view of women. William Dean Howells acutely observed that Er-ring's "sentimental excess and unbalance is true to the West, and to a new country." [5] Erring's expectations are individual and eccentric, lacking an established tradition and a realistic knowledge of human nature to build upon. In this respect,

Erring is an anticipation of the Anderson grotesque, and the novel is an early version of the buried life theme as well as the anticonformity theme.

In addition, the central point of view in Howe's novel, that of Ned Westlock, is itself representative of a crippling environment.[6] The very limitations of Ned Westlock's narrative voice mirror the sterility of Twin Mounds, but Ned Westlock *is* Howe. Joseph Kirkland told Hamlin Garland that Howe's country town "never had any existence outside of his tired brain."[7] Rather Howe's country town exists *through* his tired brain and deprived spirit. The grey, arid, barren quality of the town comes to us through Howe's editorial voice, a voice that is exactly the same in his late autobiography as in his early novel. In 1920, Howe attempted a refutation of E. L. Masters' *Spoon River Anthology* in a book entitled *The Anthology of Another Town*. What was meant to be a rebuttal seems more of a confirmation; Howe's town has less sex and violence than Spoon River, but the depiction of petty conflicts and domestic warfare jibes with Masters. The main difference is that Howe takes the dreariness of small town life as a norm and resents those who do not. What could be more indicative of intellectual and emotional sterility than to resent those who cannot rest content with Spoon River?

Howe's inability to understand the underground meanings of his own novel is widely divergent to the somewhat cold intelligence of Joseph Kirkland's *Zury: The Meanest Man in Spring County* (1887). The subtitle of *Zury* is *A Novel of Western Life*. Kirkland's well-realized intention was to write a comic novel of Midwestern life and manners. Treating subject matter similar to that of Howe and Eggleston, Kirkland's tone differs; he writes with graceful irony, avoiding the descents into sugary sweetness that spoil Eggleston's style and the clumsy bleakness of Howe's prose. Although Kirkland was brought up partly in the West, his parents were

cultured Easterners; he saw Pinckney, Michigan—the model
for Wayback, Illinois in *Zury*—through foreign eyes. His
mother, "a pioneer realist," had angered the Pinckneyites by
her literary sketches of their entertaining crudities.[8] The condescension in Kirkland's portraits of rural Illinoisans was a
family inheritance.

Kirkland, a writer more conscious of literary technique
than either Eggleston or Howe, cleverly built his book
around two points of view, each allowing him a useful
perspective from which his investigation of Midwestern life
could proceed. The first point of view is that of the novel's
hero, Zury (short for Usury), a farmer admired by his neighbors as "the meanest ma-an in Spring Caounty," [9] meanness,
in the local usage, denoting a tight hold on a dollar rather
than a quality of spite or cruelty. Through Zury, Kirkland is
able to show two sides of the Midwestern character: Zury's
petty materialism is partially offset by his colloquial wit and
shrewd good humor. Kirkland intends his character to be a
prototype of the Midwesterner.

Ann Sparrow, Kirkland's heroine and second-point-of-
view character, is brought into the book for another purpose.
Coming from the East to teach school at Wayback City, Ann
provides an outside view of the West through which Kirkland can polemicize against romantic viewpoints toward
farm life. It is Ann who is impressed by the flytrap, an
instrument that consists of two wooden boards with honey
smeared on them and hung about a foot apart. When a
number of flies have been drawn by the honey, the boards are
clapped together, strewing dead and dying flies all over the
floor. And it is from Ann's observations that Kirkland
launches into an apostrophe to the subtle aroma of farm life:
"Ammonia is the inevitable bane of all intercourse with
horses and cattle. Oh, why can we not be led by Thoreau and
Walt Whitman to glory in the breath of Nature—all the
breaths of Nature? But we cannot" (142).

The farmers and townspeople are not ennobled by contact with nature. Rather they show the "libido for the ugly" that H. L. Mencken was to attack. In Wayback City the houses are sunbeaten and ugly since no effort has been made to preserve the trees. Zury's answer to Ann's delight in the woods surrounding his farm is:

"Yes—its handy to have fire-wood clust by, n' not fur t' haul. I cal'late t' have the trees on that thar forty girdled naow, soon's I can get raound to it, so's it'll look a little more cleared up n' civilized back o' the haouse."

Ann was rather struck with the idea of forty acres of dead girdled trees as a symbol of civilization . . . (137).

Besides polemicizing against the ugliness of the farm and village, Ann serves to reveal the intolerance of the region when the townspeople suspect her (correctly) of having slept with Zury. Zury himself had had problems in the past when he was suspected of holding the heretical Universalist belief that all mankind would be saved rather than the majority's being properly damned. As with Cooper and Tocqueville, Ann "began to appreciate more than ever the despotic tyranny of a lawless and unbridled 'freedom of opinion' " (190).

Kirkland, thus effectively combined two devices in his comic social history of rural Illinois: a prototypical native hero and a sensitive female observer with an alien point of view. By means of this double perspective, Kirkland manages to both mock and glorify his region. For although the limitations and meanness of the Midwest have been clearly shown, Zury, its native product, is subtly idealized throughout the novel for his folk shrewdness. The ending of the book even foreshadows the arrant romanticism of Owen Wister's *The Virginian*, the civilized and female East mating with the practical, masculine West.

But for all of Kirkland's smooth skill, *Zury* is a less

important novel than Howe's clumsy and suggestive *tour de force*. Nothing in *Zury* matches the evoked bleakness and dreariness of *The Story of a Country Town,* and a certain tone of complacency in the novel is confirmed by the too-easy reconciliation of the ending.

Hamlin Garland's first appearance in this study was in the role of eulogist of the small town, but Garland's best work is precisely in the contrary tradition, revealing the drabness and sterility of Midwestern farm and town life. Garland had lived on farms in Wisconsin, Iowa, and the Dakotas and knew the dreary wretchedness of farm life from direct experience. In his autobiography, *A Son of the Middle Border,* he expresses his contempt for literary romanticizations of the farm: "Milking as depicted on a blue china plate where a maid in a flannel petticoat is caressing a gentle jersey cow in a field of daisies is quite unlike sitting down to the steaming flank of a stinking brindle heifer in flytime." [10] A knowledge of the usual conversational topics of farm hands might disturb "those who think of the farm as a sweetly ideal place to bring up a boy" (175). But the true qualities of prairie life did not come home to Garland until he had been in the East for some years and returned to the West with a new perspective. He now saw clearly the material and spiritual deprivation of farm and town life, perceiving tragic values in scenes that had once seemed merely dull and petty. When he reached Osage, Iowa, the farmers and townspeople, people he had previously known, seemed spiritless, futile, defeated:

Men who were growing bent in digging into the soil told me something of their desire to see something of the great western world before they died. Women whose eyes were faded and dim with tears, listened to me with almost breathless interest whilst I told them of the great cities I had seen, of wonderful buildings, of theaters, of the music of the sea. Young girls expressed to me their longing for a life which was better worth while, and lads, eager for adventure and excitement, confided to me their secret intention of leaving the farm at the earliest moment (366).

The literary result of Garland's experience was *Main-Travelled Roads*. Ironically, the book's picture of farm life was deeply resented in the West itself: "Statistics were employed to show that pianos and Brussels carpets adorned almost every Iowa farmhouse. Tilling the prairie soil was declared to be 'the noblest vocation in the world, not in the least like the picture this eastern author has drawn of it' " (415). The West believed in its own myth; what else did it have to offer? Garland truthfully replied that far from exaggerating the grimness of farm life, he had not been able to bring himself to reveal the full extent of the sufferings of the farm wife. Moreover, his book was written not out of hate but an ambivalent love: "I acknowledged a certain responsibility for the conditions of the settlers. I felt related to them, an intolerant part of them. Once fairly out among the fields of the Northern Illinois everything became so homely, uttered itself so piercingly to me that nothing less than song could express my sense of joy, of power. This was my country —these my people" (355).

The ambivalence is evident in *Main-Travelled Roads* (1891), the collection of stories the trip inspired. On the one hand, there is the ersatz glorification of small-town togetherness in "God's Ravens"; on the other, such truly bitter stories of toil and deprivation as "A Branch Road," "The Return of a Private," "Under the Lion's Paw," "A Day's Pleasure," and strongest of all, "Up the Coulee." Even in most of these stories, however, there is a certain tension between hopefulness and reconciliation that sometimes pulls too much in the direction of sentimentality.

"A Day's Pleasure" is somewhat vitiated by a sentimental ending to what was otherwise a sound story. The story begins with the pathetic eagerness of the farm wife to share her husband's trip to town, not out of any great affection for the husband, who is obtuse and dull though good natured, but simply to escape momentarily the monotony of the farm and its daily round of toil. The toll of such a life is economically drawn by recurrent mention of the dull back pain that is the permanent and only legacy of her labors. The town offers only the dubious pleasure of wandering up and down the street and sitting down to rest in a grocery store. So far, the story has been realistic, but then Garland introduces a sweet lady, who in a gratuitous impulse of pity invites the farm wife into her house for tea! The story closes with the impossibly sentimental line: "The day had been made beautiful by human sympathy." [11] The issue here is not the possibility of such an incident; we can easily imagine it happening in real life. But to end a *story* in such a way is to say implicitly that nothing is irredeemable, that all life's troubles can be solved if only people are a bit kind—and they *will* be! This was the message of the conventional fiction of Garland's time, and this ending is a cowardly evasion. For the true story is of the inescapable trap the farm woman finds herself in, with "a home of toil at one end and a dull little town at the other" (245).

Similarly marred is "A Branch Road," which until its conclusion is a parable of waste and hopelessness. Will Hannan goes West in a cloud of spite after a petty misunderstanding with Agnes, the girl he had intended to marry. Coming back years later, he finds Agnes married to the crude, brutal Ed Kinney. She has to bear with her husband's snivelling old father and malicious complaining mother— the whole brood living in a drearily ugly house and dining in the following setting: "The room was small and very hot; the table was warped so badly that the dishes had a tendency to slide to the center; the walls were bare plaster grayed with time; the food was poor and scant, and the flies absolutely swarmed upon everything like bees" (52).

As for Agnes, she shows the effects of such a life: "She was worn and wasted incredibly. The blue of her eyes seemed dimmed and faded by weeping, and the old-time scarlet of her lips had been washed away. The sinews of her neck showed painfully when she turned her head, and her trembling hands were worn, discolored, and lumpy at the joints" (48).

The implications of this description become even stronger when we note that it comes through the point of view of Will Hannan who is responsible for it all. Out of remorse, Will proposes to Agnes that they run off together, but with "infinite, dull despair and resignation in her voice" (58), she responds that it is too late, she cannot be helped. Will himself really feels this too, though with a vague desire to break out of the trap: "He felt as young people seldom do the irrevocableness of living, the determinate, unalterable character of living. He determined to begin to live in some new way—just how he could not say" (45).

The true story of "A Branch Road" is perfectly summed up in the first of the two sentences quoted above. In Chapter One we have seen that part of the charm of the myth of the town was that all tragedy was revocable, alterable, but Garland's best stories show the farm as a place where in actuality life is more relentless, less malleable than elsewhere. However, in "A Branch Road," he again weakly resolves the story with Will finally persuading Agnes to bolt with him. In one sense, this ending is rebellious in the context of its time of publication since it celebrates an adultery, however much qualified by Ed Kinney's unfeeling brutality. But in a deeper way, it conforms by finally backing away from its own premise of irrevocability. It may be questioned as to whether the ending is not legitimately affirmative rather than meretriciously so, but there are indications throughout that Garland himself does not quite believe in it. This is particularly evident in several passages that make it quite clear that Agnes has entirely lost any sexual attractiveness to Will; his motivations are entirely those of pity and guilt. In the last lines of the story, Will cannot quite carry the burden of affirmation so it is shifted conveniently to nature: "Will shuddered with a thrill of fear, she was so weak and worn. But the sun shone on the dazzling, rustling wheat, the fathomless sky, blue as sea, bent above them—and the world lay before them" (65).

Garland did write three stories that were unspoiled by false affirmation: "The Return of a Private," "Under the Lion's Paw," and "Up the Coulee." "The Return of a Private" celebrates the Midwestern farmer as a soldier who, having endured a bloody war with men, returns to fight a hopeless battle with nature and mortgages. "Under the Lion's Paw" is a Populist parable, though nowhere does the political message of the story interfere with its human values. The story is of a farmer, Haskins, who has worked furiously to build up a reserve sufficient to buy the farm he rents. Hope sustains Haskins and his wife even in the midst of their unending round of ferocious labor, and finally they have the $2,500 at which the farm was valued. Meanwhile, during their labor, the activities of the farm's "true owner," a land speculator, are described with effective irony: "He was mainly occupied now with sitting around town on rainy days, smoking and 'gassin' with the boys,' or in riding to and from his farms. In fishing time he fished a good deal. Doc Grimes, Ben Ashley, and Cal Cheatham were his cronies on these fishing excursions or hunting trips in the time of chickens and partridges. In winter they went to Northern Wisconsin to shoot deer" (205). The final confrontation between these two ways of life occurs when the landlord commits the outrageous affront of informing Haskins that the price of the farm has gone up to $5,500 because of Haskins' own improvements! After coming very close to killing the landlord, Haskins is left looking hopelessly ahead to years of unending and unrewarding labor.

This is also the essential vision of *Main-Travelled Roads.* As Garland perceived, farming is not so much work that has finite goals and clear rewards but labor—heavy physical exertion that moves in an unending cycle. Thus the vision of hopeless despair, an antithesis of the American cult of optimism that had reached an extreme in the farm and village myth. As we have seen, Garland occasionally succumbed to this myth, but when most honest, his writing is a bleak counter to it. No story better embodies the dumb despair of Midwestern farm life than "Up the Coulee," which recounts the successful actor Howard McLane's long-delayed return to his farming family. He finds his brother Grant bearing the whole load of the family and full of bitter resentment at Howard's failure to have shared his success with the family. Despite spirit and body-destroying labor, Grant has been unable to make a go of it. He sums up the family's predicament: "A man like me is helpless. . . . Just like a fly in a pan of molasses. There ain't any escape for him. The more he tears around, the more liable he is to rip his legs off" (113).

Everything about farm conditions confirms Grant's analysis, subversive as it is to the traditional American idea of the inevitable reward for effort. Garland's character Howard tries to pull the same trick that Garland himself pulled in other stories by offering Grant money for a new start. But Garland stays true to his vision of waste in Grant's response: "I mean life ain't worth very much to me. I'm too old to take a new start. I'm a dead failure. I've come to the conclusion that life's a failure for ninety-nine percent of us. You can't help me now. It's too late" (129).

It is always too late in Garland's best stories, though sometimes he is unwilling to admit it. Another defect is that his characters, though pitiable in their dumb persistence, are lacking in any further mental or emotional interest. Of course, their very poverty of consciousness is Garland's subject, but he is unable to suggest any hidden potential in his characters that would emphasize the crime done to them. In that sense, Garland is not a chronicler of the buried life so much as a life in which the only emotion, sometimes a quite open one, is that of weary despair.

More in key with the buried life theme was Mary E. Wilkins, author of the collection of stories *A New England Nun* (1891). Much more than Garland's, Miss Wilkins' [12] stories tend toward sentimental resolutions that dissolve the genuine tensions they build up in a factitious glow of brotherliness. But if the plots of many of the stories are defective, Miss Wilkins very nearly makes up for it by a sharpness of observation that isolates some significant aspect of New England character in almost every story. In "Christmas Jenny" there is a brilliant scene in which an old New Englander keeps slipping on an icy part of his walk and spilling the carefully filled bucket of water he has been trying to bring in. Finally: "When his pail was filled and he again started on the return, his caution was redoubled. He seemed scarcely to move at all. When he approached the dangerous spot his progress was hardly more respectable than a scaly leaf-slug's. Repose almost lapped over motion. The old woman in the window watched breathlessly." [13] Naturally, despite the precautions, he falls again, and this time he continues to lie there, refusing his wife's attempts to help him up.

But old Jonas Carey sat still. His solemn face was inscrutable. Over his head stretched the icy cherry branches, full of the flicker and dazzle of diamonds. A woodpecker flew into the tree and began tapping at the trunk, but the ice-enamel was so hard that he could not get any food. Old Jonas sat so still that he did not mind him. A jay flew on the fence within a few feet of him; a sparrow pecked at some weeds piercing the snow-crust beside the door. Over in the east arose the mountain, covered with frosty foliage full of silver and blue and diamond lights. The air was stinging. Old Jonas paid no attention to anything. He sat there.

The old man both correlates and contrasts with the natural scene around him. He is as emotionally frozen as the ice but lacks the dazzle. His sole governing principle is spite—at his wife and at himself. Eventually he is lured into the house by the fear that a visiting neighbor will get the bit of sausage his wife was cooking up for him.

This vignette typifies Miss Wilkins' picture of New England. Out of the economic and social main-stream, having lost much of its youth to the Midwest and South in the aftermath of the Civil War, New England is a community of oldsters whose lives, lacking sufficient outward references, have turned in on themselves, producing patterns of spite and petty selfishness. In this and other stories, Miss Wilkins emphasizes not so much the meanness of New England people as the pettiness that reveals an emotional deprivation even greater than any grand meanness could do. Despite the sentimentality of most of her stories ("Life-Everlastin' " is a marvelous exception), Miss Wilkins provides a piercing insight into a New England winter of the soul.

All of the writers thus far discussed are of considerable interest from the point of view of cultural history but none, it must be admitted, had any real literary excellence. They lack sufficient significance and universality. They did adumbrate major themes of a later American literature but without pushing these themes to their fullest development. Howe, for instance, discovered a major cultural theme—the buried life —but his own life was buried, and he was only gropingly aware of what he was doing. Unable to bring his themes to full consciousness, he was unable to effectively shape and control them.

Another group of realists wrote on the theme of the small

town with greater literary sophistication and with a deeper moral consciousness. William Dean Howells, Harold Frederic, and Stephen Crane wrote genuine masterpieces wholly or partially about the small town. These writers went beyond local color and muted evocation to universal revelations of the meaning and consequences of provincialism.

Ironically, Howells was to be one of the devil figures of the 1920's revolt, caricatured in Sinclair Lewis' Nobel Prize address as having "the code of a pious old maid whose greatest delight was to have tea at the vicarage." [14] Lewis was ignorant of Howells' early battles for realism, including his courageous advocacy of Stephen Crane's *Maggie,* and Lewis had certainly not read *A Modern Instance,* which anticipated the teens and twenties in its exposure of the mental and moral inadequacy of the small town.

Provincialism is, of course, only a secondary theme in *A Modern Instance;* the major theme is the breakdown of the institution of marriage in a society in which the traditional supports have vanished or are eroding. It might be supposed that the one place the traditions were maintained was in New England—both in its villages, characterized as they supposedly were by plain living and high thinking, and in its cultural center, Boston. To these idealized images, Howells opposes the realities of a Maine village more aptly described as drab than plain and a Boston dominated, on the one hand, by a crass commercialism and, on the other, by a bloodless gentility.

Howells concentrates more on character than on setting in his novel, but the setting, far from being a mere backdrop, is one of the essential determinants shaping the two protagonists, Marcia Gaylord and Bartley Hubbard, whose mismarriage is the main plot of the novel. Marcia's tendency toward undisciplined passion and Bartley's inclination toward cynical cleverness meet no institutional checks in the inadequate culture of Equity, Maine. Indeed, Bartley is encouraged in his cheap and arrogant displays of what he supposes to be sophisticated superiority by the local admiration for "smartness." There is little in the ironically named town of Equity to serve as a worthy object for the intellect or the emotions, and without such objects how are the intellect and emotions to be educated?

Marcia's father, Squire Gaylord, is the town leader, a position gained by his superior intelligence and firmness of character. The Squire even has a moral predominance, for though he is an outspoken "free thinker," he is, in an odd way, the town's primary defender of tradition, religious as well as moral. Equity Protestantism has embraced strange new gods: "Religion there had largely ceased to be a fact of spiritual experience, and the visible church flourished on condition of providing for the social needs of the community. It was practically held that the salvation of one's soul must not be made too depressing or the young people would have nothing to do with it." [15] In contrast, the Squire is an old-fashioned Deist in the Tom Paine mold. His bleak and morally stern infidelity has a greater affinity with the puritanism that the town had outgrown than with the new religion of bland sociality. The paradox Howells implies is that the Squire's infidelity is a position of more spiritual integrity than a Protestant vision that was not only revised but positively altered.

But if the Squire is, relatively, the best of the town, this merely illustrates its extreme limitations. Howells' descriptions of the Squire's "rusty black clothes," of his "hawk-like profile" (16), of the "bitter tang" (37) of his sardonic ironies, and of his cold and arid manner reveal a stoically self-contained man whose integrity and emotional barrenness are but two sides of the same coin. The limitations of such a type are clearly expressed when, at the end of the novel, the defeated Marcia is shown settling into the "stern aridity" (447) for which her father has provided the model.

Squire Gaylord's infidelity accounts for his bleakness but also for his individuality. If nothing else, he is his own man. Marcia has inherited the Squire's disbeliefs but without his tough good judgment. The Squire's disbelief defines him; hers is mere negation. Her limitations become most clearly apparent after her marriage with Bartley when she is unable to cope with the alien environment of Boston. Most graphically revealing is Marcia's consultation with Ben Halleck concerning the spiritual welfare of her daughter, Flavia.

"I want Flavia should belong to some particular church."

"There are enough to choose from," said Halleck with pensive sarcasm.

"Yes, that's the difficulty. But I shall make up my mind to one of them, and then I shall always keep to it. What I mean is that I should like to find where most of the good people belong, and then have her be with them," pursued Marcia. "I think, it's best to belong to some church, don't you?"

There was something so bare, so spiritually poverty-stricken, in these confessions and answers, that Halleck found nothing to say to them (281).

Thus when her marriage breaks up, it is fitting that she return to her father in Equity. Her only spiritual resource is a dry cold stoicism like that of her father's, a stoicism that staves off emotional collapse at the cost of an extreme renunciation of hope and feeling, a closing up of spiritual shop.

Although Harold Frederic's novel, *Seth's Brother's Wife* (1887), does not quite live up to its subtitle—*A Study of Life in the Greater New York*—the most interesting theme in the book is the differences set up but inadequately explored between this rural-based upstate New York life and the life of the cities. Not all the comparisons are to the favor of the city. One of the characters, for instance, who has been living in New York City makes the mistake of supposing that he can move back to his birthplace and buy his way into Congress. He fails to realize that, though local politics are "practical" and even unprincipled, they are not financially corrupt. The implication is that the country is not quite so bad as the city in this respect. Nevertheless, the country is shown as a place that offers little possibility of intellectual or spiritual sustenance. As Frederic notes, the farmhouse funeral sums up the general dreariness of rural life: "The rural life itself is a sad and sterile enough thing, with its unrelieved physical strain, its enervating and destructive diet, its mental barrenness, its sternly narrowed groove of toil and thought and companionship—but death on the farm brings a desolating gloom, a cruel sense of the hopelessness of existence which one realizes nowhere else." [16]

Country people attempt relief through gritty humor and salvationist religion: "But the bleak environment of the closed life, the absence of real fellowship among the living, the melancholy isolation and vanity of it all, oppress the soul here with an intolerable weight which neither fund of sardonic spirits nor honest faith can lighten" (34). As one of Frederic's characters claims, the nineteenth century is the century of the cities: "Perhaps there may have been a time when a man could live in what the poet calls daily communion with Nature and not starve his mind and dwarf his soul, but this isn't the century" (33).

However, this indictment is delivered by a vain, selfish, citified woman which somewhat qualifies its import. In fact, Seth Fairchild, Frederic's hero, finally rejects this woman, his brother's wife, after having very nearly drifted into an affair with her, and marries a sweet country girl. Such ambiguities very nearly form a pattern in Frederic's novel with the editorial comments, whether by Frederic himself or one of his characters, almost always damning the country while the plot favors the country. Unfortunately, what might have been an interestingly ambiguous story finally becomes too involved with the merely conventional mystery story of the murder of Seth's brother, a murder that has no real symbolic significance. The story fails to enforce the editorial comments on the hopelessness of rural life since all of its more attractive characters end successfully.

Perhaps the main interest of *Seth's Brother's Wife* is in its somewhat sketchy anticipation of the themes of Frederic's masterpiece, *The Damnation of Theron Ware* (1896), a powerful story of the tensions brought on provincialism when faced with unsettling new challenges. At first, this story seems a simple attack on the dreariness of village life. The reader cannot help but sympathize with the Reverend Theron Ware who has been assigned to the dreary Methodist post of Octavius, New York. As a welcome, a delivery boy informs the Wares that the trustees will not stand for their taking milk on Sundays, inspiring Mrs. Ware to quote Wendell Phillips: "The Puritan's idea of hell is a place where everybody has to mind his own business!" [17] The arrival of the trustees does nothing to brighten the picture. Frederic's portrayal of two of these trustees is a precise evocation of American village types:

The obvious leader of the party, Loren Pierce, a rich quarry-man, was an old man of medium size and mean attire, with a square, beardless face as hard and impassive in expression as one of his blocks of limestone. The irregular, thin-lipped mouth, slightly sunken, and shut with vice-like firmness, the short stub nose, and the little eyes squinting from half-closed lids beneath slightly marked brows, seemed scarcely to attain to the dignity of feature, but evaded the attention instead, as if feeling they were only there at all from plain necessity, and ought not to be taken into account. Mr. Pierce's face did not know how to smile,— what was the use of smiles?—but its whole surface radiated secretiveness. Portrayed on canvas by a master brush, with a ruff or red robe for masquerade, generations of imaginative amateurs would have seen in it vast-reaching plots, the skeletons of a dozen dynastic cupboards, the guarded mysteries of a half a century's international diplomacy. The amateurs would have been wrong again. There was nothing behind Mr. Pierce's juiceless countenance more weighty than a general determination to exact seven per cent of his money. . . . But Octavius watched him shamble along its sidewalks quite as the Vienna of dead and forgotten yesterday might have watched Metternich.

Erastus Winch was of a breezier sort,—a florid, stout, and sandy man, who spent most of his life driving over evil country roads in a buggy, securing orders for dairy furniture and certain allied lines of farm utensils. . . . To look at him, still more to hear him, one would have sworn he was a good fellow, a trifle rough and noisy perhaps, but all right at bottom. But the county clerk at Dearborn County could have told you of agriculturalists who knew Erastus from long and bitter experience, and who held him to be even a tighter man than Loren Pierce in the matter of a mortgage (26–27).

The symbolism of the names is obvious: Pierce and Winch. Every detail of description reveals Pierce as the "economic man"; Pierce has no attributes that exist without monetary function. Following the physical description is a mock-heroic reduction of the universal will to power to an American villager's will to 7 per cent interest. *Mean* is the resonant word; Pierce's ambitions are as mean as his attire. He has power without personality or intellect, power purely negative and repressive; he represents everything counter to life.

If Loren Pierce is a small-town Rockefeller (note how the description tallies), the archetype of the old-fashioned bank president or financial overlord, the more modern Erastus Winch is the salesman *par excellence.* He is a Babbitt but more sinister, the apostle of P. R., the good fellow whose good fellowship is as hollow as the pasteboard smile in a thousand and one cigarette advertisements. His mask of rough unpretentiousness is a stock American persona.

Pierce and Winch represent a form of Protestantism that has become a mere propaganda machine for the idealization of business traits. Avarice has been dropped from the list of the vices, and the businessman's indifference or hostility to aesthetic qualities that might distract him from the pursuit of gain is translated as otherworldliness and resistance to the temptations of the flesh:

"We are a plain sort o' folks up in these parts," said Brother Pierce. . . . His voice was as dry and rasping as his cough, and its intonations were those of authority. "We walk here," he went on, eyeing the minister with a sour regard, "in a meek an' humble spirit in the straight and narrow way which leadeth unto life. . . . No new-fangled notions can go down here. Your wife'd better take them flowers out of her bunnit afore next Sunday" (29).

Theron's religion is very different from that of Octavius. Loren Pierce complains about the sermons Theron gave at the Methodist conference as being too intellectual and, as we have seen, Alice Ware admires anti-Puritan Wendell Phillips. When Pierce calls for hell-fire sermons including descriptions of the fearful deathbeds of Voltaire "with the Devil right there in the room, reachin' for 'em, and they yellin' for fright" (29–30), Theron is tempted to admit his contempt for such old wives' tales. In many respects, Theron typifies (his ignorance of the higher criticism excepted) certain modern Protestant ministers—optimistic, liberal, mildly addicted to comfortable clichés, with an attenuated Emersonian belief in the beneficence of the universe and the beauty of nature. It was not so much the narrow, self-sufficient, primitive religion that was typical of Octavius as it was Theron's more idealized, but also more tenuous, kind of belief that suffered the full destructive effects of twentieth-century knowledge. As Frederic's novel proceeds, it becomes evident that it is the inadequacy of *this* kind of religion and culture—"God without thunder"—even more than the Primitive Methodist mentality of such as Pierce that is Frederic's true target. As John Henry Raleigh notes, Theron

Ware represents "the vestigial remains of the consciousness of the early nineteenth century, once powerful, now vulnerable." [18]

A provincial mentality, armed only with an unexamined belief in the goodness of life and an untested belief in his own innate decency, Theron Ware can survive the crude onslaught of Pierce and Winch but is utterly overwhelmed by the seemingly beneficent trio of Father Forbes, Doctor Ledsmar, and Celia Madden, who represent, respectively, a more sophisticated religious idea ("this Christ-myth of ours") (74), scientific rationalism, and a sexually tinged Walter Pater-type aestheticism—all European imports that were only just now reaching the American cities, much less such backwaters as Octavius. This is, indeed, a brave new world, and Theron is as unequipped for it as Huxley's savage. Theron is ambiguously illumined and damned by his new knowledge.[19] Eventually, his new friends, who had looked on him as a "real acquisition," a sort of early American piece in their collection, abandon him when he commits the *gaffe* of vitiating his antique qualities by attempts at sophistication. Seeing the contempt in which others hold him and full of self contempt, Theron fully enters the twentieth-century cosmos: "The world was all black again—plunged in the Egyptian night which lay upon the face of the deep while the earth was yet without form and void. He was alone in it,—alone among awful planetary solitudes which crushed him" (333).

In the end, Theron is saved from complete destruction by the pragmatic Sister Soulsby, who assures him that, mean as he is (and Theron becomes painfully mean—in the sense of small-souled—in the course of the book), he is no worse than the average run of humanity. Theron *is,* in fact, average and representative: a provincial mind faced with the complexities of a new era and not muddling through very successfully. Attacking the central image of American innocence, the small-town man, *The Damnation of Theron Ware* portrays an innocence that is really ignorance, which leaves the "average" American unprepared to cope with the mediocrity and corruptibility of his own spirit and destines him to forms of sophistication that are merely excuses for corruption.

The vision of small-town failure is no less cold and clear in Stephen Crane's "The Monster" (1897). "The Monster" is the first of a number of stories Crane set in Whilomville, based on Port Jervis, New York, where he had spent some of his childhood. The later stories are about children and their curious social rituals. The town is merely an unimportant backdrop for the childhood world, a world that Crane treats not so much with sentimentality as with nostalgia and indulgent irony. An example is the following passage revealing the resentment aroused by the "professional bright boy" of the Sunday school class: "The other boys, sometimes looking at him meditatively, did not actually decide to thrash him as soon as he cleared the portals of the church, but they certainly decided to molest him in such ways as would re-establish their self-respect. Back of the superintendent's chair hung a lithograph of the martyrdom of St. Stephen." [20] For Crane, this kind of writing is poor stuff. It appeals to a stock response of warmly remembered, aggressive boyhood, and it uses irony to dispel rather than create tension, though it does present insights into the more brutal aspects of the childhood mind unusual in this era.

In "The Monster," the child world is at the periphery, and a harder, more complicated irony is at the center. "The Monster" begins deceptively, however, like the later Whilomville stories: "Little Jim was, for the time, engine Number 36, and he was making the run between Syracuse and Rochester. He was fourteen minutes behind time, and the throttle was wide open. In consequence, when he swung around the curve at the flower-bed, a wheel of his cart destroyed a peony. Number 36 slowed down at once and looked guiltily at his father, who was mowing the lawn." [21] The indulgent, facetious, ironic tone is compounded with a description evoking the mellow serenity that the myth of the small town held to be its distinguishing characteristic: "The doctor was shaving the lawn as if it were a priest's chin. All during the season he had worked at it in the coolness and peace of the evenings after supper" (4). This beginning is done quite straight without any intention of undercutting.

But in the myth of the small town, serenity of scene is supposed to be just one aspect of a general quality of peacefulness, goodness, whatever is normal and decent. This quality, the myth holds, defines the people as well as the place. Conventional, small-town people may be, but the essence of the myth is that the conventional thought patterns and moral judgments are *right*. What most people believe is, in fact, true, and the way they behave is, in fact, the way they (and everyone else) ought to behave.

Crane, however, based his whole literary ironic style on the conviction that the conventional is always wrong. Much of Crane's irony can be simply described as the shock that results when personal vision compares notes with conventional expectations. Crane is as much concerned with *the way it is not* as with *the way it is*. In "The Monster," conventional responses are the grounds of moral failure.

The story is not anything so simple as a mere flouting of contrast between nonconformity and conventionalism—the sort of thing done with wearisome stereotype in such contemporary novels as *One Flew Over The Cuckoo's Nest*. Rather, there are a careful series of gradations of the conventional, some of them innocuous, some decent, some vicious. The conventionality of "smart" conversation is surely innocuous: "The band played a waltz which involved a gift of prominence to the bass horn, and one of the young men on the sidewalk said that the music reminded him of the new engines on the hill pumping water into the reservoir. A similarity of this kind was not inconceivable, but the young man did not say it because he disliked the band's playing. He said it because it was fashionable to say that manner of thing concerning the band" (17–18).

The performance of the volunteer firemen at the Trescott fire is heroic but in a thoroughly conventional manner, but the heroism of the Trescott's Negro hostler, Henry Johnson, is not conventional. He rushes in to save Jimmie Trescott, not because he wants to make a show of heroism (in contrast to most Crane characters, those petty posturers), but out of the impulse of his close friendship with Jimmie, an act that genuinely transcends self. Yet this heroism is just what the public wants and admires, so the public response to it can be perfectly conventional: "The morning paper announced the death of Henry Johnson. There was also an editorial built from all the best words in the vocabulary of the staff. The town halted in its accustomed road of thought, and turned a reverent attention to the memory of this hostler. In the breasts of many people was the regret that they had not known enough to give him a hand and a lift when he was alive, and they judged themselves stupid and ungenerous for this failure" (41).

This generous stock response comes easily because of the stock situation that precipitated it. But when Henry Johnson turns out to be alive, horribly disfigured and reduced to idiocy, the responses are more variable and confused though equally stock. A hero is supposed to either survive with medals and minor injuries or gloriously die. He is not supposed to live on as a physical and mental wreck, a testimony to fate's proclivity toward absurdity, half way between a horror—

"Well, what makes him so terrible?" asked another.

"Because he hasn't got any face," replied the barber and the engineer in duet. . . .

and a joke—

"He has no face in the front of his head,/In the place where his face ought to grow" (61).

While the chorus of townspeople in Reifsnyder's barber shop generally agree that Doctor Trescott was right to preserve Johnson's life—

"Supposing you were in his place," said one, "and Johnson had saved your kid, what would you do?"

they cannot fit the faceless former hero himself into their conventions. To his embodied symbolization of the irrational and awful, they oppose their primitive responses of repulsion and hysteria.

Doctor Trescott is resented for his sponsorship of this strange, frightening "monster." Mrs. Hannigan, who has caught her son and others proving their courage by approaching the oblivious and moaning monster, "stared with a bitter face at the Trescott house, as if this new and handsome edifice was insulting her" (89). Such unearned indignations are among the emotional luxuries of life. Is it a psycho-sociological law that, the more simple and unearned the response, the more intense and satisfying it is? The psychology of resentment is further shown in Jake Winter's self-righteous rage at Doctor Trescott after Winter's daughter has had a nervous shock from seeing Johnson's face. Trescott calmly leaves Winter's house when he finds his medical attentions are not wanted: "This placid retreat seemed to suddenly arouse Winter to ferocity. It was as if he had then recalled all the truths which he had formulated to hurl at Trescott. So he followed him into the hall, and down the hall to the door, and through the door to the porch, barking in fiery rage from a respectful distance. As Trescott imperturbably turned the mare's head down the road, Winter stood on the porch, still yelping. He was like a little dog" (94).

Such resentment is based on a chimera but becomes self-justifying and grows fatter by feeding on itself.

In the scene immediately following, two female gossips vicariously feast on what has by now been transformed into a heroic act of defiance on Jake Winter's part. Their pleasure, of course, is not in Winter's rise but Trescott's fall. But a third, more independent, gossip exposes the chimerical aspect of the whole affair:

> Martha, at her work, had been for a time in deep thought. She now interrupted the others. "It don't seem as if Sadie Winter had been sick since that time Henry Johnson got loose. She's been to school almost the whole time since then, hasn't she?"
>
> They combined upon her in immediate indignation. "School? School? I should say not. Don't think for a moment. School!"
>
> Martha wheeled from the sink. She held an iron spoon, and it seemed as if she was going to attack them. "Sadie Winter has passed here many a morning since then carrying her schoolbag. Where was she going? To a wedding?" (96)

Crane knows that people arrange their beliefs to support their emotions. Martha seems an exception, but earlier we were told that Martha was "the most savage critic in town" (80), whose opinion on a local flirtation was that "Mrs. Minster and young Griscom should be hanged side by side on twin gallows" (78). This time, perhaps out of an instinct of opposition to the two other gossips, she happens to argue for the right cause.

Most of the town, however, is not so contrary as Martha. Dr. Trescott is approached by a delegation of leading citizens who suggest to him that he shuttle Johnson off to some isolated farm or into an institution, but this overt pressure is the least of it. The story ends with a powerful suggestion of what lies ahead for the Trescotts. The town has closed ranks. Only one woman has shown up for Mrs. Trescott's accustomed Wednesday tea; fifteen more were expected. The Trescotts face the economic and social reprisals of a town united in stupidity and dishonor. They face the unbearable prospect of a complete isolation, the kind of isolation that freezes the soul and sometimes causes its victims to doubt their inmost convictions in the face of a united public opinion that pronounces them wrong.

But the story has a hero, Doctor Trescott, whose courage and decency are proved by his inarticulateness and uncertainty. The thought that Henry ought to be allowed to die occurs to Trescott *before* anyone else, and he can justify his care for Johnson only by stammering repetitions of the obvious—"but, by God! He saved my boy" (45). Trescott knows, however inexpressibly, what he must do as a human being, and his courage is in doing it, without the support of convention, indeed, in the face of the general disapproval of the town of Whilomville, which is, of course, collectively, the "monster" Crane's title denotes. Only one writer before the second revolt of the teens and twenties exposed the herd mind of the small town with an effectiveness equal to Crane's. That was Mark Twain.

3. Mark Twain: The Southwest and the Satirist

Mark Twain, even more than Howells, Frederic, and Crane, attacked the myth of the small town as an adequate image of American values. There is, of course, a popular image of Twain as the representative of an innocent and pastoral America, the reassuring symbol of the vanished small-town paradise that so many Americans long to return to. This image is perfectly developed in Charles Neider's introduction to Twain's autobiography: "It brings back the tone and flavor of an America which was young and optimistic, a homespun, provincial America but an America with greatness in its heart. Thoreau's America may have contained many lives of quiet desperation. Mark Twain's decidedly did not." [1] Twain once responded to a boyhood chum's self-pitying evocation of childhood joy and innocence with the following outburst: "Man, do you know that this is simply mental and moral masturbation." [2]

But Twain himself bears some responsibility for the distortions he has been subjected to. The Walt Disneyfied image of small-town life is, after all, a technicolor not-too-revised version of Twain's St. Petersburg with, perhaps, an occasional Uncle Remus introduced to demonstrate how benign the Negro used to be in the good old ante-bellum days when everybody loved each other.

In fact, in Twain's work, there are two quite different

64

images of the small town, reflecting two sets of ambivalences on Twain's part: his ambivalences toward his native Southwest and those toward the middle-class culture he wrote in and (sometimes all too much) for. These ambivalences were originally observed in Van Wyck Brooks's brilliant and controversial study *The Ordeal of Mark Twain.* (Brooks himself was an important contributor to the second revolt from the village, and the place of *The Ordeal* in Brooks's over-all theory of American culture will be considered in Chapter 4.) For the purposes of this section, it is necessary only to extract two notions from Brooks's book. The first is that Hannibal and its culture were drab and stultifying, combining a prudish puritanism with a materialistic emphasis on practical pioneering, these two forces working to produce a spiritually desiccating atmosphere of uncritical conformity and emotional sterility. The East was characterized by a genteel version of the same phenomena; art was more valued than in the West, but only provided that it stayed safely detached from life. Thus, both East and West militated against free artistic creativity and intellectual criticism. The result of these pressures was that Twain, a natural satirist, dissipated much of his talent in a conformist humor rather than a liberating satire.

It should be admitted that, even in this simplified restatement, some defects in Brooks's argument are apparent. Yet along with Bernard De Voto's *Mark Twain's America,* a lengthy attack on Brooks and a defense of the West, *The Ordeal* is the foundation of modern Twain criticism. Brooks and De Voto established two of the major problems of this criticism. Since Brooks, there have been penetrating studies of the causes of Twain's despair and literary breakdown (De Voto, ironically, wrote one of the best);[3] since De Voto, there has been exhaustive study of Twain's debts to American humor and other sources. Moreover, Brooks and De Voto raised an important cultural issue: did the provincial culture of the West ruin Twain or did it, on the contrary, inspire him?

Brooks's villains, the twin forces of puritan and pioneer that supposedly ruined Mark Twain (among other American artists), are, for the most part, figments of his imagination, historical myths. De Voto was quite correct in complaining, "Abstractions became entities and objectively existed. The Frontier, the American, the Puritans, the Pioneer, the artist, the American artist . . . and a score or two of other clichés began by embodying the sentiments of critics about ideas they disliked and ended as actual independent existences." [4] Actually, by "pioneer," Brooks meant businessman, and by "puritan," he meant anyone of narrow and repressive religious viewpoints. Brooks's ally, Randolph Bourne, even admitted that "If there were no puritans we should have to invent them." [5] De Voto, a Westerner, was not interested in puritans, but Brooks's invention of the pioneer infuriated him. In *Mark Twain's America,* he cited an abundance of Western humor and history to prove that, although Easterners may have been repressed, pioneers certainly were not. The West, in fact, was wild, boozing, brawling, full of beans. The pioneers had "dances, hoedowns, roof raisings, fanning bees, bobsled rides, barbecues, fiddling matches," [6] and they also had lots of sex.

De Voto's pioneers may be slightly less fictive than Brooks's, but they certainly have nothing to do with Mark Twain. Hannibal was a town, if a new one, and not a wilderness settlement; the people in Hannibal were small-townsmen, not pioneers. Although there was not infrequent violence in Hannibal, the official culture of the town was, as we see it in Dixon Wecter's excellent study, Victorian and prudish, far closer to Brooks's puritanically repressed environment than to De Voto's bouncing and bumptious West. As Wecter shows, the Hannibal that Twain grew up in had repudiated the sexual frankness of the frontier and was tending toward an exaggerated delicacy and refinement. Brooks had attacked Twain's subservience to the genteel worship of women and had speculated that Twain's semi-private bursts of verbal obscenity were the logical counterpart of his repressions. Wecter, in turn, notes that "Deeply grounded was the ideal of woman as a paragon of purity, the Divinely-appointed civilizer of the coarse masculine clay. The lady in her conventional role—and she was nothing if not conventional—occupied that niche of reverent adoration from which the Protestant forebears had expelled the Virgin Mary." [7]

Even De Voto later noted the almost complete absence of sex in Twain's published works.[8] And some of Twain's own statements about Hannibal seem almost to confirm Brooks's desolate portrait.

Twain showed St. Petersburg as one side of a small town —but he recognized E. W. Howe's Twin Mounds as another. Twain wrote to Howe: "Your pictures of that arid village life and the insides and outsides of its people, are vivid, and what is more true; I know, for I have seen it all, lived it all." [9] In the *Autobiography,* Twain comments that kissing in his family was limited to the deathbed: "Our village was not a kissing community." [10] Dixon Wecter notes that Twain's unpublished manuscripts record several affecting instances of lives buried in quiet desperation in "The Spoon River that was Hannibal." [11] In fact, though Brooks's study was wrong in most of its details, naïve in its psychology, and ignorant in its historical generalizations, none of the many thoroughly documented and intelligently researched refutations have altogether succeeded in exorcising the faint, vestigial, ghostly presence of Brooks's frustrated and despairing Twain, the satirist who did not publish all of his satire, the obscene joker whose novels have far less recognition of sex in them than those of William Dean Howells, the philistine celebrator of industrial progress who privately developed an elaborate pessimistic philosophy.[12]

Indeed, Justin Kaplan's recent biography, *Mr. Clemens and Mark Twain,*[13] presents us (though without acknowledgement) with a modernized version of Brooks's Twain. Certainly De Voto's contrast of pioneer vigor with Eastern effeteness has become dated more than Brooks's portrait of a radically disturbed and divided man.

There is, however, a basic inconsistency in Brooks's study: if Twain's failure could be attributed, as Brooks claimed, to the inadequacies of a materialistic American culture that was characterized by the anti-intellectual West and the genteelly proper East, what about his success? The value of De Voto's book was that it showed the major debts of both theme and technique that Twain owed to his childhood in Hannibal and to the American humor of his time.

However, a recognition of Twain's debt to Hannibal and to native humor must be coupled with the recognition that he became an important writer only by transcending his sources. Most American humor is completely witless and unreadably dull. Constance Rourke's *American Humor,* as an instance, is far more entertaining and interesting than most of the sources she draws on. It is true that the Western genre of tall tale has bursts of wildly exuberant imaginative language, but even the best of such writings are overly repetitious, lacking in variety; more than a few pages of ringtailed roaring is too much of a good thing.

Southwestern humor offers some exceptions. Augustus Baldwin Longstreet's *Georgia Scenes* (1835) and George Washington Harris' *Sut Lovingood* (1867) are consistently live and interesting. At the same time, these two books, the best of Southwestern humor, clearly reveal the limitations of the genre. Longstreet, like most Southwestern humorists, was cultivated and conservative, a self-conscious gentleman, a Whig in politics, but the best stories in *Georgia Scenes* are about low-life characters who speak a colorful colloquial dialect. Longstreet keeps his distance from such characters;

the stories are introduced and sometimes ended by the self-controlled, urbane narrator whose own language is formal and Addisonian. As Kenneth Lynn notes, the narrator emphasizes his distance from the lower orders whose antics he describes with an amused condescension, sometimes even explicitly comparing his own respectable values with the scenes of sadistic carnage he has just described in careful detail.[14] Such a use of narrative point of view is meretricious, somewhat like the Hollywood device of tacking on a moralistic conclusion to an essentially salacious and corrupt movie. Longstreet is in complicity with the sadism he condemns, as the detailed texture of his style reveals.

George Washington Harris, on the other hand, obviously identifies with the point of view of his East Tennessee hero, Sut Lovingood. Unlike Sut, his creator is educated, but otherwise there is a meeting of the minds. Sut Lovingood is characterized by the editors of a recent collection of Southwestern humor as playing three roles: "advocate of healthy animal spirits, satirist, and scourge."[15] The editors evidently disagree with Edmund Wilson's earlier interpretation (cited in their bibliography) of Sut as a vicious sadist, "a peasant squatting in his own filth."[16] There is no need to mediate between these opposed judgments. Wilson's view of Sut is completely confirmed by an unbiased reading of Harris; Wilson states that *Sut Lovingood* "is by far the most repellent book of any real literary merit in American literature."[17] The book has considerable literary merit in its luridly brilliant expression of animal spirits, but the animal spirits expressed are not entirely healthy. Harris has been praised for a supposedly frank depiction of sex, but most of the sex in his book is in the sniggering, voyeuristic style of the crude dirty joke and the modern "sex" magazine, and, not unlike the aforementioned "sex" magazines, sadism is really a more important motive than lechery. Thus, in "Mrs. Yardley's Quilting," there is a long passage praising the beauty and susceptibility of widows, but Sut's mind is immediately distracted from thoughts of sexual conquest into a murderous practical joke.

One very popular current of modern criticism would praise such characters as Sut precisely because of their unregenerateness. The trouble with modern liberals, in this view, is that they have a harmfully naïve belief in the goodness of human nature; writers like Harris are actually moral and religious in showing the existence of original sin. This view seems to rest on a basic misconception. Harris' book is an exemplification and justification of the hinder part of man rather than a moral vision of it. To equate Harris with, say, Faulkner [18] on the grounds of their orthodox representation of sinfulness is somewhat like equating Al Capone with Karl Barth. The modern emphasis on sin has not always escaped the pitfall of evolving into a new form of sentimentality, and the spectacle of our moral professors of literature earnestly defending a swine like Sut is not without comedy.

Longstreet, the Southern gentleman, was in unconscious emotional complicity with the poor white sadists he wrote about. Harris, more honest, openly identified with the race hatred and frustrated aggression of his protagonist. Longstreet is valuable as a vivid record. Harris is much more valuable for his perfect rendering of a still extant type of American mentality and for the twisted, neurotic, savage poetry of his dialect tales. But neither Longstreet nor Harris have a rudimentary trace of the moral insight that makes great literature possible. Twain's greatness lay in his ability to both draw on *and* transcend native American humor and his own provincial background. It is this crucial point that neither Brooks nor De Voto ever really clarified. Twain had major limitations—there are not inconsiderable traces of sadism and masochism in his writings (this is true of most important humor and satire), and he never altogether outgrew a provincial shallowness of thought—but in his greatest writings an intense moral vision operates. The difference between Longstreet and Twain may be conceived by imagining the Boggs-Sherburn episode as Longstreet would have told it; in Longstreet the episode would be reduced to a vividly described spectacle with, perhaps, an irrelevant moral comment added on. Harris cannot be dismissed so easily. Like Twain, he went beyond most Southwestern humorists by creating a world through the language and in the image of his vernacular persona.[19] But Twain's world is a sustained illusion of a recognizable society, Harris' a comic (sometimes not so comic) hell; Twain's characters are all too human, Harris' either the dehumanized objects of Sut's jokes or mountain men blown up by verbal extravagance into mythological masculine principles (Wirt Staples). As for Huck and Sut, they are opposites: Huck is too pragmatic, too knowing to be sentimental, but he is essentially humane, one of the recurrent emotional rhythms in *Huckleberry Finn* being his sickened response to cruelty and violence; Sut is subhuman and his greatest pleasure is the enjoyment of other's pain.

The sum of the differences between Twain and the Southwestern humorists is that Twain was capable of a moral insight, a basic decency, and an intellectual and emotional richness not to be found in the earlier comic depictions of the South. In fact, Twain's whole perspective was qualitatively different from the Southwestern writers. Both Brooks and De Voto saw Twain as a Midwesterner, Brooks attacking the sterility of his background, De Voto defending its literary possibilities. But Twain was more Southern than Western, and the Brooks–De Voto controversy can be solved by the clear recognition that Twain's greatest book could only have been written by a man who had come *from* a Southwestern small town *to* the cities of the Northeast. Only a man who had lived in the South could have so beautifully recreated the slave-holding culture of the Mississippi River, giving full value to its dense texture; only a man with "Northern" sympathies concerning slavery could have so harshly judged the region on moral and intellectual grounds. Crippling though Twain's background may have been, his best, as well as his worst, work is inconceivable without it. Equally inconceivable is that Twain's genius could have flowered had he remained in the South. Twain's complex perspective is essential to his greatness: an antislavery (Twain had accepted slavery without much question in his youth) former Southerner writing about a region remembered with immense nostalgia and immense contempt. One might summarize these dichotomies by noting that Twain somehow combines the Northern liberal and Southern agrarian points of view. Twain's career both proves and disproves Van Wyck Brooks's case against American culture. Almost all of the negations Brooks saw did, indeed, exert a malign influence on Twain, but Twain and his culture together produced *Huckleberry Finn.*

Before writing the almost flawless satire *The Adventures of Huckleberry Finn,* Twain had written the almost flawless example of reassuring humor, *The Adventures of Tom Sawyer.* To say this is in no way to deny that Tom Sawyer is a small classic, a book of great charm, but it is a *small* classic, its charm dependent on its unreality. It is essentially an escapist book, an escape from adult society, and thus one that makes no real judgments, offers no genuine strictures. It rather affectionately and complacently indulges the quirks and foibles of the village of St. Petersburg, which if "poor" and "shabby" is also "bright and fresh and brimming with life" and offers a vista "dreamy, reposeful, and inviting." [20] There is some satire, but none of the subjects of satire are anything Twain's middle-class readers had a real stake in; the humor is rather a nostalgic remembrance of the shared-in absurdities of the writer's and reader's presumed common past. The congregation's response to the minister's weird hymn style is an example: "He was regarded as a wonderful reader. At church 'sociables' he was always called upon to read poetry; and when he was through, the ladies would lift up their hands and let them fall helplessly in their laps, and 'wall' their eyes, and shake their heads, as much as to say, 'words cannot express it; it it is too beautiful, *too* beautiful for the mortal earth' " (45). This is a sharp and witty observation. It is also harmless humor, just as its target is *harmless* affectation. More aggressive is the assault on the sentimental citizens who had petitioned the governor to pardon Injun Joe: "Many tearful and eloquent meetings had been held, and a committee of sappy women been appointed to go in deep mourning and wail around the governor, and implore him to be a merciful ass and trample his duty under foot. Injun Joe was believed to have killed five citizens of the village, but what of that? If he had been Satan himself there would have been plenty of weaklings ready to scribble their names to a pardon petition and drip a tear on it from their permanently impaired and leaky waterworks" (269–70). This has, of course, all the courage and satirical energy of the usual editorial page. As Van Wyck Brooks put it, "If the real prophet is he who attacks the stultifying illusions of mankind, nothing, on the other hand, makes one so popular as to be the moral denouncer of what everybody else denounces." [21] The villain of the book is a monstrous outsider, Injun Joe, and with his death, the village is again at peace, for it has no internal oppositions or morbidities.

True, there is some childhood rebellion in this village. Against what? The restraint of "whole clothes and cleanliness" that galls Tom Sawyer of a Sunday. And Tom Sawyer, as Leslie Fiedler and Dwight Macdonald have pointed out, is the adult's idea of the perfect good-bad boy, not so good as to be a sissy but basically a conformist beneath all his rebellions and whose very limited badness actually fulfills adult expectations of what a boy should be.[22]

Much of this brand of humor, to be sure, carries over into

Huck Finn. But *Huck Finn* is *in toto* genuine and very powerful satire. Indeed, even some of the carry-over from *Tom Sawyer* is qualitatively changed by its reappearance in *Huck Finn*. Even the seemingly superficial humor of Huck's complaints about the cramping effects of "civilized" clothing and manners becomes symbolic of an effective root critique of society in *Huck Finn*. Clothes there symbolize the cramping effects of custom and conformity, subservience to which Twain sees as the universal human slavery. As Henry Nash Smith demonstrated, if the basic metaphor of the book is Negro slavery, the basic idea is universal human slavery. As in the later writings of Mencken, Lewis, and Stribling, humanity is enslaved by the mind-forged manacles of conventional ideas and customary practices: "Customs are not enacted, they grow gradually up, imperceptibly and unconsciously, like an oak from its seed. In the fullness of their strength they can stand up straight in front of a world of argument and reasoning, and yield not an inch. . . . Custom is custom; it is built of brass, boiler iron, granite; facts, reasonings, arguments have no more effect upon it than the idle winds have upon Gibralter." [23]

Twain knew that two logically contradictory ideas can be maintained without conflict if both are based on convention. Thus, in the Grangerford-Shepherdson episode, two feuding families attend the same church, hear and approve a sermon on brotherly love, then go back to fighting. Religion is one convention, feuding another. Ideas and ideals exist in compartments without reference to each other or to reality. Only Kentucky hogs find pragmatic values in church: "there warn't anybody at the church, except maybe a hog or two, for there warn't any lock on the door, and hogs like a puncheon floor in summer-time because its cool. If you notice, most folks don't go to church only when they've got to; but a hog is different." [24] The inertia of custom may be comic but it leads to pure horror: "All of a sudden, bang! bang! bang!

goes three or four guns—the men had slipped round
through the woods and come in from behind without their
horses! The boys jumped for the river—both of them hurt
—and as they swum down the current the men run along the
bank shooting at them and singing out, 'Kill them, kill
them!' " (154). The ultimate revelation of custom: "Kill
them, kill them!" As Huck and Jim escape, "We said there
warn't no home like a raft, after all. The other places do
seem so cramped up and smothery . . ." (156).

On the universal level the Grangerford-Shepherdson feud
is a criticism of mental inertia and slavery to convention. On
a more particular level, it is a criticism of the South, "a
tissue-cuticled semi-barbarism which set itself up for a lofty
civilization." [25] The feuding Grangerfords are not illiterate
backwoods people but affluent and pretentious slaveholders.
Moreover, although *Huckleberry Finn* is set in the 1840's,
Twain's attack is as much on the South of the eighties as on
the ante-bellum South. Louis Budd points out that Republican newspapers of the eighties began to play up Southern
feuds and homicides for political purposes. The Boggs-Sherburn episode takes place in Arkansas, which, as Budd notes,
became a favorite target for the Republicans because it remained as unreconstructed as other former rebel states while
lacking their aura of plantation-myth glamour. [26]

As the Boggs-Sherburn episode proceeds, Twain again
moves from the topical to the universal, from small-town
Southern loafers to the "god damned human race." The town
itself is an exactly described Southern slum: "The stores and
houses was most all old, shackly, dried-up frame concerns
that hadn't ever been painted. . . . The houses had little
gardens around them, but they didn't seem to raise hardly
anything in them but jimpson weeds, and sunflowers, and
ashpiles, and old curled-up boots and shoes, and pieces of
bottles, and rags, and played-out tin-ware" (181).

Nothing could be more particularized: this is Arkansas in

the 1840's (modern improvements would be old tires and rusting car bodies added to the other front yard ornaments). But in the aftermath of Sherburn's shooting down of Boggs, human qualities are unmasked which are as universal as human nature itself:

One long lanky man, with long hair and a big white fur stove-pipe hat on the back of his head, and a crooked-handled cane, marked out the places on the ground where Boggs stood, and where Sherburn stood, and the people following him around from one place to t'other and watching everything he done, and bobbing their heads to show they understood, and stooping a little and resting their hands on their thighs to watch him mark the places on the ground with his cane; and then he stood up straight and stiff where Sherburn had stood, frowning and having his hat-brim down over his eyes, and sung out, "Boggs!" and then fetched his cane down slow to a level and says "Bang!" and then staggered backwards, says "Bang!" again, and fell down flat on his back. The people that had seen the thing said he done it perfect; said it was exactly the way it all happened. Then as much as a dozen people got out their bottles and treated him (188).

The satire here is on generalized human nature. Twain brilliantly reveals the terrible human fascination with sensational events and vicarious experiences of violence. The observation is painful. In the lanky man's recreation of violence, we cannot fail to recognize universal human qualities; the people in the crowd bob their heads to show understanding; they were there, they saw it, they confirm their importance. Twain himself tells us with haunted exactness the details of the killing, reliving the traumatic experience of witnessing Frank Owsley's killing of Sam Smarr in Hannibal, Missouri, a murder that occurred when Twain was nine years old. Of course, there are qualitative differences in the universal fascination with violence that Twain himself, like his characters, reflects. The lanky man is frivolous and insensitive, whereas Twain himself brings complex emotions and a moral vision to bear on both the murder and its compulsive re-enactment. For Twain and his reader the murder is a traumatic visitation, a morally significant event, rather than merely the God-granted temporary thrill experienced by the lanky man and his audience.

In *Tom Sawyer,* horror is a melodramatic and external threat to the peace of the village; in *Huckleberry Finn* it is a commonplace, (intentionally) banal internal component of the village. But more horrifying than Bricksville is the pervasive atmosphere of a slave culture. Like all satirists and humorists, Twain's theme was incongruity, and where could more incongruities be found than in the combination of genteel middle-class democracy with chattel slavery? Twain had no need to search out material:

As I have said, we lived in a slaveholding community; indeed, when slavery perished, my mother had been in daily touch with it for sixty years. Yet, kind-hearted and compassionate as she was, I think she was not conscious that slavery was a bald, grotesque, and unwarrantable usurpation. She had never heard it assailed in any pulpit, but had heard it defended and sanctified in a thousand; her ears were familiar with Bible texts that approved it, but if there were any that disapproved it they had not been quoted by her pastors; as far as her experience went the wise and good and the holy were unanimous in the conviction that slavery was right, righteous, sacred, the peculiar pet of the Deity and a condition which the slave himself ought to be daily and nightly thankful for. Manifestly, training and association can accomplish strange miracles.[27]

In Henry Nash Smith's brilliant essay on *Huckleberry Finn,* he points out that even Huck has no *intellectual* objections to slavery. *Huckleberry Finn,* as Twain himself said, was a book "where a sound heart and a deformed conscience come into collision and conscience suffers defeat." [28] Huck's "conscience" is thoroughly conventional and speaks always in the clichés of the Southern protestant rhetoric which are the only abstract moral precepts he knows. At one point, Huck's conscience nearly drives him to betray Jim, but a series of images of their trip down the river come into his mind and prove irresistible. Heart and imagination overcome the cultural super-ego, and Huck, in full belief that he is doing evil, decides to chance Hell. Paradoxically, it is the romantic imaginative associations of the very Southern river down which slaves were sent that enriches Huck Finn's consciousness to the point that he is able to disobey the community superego. What could better demonstrate the ambiguities of Twain's relation to Southwestern culture?

If, in *Huckleberry Finn,* the society-molded conscience speaks in clichés, the imagination speaks in the poetry of the vernacular, a poetry that varies between the satirical and the romantic. The imaginative texture of Huck's language becomes Twain's method for both unmasking the fake and revealing the authentic. None of Twain's fiction after *Huckleberry Finn* has such depth and beauty of texture. *Puddn'head Wilson* (1894) has an effective theme that the plot sometimes brilliantly supports and sometimes seems to disremember, but it has almost no texture at all. Twain's description of Bricksville in *Huckleberry Finn* uses physical shabbiness as a symbol of moral shabbiness, but there is also a textural succulence in Bricksville's shabbiness, a delight in the grittiness of immediate reality, this charm of texture being one of the qualities that makes *Huckleberry Finn* a romance as well as a satire. In *Puddn'head Wilson,* the description of Dawson's Landing is entirely at the service of satirical unmasking; there is not the slightest element of the romantic nostalgia that complicated and enriched other Twain works.[30] The houses are described as "snug," "whitewashed," and "pretty"; the town is "sleepy and comfortable and contented."[31] But these qualities are the town's facade; its reality is that "Dawson's Landing was a slaveholding town."

(13) Not that the townspeople are consciously hypocritical; they are quite "innocent" of the notion that slaveholding is any degree immoral. It is just this entirely "innocent" complicity in a vast structural social evil that is the main target of Twain's satire. It is the town's very acceptance of slavery as something unquestionably natural and right, an institution based on absolute and innate differences between two unmixable races that allows it to be duped by the substitution of a Negro baby for a white one. The switch subverts the official Southern slaveholding version of reality on two grounds: (1) A Negro brought up as a white will easily pass for one if he physically appears white, this demonstrating that race differences are cultural not biological. (2) Some Negroes can physically pass for whites because genetically they are mostly white, this affirming the officially denied reality of race mixing. Twain sardonically plays on blood lines in the names of his central characters, York Leicester Driscoll, Pembroke Howard, and Percy Northumberland Driscoll, all of whom uphold an ideal of gentlemanliness associated with their F.F.V. ancestry, the blackly humorous joke of the book being that the switched Negro legitimately makes the same claim in his *true* identity as well as his false since he is in fact the result of "miscegenation" between the one-sixteenth Negro slave Roxana and Cecil Burleigh Essex, F.F.V. The book then shows these structural realities of Southern small-town culture: (1) Innocence (i.e., moral unawareness) is really the worst form of guilt. (2) Social identity is a purely arbitrary convention.

Needless to say, the delusions of small-town identity do not apply merely to the slaveholding South; the slaveholding South merely provides the most striking symbol for Twain's fable of identity. Indeed, the main weakness in the story comes when Twain tries to juice up his geometrically abstract fable with dialect or humorous digression. Twain's language in *Puddn'head Wilson* has become most convincing when most bare and direct; satirical bitterness has so replaced romantic sensuous immediacy and indulgent humor that attempts at the latter invariably ring false.

"The Man That Corrupted Hadleyburg" (1899) is better written than *Puddn'head Wilson* precisely because it has less local texture; the town might be in the Midwest or the Southwest. There is little physical description of the town, and the characters never speak in dialect. Twain's imagination no longer functions in this way. "The Man That Corrupted Hadleyburg" is a fable and its abstractness is proper to its form. If there has been a loss of sensuous immediacy and richness of complication from Twain's depiction of the small town, there has been a gain in sardonic ferocity and unmasking perceptiveness that shows in yet another devastating treatment of small town "innocence."

The substance of the fable is condensed in Twain's characterization of the Richardses. This old couple, still in love with each other, is the very image of small-town sweetness. Under one name or another, they still turn up in Hollywood's or television's periodic outpourings of sentimentality about the "vanished America," usually cast in the role of benevolent grandparents. The Richards stereotype, in fact, represents one of our culture's various substitutes for morality. Instead of facing a social problem directly, recourse is had to the values represented by good, simple old people in a country town. But Twain knows well that the Richardses and their small town are a negation; theirs is a fugitive and cloistered virtue, protected by its insulation from experience. They are good because of what they *do not* do. The temptation such people are open to is the greed for money, and this temptation becomes well nigh irresistible if it is certain that a dishonest act is safe, that none of the neighbors will know. For public opinion is the secret ruler of the small town.

The Richardses are completely unmasked when they discuss Reverend Burgess, about whose name hangs an undefined aura of scandal. First, Mrs. Richards enjoys herself by being indignantly moral about Burgess' supposed misdeeds, and then she is dumbfounded when her husband admits that he knows Burgess to be innocent but was never man enough to face the wrath of the town by defending its scapegoat. Mrs. Richards now finds it necessary to stumble her way through feeble rationalizations: "One mustn't—er—public opinion—one has to be so careful—so—" [32] Even more revealing is her response to Mr. Richards' assurance that Burgess does not know that Richards could have saved him:

"Oh," exclaimed the wife, in a tone of relief, "I am glad of that. As long as he doesn't know that you could have saved him, he—he—well, that makes it a great deal better. Why, I might have known he didn't know, because he is always trying to be friendly with us, as little encouragement as we give him. More than once people have twitted me with it. There's the Wilsons and the Wilcoxes, and the Harknesses, they take a mean pleasure in saying, *"Your friend* Burgess," because they know it pesters me. I wish he wouldn't persist in liking us so . . ." (11).

Mrs. Richards' hesitations in her first sentence show her unwillingness to admit even to herself that her moral code is mere public opinion. Her final sentence completely unmasks her. Later, the Richardses receive a letter that purports to supply the sentence that is the key to the forty-thousand-dollar sack; "YOU ARE FAR FROM BEING A BAD MAN: GO, AND REFORM" (26). The Richardses' response to their supposed good fortune is captured with deadly satire: "It was a happy half-hour that the couple spent there on the settee caressing each other; it was the old days come again—days that had begun with their courtship and lasted without a break till the stranger brought the deadly money." What could be more satisfying to American sentimentalities? A simple, fine, unpretentious old couple, still in love. No George and Martha here! But we remember that the old couple's happiness is newly based on forty thousand dollars.

The writer of the letter claims that the golden phrase had been said by the late Goodson; the writer is passing it on to

Mr. Richards because Goodson said "you—I *think* he said you —am almost sure—had done him a very great service once, possibly without knowing the full value of it. . . ." The vagueness of the letter is satanically calculated to set poor Richards' rationalization mill going, in search of the nonexistent service:

It had to be a service which he had rendered "possibly without knowing the full value of it." Why, really, that ought to be an easy hunt. . . . And sure enough, by-and-by he found it. Goodson, years and years ago, came near marrying a very sweet and pretty girl, named Nancy Hewitt, but in some way or other the match had been broken off; the girl died, Goodson remained a bachelor, and by-and-by became a soured one and a frank despiser of the human species. Soon after the girl's death the village found out, or thought it had found out, that she carried a spoonful of Negro blood in her veins. Richards worked at these details a good while, and in the end he thought he remembered things concerning them which must have gotten mislaid in his memory through long neglect. He seemed to dimly remember that it was *he* that found out about the Negro blood; that it was he that told the village; that the village told Goodson where they got it; that he thus saved Goodson from marrying the tainted girl . . . (32–33).

A. C. Spectorsky tells of a party game that grew up in the suburbs in the 1950's. "It" was told that, while "It" was out of the room, the company would make up an outlandish story that "It" was to try to piece out through asking leading questions. Actually the company will answer *"no"* to any question ending in a consonant, *"yes"* to any question ending in a vowel, and *"maybe"* to a question ending in *y*. "It," then, is forced to make up a story that unknowingly discloses unconscious fantasies by free association. "Once there was a girl from whose unconscious appeared a story about a circus-train which was wrecked and spewed forth freaks who raped all the women living in houses beside the railroad track. When she was told it was her story, that she alone had supplied the details, she burst into tears and fled alone into the night." [33]

The girl's conventional enough Freudian fantasy is not so shocking. Twain, playing the jokesmith in "The Man That Corrupted Hadleyburg," forces his character into a far more horrifying revelation of the meanness of his imagination. The implication is that Richards probably never *really* did say anything about the girl—but he can *imagine* himself exposing the girl and can imagine its being a worthy deed in the face of a need to find a reason for the forty thousand dollar reward. Twain ends his sadistic joke by having the Richards literally frightened to death by the mistaken fear that their dishonesty and spiritual poverty have been discovered and proclaimed.

The American small town has long been the image of communal virtue and of old-fashioned individualism. Twain's perception is that what holds the small town together is communal fear. In the course of developing the perception, Twain does the most brilliant demolition job on the sentimental image of the small town to be found in our literature. It may seem that the point of Twain's fable is dated. The twentieth century has made refinements in the arts of frightfulness and discoveries in the realm of evil that make the citizens of Hadleyburg, with their abstract avarice, appear almost innocent in comparison. Mr. Richards, after all, is FAR FROM BEING A BAD MAN. But then we realize that the Richardses—perfect images of the conventional American idea of small-town goodness—adumbrate the spiritual qualities of the decent, Christian, middle-class people of our own time who in various countries, have participated in, or at least condoned, every imaginable viciousness and atocity. Twain could not have better revealed the underlying bankruptcy of purely conventional middle-class morality. No later writer surpassed the ferocity on Twain's assault of the conformist mass mind.

4. Willa Cather: The Home Place, Stultification and Inspiration

The first revolt from the village was part of the more general realistic movement that began in the seventies and ran aground in the nineties. The second revolt from the village can be reasonably dated from 1915 to 1930. But, with a characteristic independence of spirit, Miss Willa Cather of Red Cloud, Nebraska, started her revolt early, though, of course, it was carried on into the teens and twenties. Her work forms a bridge between the two revolts. Like Garland, she emphasizes the deprivations of farm life, and like the twenties writers, she attacks the materialism and spiritual deadness of the small town. She has her own version of the two major themes of the revolt: her pioneer or artist heroes and heroines realize the buried inner life of creative vitality, in the one case, by a transformation and ordering of the wild landscape and, in the other, by the free realization of the spirit in works of art. Both pioneer and artist find themselves opposed to the spirit-blighting conformity and mediocrity of the herd.

But does Miss Cather really belong to the revolt from the village? Carl Van Doren did not consider Miss Cather to be a part of the movement that he christened; he believed she had no desire for revenge against her environment.[1] Edward Wagenknecht, writing in 1929, saw Miss Cather as a thankful alternative to the unpleasantness of Lewis and others:

"There is no trace in Miss Cather of what has been called in recent literature the 'revolt from the village,' none of the bitter superciliousness of Mr. Sinclair Lewis's attitude toward Main Street." [2] T. K. Whipple's view differs sharply: "I cannot agree with Van Doren that she has few revenges to take on her environment. On the contrary, her scarification of it, repeated again and again is as vitriolic as that of any contemporary. The American community, whether family or town or neighborhood, is always the villain of the piece. It is the foe of life; it is worse than sterile—deadly poisonous, adverse to human growth, hostile to every humane quality." [3]

Willa Cather's early and only recently collected stories bear out Mr. Whipple. Not untypical is a passage from "On the Divide" (1896): "Insanity and suicide are very common things on the Divide. They come on like an epidemic in the hot wind season. These scorching dusty winds that blow up over the bluffs from Kansas seem to dry up the blood in men's veins as they do the sap in the corn leaves. . . . It causes no great sensation there when a Dane is found swinging to his own windmill tower, and most of the Poles after they have become too careless and discouraged to shave themselves keep their razors to cut their throats with." [4]

In her first collection of stories, *The Troll Garden* (1905), Miss Cather's negative evaluation of the Nebraska environment holds firm. "A Wagner Matinee" tells the story of Aunt Georgiana who returns to her native city of Boston after thirty years on a Nebraska homestead. The narrator of the story, her nephew, meets her "with that feeling of awe and respect with which we hold explorers who have left their ears and fingers north of Franz-Joseph-Land, or their health somewhere along the Upper Congo." [5] Her appearance fits this image of deprivation: "Originally stooped, her shoulders were now almost bent together over her sunken chest. She wore no stays, and her gown, which trailed unevenly behind, rose in a sort of peak over her abdomen. She wore ill-fitting false teeth, and her skin was as yellow as a Mongolian's from constant exposure to a pitiless wind and to the alkiline water which hardens the most transparent cuticle into a sort of flexible leather" (198–99). The greatest deprivation, however, had been the enforced burial of her aesthetic sense, which gradually and painfully reawakens in the course of the concert. The "conquest of peace," the Nebraska homestead and cornfield, has been "dearer bought than those of war" (205). The implication is clear that the sacrifices had not been worth it.

If farm life is wretched, the life of the small town is no more attractive. "The Sculptor's Funeral" is a polemic against the Midwestern small town. The body of Harvey Merrick, a great sculptor, has been sent back to his Kansas home for burial. The townspeople reveal themselves as they sit about trimming their nails, chewing toothpicks, and reminiscing:

"Harve never was much account for anything practical, and he shore was never fond of work," began the coal-and-lumber dealer. "I mind the last day he was home; the day he left . . . Harve, he come out on the step and sings out, in his ladylike voice: "Cal Moots, Cal Moots! please come and cord my trunk."

"That's Harve for you," approved the Grand Army man gleefully. "I kin hear him howlin' yet when . . . his mother used to whale him with a rawhide in the barn for lettin' the cows get foundered in the cornfield. . . . He killed a cow of mine that-away-onct. . . . Harve, he was watchin' the sunset acrost the marshes when the anamile got away; he argued that sunset was oncommon fine."

"Where the old man made his mistake was in sending the boy East to school," said Phelps. . . . "What Harve needed . . . was a course in some first-class Kansas City business college" (76–77).

Christina Rossetti's verses are quoted opposite to the title page of *The Troll Garden:*

> We must not look at Goblin men,
>   We must not buy their fruits;
> Who knows upon what soil they fed
>   Their thirsty hungry roots? [6]

To Willa Cather, in her early stories, the West is a goblin land, a blighting soil stunting human growth. In the Sand City of "The Sculptor's Funeral," the only standard of value is monetary, and the only life the townspeople understand is a life devoted to money getting. The "frontier humor" of the townspeople is really a mechanism to promote conformity directed as it is against all pretensions beyond the practical and materialistic, against any expression of the inner life. An artistic temperament caught in such an environment must either succumb or escape to the East. The effect of Cather's indictment of the small town is marred, however, by her sentimentalized portrait of an artist; Harvey's mooning at the sunset instead of bringing in the cows is pure bathos. It is hard to believe that Harvey was an artist; he seems more like a choreographer or fashion designer.[7]

"Paul's Case," a beautifully told story, extends Miss Cather's criticism from town to city. Pittsburgh is as physically ugly and as banal in its values as Sand City—but with one difference: the theater and the opera provide an escape not found in Sand City for the poetic temperament. If Miss Cather's victim-hero, Paul, has a poetic temperament, he is certainly no poet; as John H. Randall points out, he wants to enjoy rather than create and even his enjoyment is passive. The music or the play is merely a stimulus to day-dreams. His response to art is that of a nineties decadent.[8] Willa Cather suggests a cause for this pathological interest in art: "Perhaps it was because, in Paul's world, the natural always wore the guise of ugliness, that a certain element of artificiality seemed to him necessary in beauty" (231–32).

"A Sculptor's Funeral" and "Paul's Case" form a dilemma.

The native environment is bleak, ugly, hostile to art, but an art disconnected from experience is sterile and third-rate. This dilemma seeks resolution in *O Pioneers!* (1913) in which Miss Cather shows the possibility of the aesthetic sense fulfilling itself in an organic relation to the environment. The "wild land" of Nebraska seems, at first, unalterably hostile to human life: "One January day, thirty years ago, the little town of Hanover, anchored on a windy Nebraska table-land, was trying hard not to be blown away. . . . The dwelling-houses were set about haphazard on the tough prairie sod; some of them looked as if they had moved in overnight, and others as if they were straying off by themselves, headed straight for the open plains. None of them had any appearance of permanence, and the howling wind blew under them as well as over them." [9] But Alexandra Bergson's strength of will and identification with the soil combine with her creative vision to bring about the taming of the land.

Alexandra's conquest marks a new artistic use of Willa Cather's Nebraska childhood. Her stories can now celebrate, as well as react against, Nebraska. It should be remembered, nevertheless, that if *O Pioneers!* is a celebration, it also contains the polemical elements rarely absent from Cather's fiction. More typical of the frontier than Alexandra are her two brothers, with their stupidity, conformity, and fear of public opinion. Even the dilemma between a sterile culture and the need for a rooted aesthetic is not entirely overcome. Alexandra, it is true, quite literally creates a "culture" from the ground up. But the relation never extends further than between her and the soil; her stupid relatives and dull neighbors are not material for the development of a native social culture. After her conquest of the land has been accomplished, Alexandra begins to feel dissatisfied. All she can now do with her land is make money from it. How uncreative! Willa Cather quite obviously does not know what to do with a successful pioneer.

In Miss Cather's next novel, *The Song of the Lark,* she returned to the artist as her symbol of the creative will. Again, as in the stories of *The Troll Garden,* the artist is opposed to a narrow, conformist, petty society. Like John Dos Passos, Willa Cather saw America as two nations, but her nations are the creative and the impotent rather than the wealthy and the poor. She interprets life not in Marxist terms, as a battle between economic classes, but in ethical terms similar to those of Van Wyck Brooks (see Chapter 5), as the narrow and acquisitive life opposed to the creative and the humane life. Artists, like Thea Kronborg, are not the only ones on the side of the angels; Miss Cather also admired two other character types that recur throughout her stories: people like Howard Archie, who are intelligent, easy going, and generous; and people like Spanish Johnnie and Ray Kennedy who are loyal and simple-hearted. (Simple-minded too, if the truth be known.)

Contrasted to these are the more representative natives of Moonstone, Colorado: Mrs. Archie, Thea's own brothers and sister. Mrs. Archie "was one of those people who are stingy without motive or reason, even when they can gain nothing by it." [10] She shuts her house in the daytime to keep the dust from coming in. "Such little, mean natures are among the darkest and most baffling of created things. There is no law by which they can be explained. . . . They live like insects, absorbed in petty activities that seem to have nothing to do with any genial aspect of human life" (34–35). The portrait is not ineffective, but Mrs. Archie is not that mysterious; Freud would have understood her perfectly.

Saddest of all, Thea's own sister, Anna, is the prototype of an evangelical prig, taking her opinions second-hand from newspapers and Sunday-school talks, thinking at length of the wickedness of Denver, Chicago, and even Moonstone, indulging in "the kind of fishy curiosity which justified itself by an expression of horror" (131–32). Anna and Thea's brothers bitterly resent Thea's nonconformity, particularly her association with the lower-class Mexicans, the only group in town that appreciates her singing ability. Thea is forced to an unpleasant realization; she had always supposed "that though they had no particular endowments, *they were of her kind,* and not of the Moonstone kind." But now, "she saw that Anna and Gus and Charley were among the people whom she had always recognized as her natural enemies" (239–40). (Willa Cather's italics.) From the "Moonstone kind," "her natural enemies," Thea turns to the Mexicans, to the talented and educated Howard Archie, and to the atheistic railway brakeman, Ray Kennedy. In a literal *deus ex machina,* Ray Kennedy is killed in a railroad accident, leaving Thea the beneficiary of his insurance policy on condition she use the money to study music in Chicago.

In Chicago, Thea is shocked to find the same prevailing mediocrity as in Moonstone. She fairly wears herself down with hate, explaining, "If you love the good thing vitally, enough to give up for it all that one must give up for it, then you must hate the cheap thing just as hard. I tell you there is such a thing as creative hate! A contempt that drives you through fire, makes you risk everything and lose everything, makes you a long sight better than you ever knew you could be" (458–59).

The objects of Willa Cather's hate (Thea is a direct spokesman for Miss Cather in this passage) are materialism, narrow evangelism, conformity, self-satisfied mediocrity, pettiness. The "good thing" complementary to these negations is less easy to define. Creativity and generosity are part of what she means, but she best symbolizes it in terms of place, her main symbol being, as Philip L. Gerber has shown, the big red rock, variously projected as a mesa and as an old Indian cliff village.[11]

In *The Song of the Lark,* the big red rock is Panther Canyon, which restores Thea at a time of discouragement in her artistic career. Her emotional sources have dried up in Chicago. As inimical as Moonstone may have been to artistic talent, in the end it provides a reservoir of emotional strength through Thea's memories, and her art has organic connections with the place—the usual dilemma of Miss Cather's fiction. It should be emphasized, however, that Miss Cather is not compromising with the small town; it is rather the physical environment that Thea responds to. Panther Canyon provides a substitute source for emotional refreshment:

The faculty of observation was never highly developed in Thea Kronborg. A great deal escaped her eye as she passed through the world. But the things which were for her, she saw; she experienced them physically and remembered them as if they had once been a part of herself. . . . There were memories of light on the sand hills, of masses of prickly-pear blossoms she had found in the desert in early childhood, of the late afternoon sun pouring through the grape leaves and the mint bed in Mrs. Kohler's garden, which she would never lose. . . . In Chicago she had got almost nothing that went into her subconscious self and took root there. But here, in Panther Canyon, there were again things that seemed destined for her (301).

The canyon is like the abandoned village in Robert Frost's poem "Directive," a place where one can "Drink and be whole again beyond confusion." [12] It has the appeal of the simple and primitive: "Here everything was simple and definite, as things had been in childhood. Her mind was like a ragbag into which she had been frantically thrusting whatever she could grab. And here she must throw this lumber away. The things that were really hers separated themselves from the rest. Her ideas were simplified, became sharper and clearer. She felt united and strong" (306).

The Song of the Lark is disguised autobiography. Ostensibly based on Olive Fremstad, its true heroine is Willa Cather, an artist who has a creative hate of Western towns but whose art must draw on the images of childhood. The Panther

Canyon scene is altogether extraneous to the plot of *Song,* yet it is one of the most memorable episodes in the novel. This is because Willa Cather had been emotionally aroused by the Southwestern cliff villages. Thea is not a character at all but a mere vessel for Willa Cather's emotions, the personal emotions and personal prejudices that are always at the center of Miss Cather's writing. John H. Randall has defined Miss Cather's novels as "extended lyrics in prose; instead of the presentation and resolution of a conflict we get the distillation of an emotion. . . . Each book is the dilation of a mood." [13] Willa Cather's novels are built around two dominant emotions: creative hate and celebratory love, both usually centered on a Midwestern or Southwestern environment that was modeled after Red Cloud, Nebraska, and its environs or on Miss Cather's second spiritual home, the big red rock. These two emotions of hate and love are not generally put into dramatic conflict but are posed as static opposites, conceived emotionally rather than intellectually. Her best passages are of description or invective, and she shows no great ability or interest in analytic or dramatic prose. Her books fit less into the prose fiction genres of novel, romance, confession, and anatomy-satire than into the more poetic forms of panegyric, idyll, elegy, and invective.[14] What she loved, she celebrated; what she hated, she raged at.

Of course, most novelists use poetic forms and all writers express personal emotion, but Willa Cather's emotion is often *merely* personal, an individual prejudice rather than an individually grasped universality. This is less true, however, in the objects of her hate than in the objects of her love. Her attacks on the conformity and the emotional and intellectual sterility of the village are on target, particularly in *The Song of the Lark.* But her images of value, even when embodied in the big red rock, become less and less convincing as her career progresses (the exception, we shall see, is *A Lost*

Lady), particularly as she begins to turn away from the present toward increasingly glorified images of the past.

Throughout Miss Cather's writings it is difficult to share her emotions regarding the Nebraska landscape and immigrant pioneer women. Miss Cather's panegyrics call too frequently for a stock response; those who have never lived in Nebraska or who do not feel a surge of conventional piety at the thought of "pioneer" may have difficulty maintaining interest in Miss Cather's novels. The problem is not merely that Miss Cather writes of things outside our experience. Mississippi is a state (and a state of mind) outside most people's experience, yet Faulkner's scenes and characters remain indelibly printed on the memory. Faulkner *creates* our interest in his scenes and characters whereas Willa Cather is somewhat dependent on our prior sympathy.

Her failure is one of expression. Her stories are built around intense emotions toward objects or people that are not shown to justify such emotions. In more technical terms, the objective correlatives to her emotion are inadequate. We are apparently supposed to value Thea, Alexandra, and the big red rock because Miss Cather does—this is not a good reason. To be sure, her characters are supposed to embody certain values—creativity, strength, etc. But they do so in too simplified terms; they do not convince—although their enemies, the sterile conformists, are often thoroughly convincing. Worst of all, they never achieve autonomy; they are mere functions of Miss Cather. The psychological critic might object that the greatest of novelists create characters who are in some degree projections of the author's fragmented psyche; Proust is not only his narrator, Marcel, but also Swann and the Baron de Charlus. Such a comparison only serves to clarify Miss Cather's failure. For although Proust's people have a common origin in his creative psyche, they emerge as distinctly individual characters. They may reflect Proust, but they never seem limited to this reflection; they give the illusion of living and acting in their own right, but Willa Cather's characters are limited to acting as either the mouthpieces or receivers of her emotion.

This is particularly evident in *My Ántonia* (1918). Even Miss Cather's admirers feel distressed over her narrator, Jim Burden. Jim rebels against the White Anglo-Saxon Protestant culture and the genteel dullness of Black Hawk, Nebraska, but for a young man, his rebellion is extremely mild; he merely goes to dances in order to be near the vitality of the immigrant country girls. Although he condemns the town boys for their lack of virility in allowing the desire for respectability to triumph over their sexual desires for the immigrant girls, Jim's own interest in the immigrant girls seem academic. They represent something to him rather than sexually arouse him. He does later have an affair with Lena Lingard which is notable mainly for its tepidness. The trouble is that Jim Burden is not real. Cather does not set up a fully imagined character and let him tell the story, but rather she sets up a ventriloquist's dummy and tells the story through it. If the reader realizes Jim Burden is only a device and accepts Willa Cather as the real narrator, the language and sentiments seem less stilted.

E. K. Brown suggests that "what is excellent in *My Ántonia* does not depend on a masculine narrator. It inheres in the material itself and in appreciation of it, which might have been just as sensitive, just as various, if Willa Cather had presented her story omnisciently." [15] Willa Cather, however, needed a narrator precisely because the excellencies of *My Ántonia* do not inhere in the material itself. Ántonia, the focus of the novel's values, is not unbelievable but neither is she very interesting. Her characterization never justifies the emotional weight Cather brings to bear upon her. Thus someone must be in the book to tell the reader how important Ántonia is; the evaluator must be a character so the reader can at least believe that the *character* feels the emotion although the reader himself is unable to. Jim Burden accounts for the presence of the emotion in the book although he cannot transfer it. The very title of the novel shows the necessity of Jim Burden. *His* Ántonia.

Ántonia does not justify the weight of emotion Miss Cather puts upon her, but she and the other immigrant girls in their vitality and freedom do serve as an effective foil to the narrowness and sterility of the self-complacent Anglo-Saxon citizens of Black Hawk, Nebraska. The real energy of Miss Cather's novel is in her rejection of the official culture of the town. True, the town is no Bricksville, Arkansas, but rather "a clean well-planted little prairie town." [16] There is a curious social situation in this town. The young men of the town are all attracted to the immigrant girls who come into town to work as maids, working to help their fathers out of debt and to send the younger children in the family to school. "Those girls had grown up in the first bitter-hard times, and had got little schooling themselves. But the younger brothers and sisters, for whom they made such sacrifices and who have had advantages, never seem to me, when I meet them now, half as interesting or as well educated. The girls, who helped to break up the wild sod, learned so much from life, from poverty, from their mothers and grandmothers; they had all, like Ántonia, been early awakened and made observant by coming at a tender age from an old country to a new" (225). The immigrant girls are interesting for two reasons: they make a fresh individual response to their new country, and they retain vestiges of old world culture. In their individual response to the new world, they come closer to having an organic relation to it than the older, more conventionalized English settlers. Their freedom is compared with the narrowness and lack of vigor of the town girls:

Physically they were almost a race apart, and out-of-door work had given them a vigor which, when they got over their first shyness on coming to town, developed into a positive carriage and freedom of movement, and made them conspicuous among Black Hawk women.

That was before the day of High-School athletics. . . . There was not a tennis-court in the town; physical exercise was thought rather inelegant for the daughters of well-to-do families. Some of the High-School girls were jolly and pretty, but they stayed indoors in winter because of the cold, and in summer because of the heat. When one danced with them, their bodies never moved inside their clothes; their muscles seemed to ask but one thing— not to be disturbed. . . .

The daughters of Black Hawk merchants had a confident, uninquiring, belief that they were "refined," and that the country girls, who "worked out," were not (226–27).

The townspeople feel innately superior to the immigrants through mere pride of race: "If I told my schoolmates that Lena Lingard's grandfather was a clergyman, and much respected in Norway, they looked at me blankly. What did it matter? All foreigners were ignorant people who couldn't speak English. There was not a man in Black Hawk, who had the intelligence or cultivation, much less the personal distinction, of Ántonia's father. Yet people saw no difference between her and the three Marys; they were all Bohemians, all 'hired girls' " (228). It is this feeling of superiority that prevents intermarriage between the immigrants and the English-speaking people:

The Black Hawk boys looked forward to marrying Black Hawk girls, and living in a brand-new little house with best chairs that must not be sat upon, and hand-painted china that must not be used. But sometimes a young fellow would look up from his ledger, or out through the grating of his father's bank, and let his eyes follow Lena Lingard, as she passed the window with her slow, undulating walk. . . .

The country girls were considered a menace to the social

order. Their beauty shone out too boldly against a conventional background. But anxious mothers need have felt no alarm. They mistook the mettle of their sons. The respect for respectability was stronger than any desire in Black Hawk youth (229).

Later the vigorous dancing of the Bohemian girls at the Firemen's Hall is compared with the utter deadliness of the typical town life, a deadliness Willa Cather sums up in a descriptive passage:

On starlight nights I used to pace up and down those long cold streets, scowling at the little, sleeping houses on either side, with their storm windows and covered back porches. . . . The life that went on in them seemed to me made up of evasions and negations; shifts to save cooking, to save washing, and cleaning, devices to propitiate the tongue of gossip. This guarded mode of existence was like living under a tyranny. People's speech, their voices, their very glances, became repressed. Every individual taste, every natural appetite, was bridled by caution. The people asleep in those houses, I thought, tried to live like the mice in their own kitchens; to make no noise, to leave no trace, to slip over the surface of things in the dark. The growing piles of ashes and cinders in the backyards were the only evidence that the wasteful, consuming process of life went on at all (249–50).

It is this kind of life that is the background for Ántonia's spontaneity. The contrast of immigrant vigor with native sterility and conformity is a trick that Willa Cather uses as well as H. L. Mencken (see Chapter 5). She had a great deal of feeling for the immigrants, desiring to celebrate those who had conquered and to mourn those who had been broken in the new world. The village rebels were apt to look kindly on almost any variation from the native American type of middle-class Protestant English or Scotch-Irish ancestry. Thus in *Spoon River Anthology,* Masters, no Catholic, praised the Catholic priest in Spoon River, speaking in *propria persona* rather than through an epitaph. In Willa Cather's novels, immigrants always are more in touch with both life and art than the native born. In *The Song of the Lark,* Miss Cather had concentrated on the immigrant's spontaneous response to art; in *My Ántonia,* she concentrated on the immigrant's spontaneous response to life.

One of Ours (1922) has an even more coercive title than *My Ántonia.* In this novel, Miss Cather avoided descriptive passages because of a mistaken fidelity to the point of view of her hero, Claude Wheeler: "I have cut out all picture-making because that boy does not see pictures." [17] The stuffy self-righteousness of "that boy" gives the show away; her hero is sentimentally conceived. The avoidance of descriptive passages force her into a greater use of direct rhetoric. Willa Cather's idealism always shows best when somewhat vaguely embodied in a person or place; the direct expression of her values reveals their intellectual poverty. For instance, she dislikes machines: "The farmer raised and took to market things with an intrinsic value; wheat and corn as could be grown anywhere in the world, hogs and cattle that were the best of their kind. In return he got manufactured articles of poor quality; showy furniture that went to pieces, carpets and draperies that faded, clothes that made a handsome man look like a clown. Most of his money was paid out for machinery, —and that, too, went to pieces. A steam thrasher didn't last long; a horse outlived three automobiles." [18]

This is nonsense. The automobile and mechanical devices have revolutionized farm life by making it nearly bearable. The type of person who responds to such agrarian sentiment is generally a country squire living in an antique-filled converted farmhouse (with indoor toilets and central heat) in Connecticut and deriving his income from New York City. Mechanical civilization has its horrors, but the only way to have avoided the necessity of it would have been for people to have stopped having babies some time ago—and that would have been unnatural. Willa Cather was oppressed by the shoddiness of modern mechanical products as opposed to the well-made handicraft goods.[19] When was the handicraft era? We might remember Huckleberry Finn's description of the interior decoration of a fine old-fashioned Kentucky double log-house of the 1840's:

Well, there was a big outlandish parrot on each side of the clock, made out of something like chalk, and painted up gaudy. By one of the parrots was a cat made of crockery, and a crockery dog by the other; and when you pressed down on them they squeaked, but didn't open their mouths nor look different nor interested. They squeaked through underneath. There was a couple of big wild-turkey-wing fans spread out behind these things. On the table in the middle of the room was a kind of lovely crockery basket that had apples and oranges and peaches and grapes piled up in it which was much redder and yellower and prettier than real ones is, but they warn't real because you could see where pieces had got chipped off and showed the white chalk, or whatever it was, underneath.[20]

Every era has its own form of shoddiness. There is a case to be made against a machine civilization, but Miss Cather lacked the intellectual ability to make it.

More effective is Miss Cather's polemic against the limitations of Claude's farm and small town environment. Claude has vague yearnings to find "something splendid about life" (52) that farm work and family do not provide. In fact, so inimical to any spiritual striving or intellectual excellence are his surroundings that he "had come to believe that things and people he most disliked were the ones that were to shape his destiny" (31). His father is not a vicious man but is insensitive and even cruel in his practical jokes. His mother is sympathetic and well-meaning, but narrow: "She thought dancing and card-playing dangerous pastimes—only rough people did such things when she was a girl in Vermont—and 'worldliness' was only another word for wickedness. According to her conception of education, one should learn, not think; and above all, one must not inquire. The history of the human race, as it lay behind one, was already explained; and so was its destiny, which lay before. The mind should remain obediently within the theological concept of history" (25). The mother's narrowness and the father's stinginess and contempt for intellectual distinction limit Claude's education to a small denominational college rather than allowing him to go to the state university. The college does, however, have one good, though unplanned, result:

> If anything could cure an intelligent boy of morbid, religious fears it was a denominational school like that to which Claude was sent. Now he dismissed all Christian theology as something too full of evasions and sophistries to be reasoned about. The men who made it, he felt sure, were like the men who taught it. The noblest could be damned according to their theory, while almost any mean-spirited parasite could be saved by faith. "Faith," as he saw it exemplified in the faculty of the Temple school, was a substitute for most of the manly qualities he admired. Young men went into the ministry because they were timid or lazy or wanted society to take care of them; because they wanted to be pampered by kind, trusting women like his mother (50).

Although Claude remains a Christian, his faith is vague, liberal, and modern rather than definite and old-fashioned. His brother, Bayliss, is the perfect expression of village evangelism, a weak, prissy type who is a prohibitionist mainly because he hates to see people enjoy themselves. Ralph, his older brother, is amiable but machine-mad. Claude finds a suggestion of the possibilities of self-realization only in an immigrant family, the Ehrlichs, whom he meets in Lincoln. The Ehrlichs are everything his own family is not: sophisticated, open, articulate, unpretentiously intellectual. "He had never heard a family talk so much, or with anything like so much zest. Here there was none of that poisonous reticence he had always associated with family gatherings, nor the awkwardness of people sitting with their hands in their laps, facing each other, each one guarding his secret or his suspicion, while he hunted for a safe subject to talk about" (41). The articulateness of the family amazes Claude as he had been brought up to feel there was something conceited about thinking things out and discussing them at length: "It wasn't American to explain yourself; you didn't have to! On the farm you said you would or you wouldn't; that Roosevelt was all right, or that he was crazy. You weren't supposed to say more unless you were a stump speaker,—if you tried to say more, it was because you liked to hear yourself talk. Since you never said anything, you didn't form the habit of thinking. If you got too much bored, you went to town and bought something new" (44).

Claude's marriage to Enid Royce puts him even further away from his vague goal. In a way, his trap is self-made. When Enid visits him in his bedroom during an illness, Claude supposes that her breach of decorum is the result of personal interest whereas she is merely being impersonally and dutifully charitable. Later he disregards a veiled warning from Enid's father about her evangelicism and vegetarianism. Claude's friend, Gladys Farmer, feels sure of what the result of the marriage will be:

Claude would become one of those dead people that moved about the streets of Frankfort; everything that was Claude would perish, and the shell of him would come and go and eat and sleep for fifty years. . . . She had worked out a misty philosophy for herself, full of strong convictions and confused figures. She believed that all things which might make the world beautiful —love and kindness, leisure and art—were shut up in prison, and that successful men like Bayliss Wheeler held the keys. The generous ones, who would let these things out to make people happy, were somehow weak and could not break the bars. Even her own little life was squeezed into an unnatural shape by the domination of people like Bayliss. She had not dared, for instance, to go to Omaha that spring for the three performances of the Chicago Opera Company. Such an extravagance would have aroused a corrective spirit in all her friends, and in the school board as well, they would probably have decided not to give her the little increase in salary she counted upon having next year.

There were people even in Frankfort, who had imagination and generous impulses, but they were all, she had to admit, inefficient—failures. There was Miss Livingstone, the fiery, emotional old maid who couldn't tell the truth; old Mr. Smith, a lawyer without clients, who read Shakespeare and Dryden all day long in his dusty office; Bobbie Jones, the effeminate drug store clerk, who wrote free verse and "movie" scenarios, and tended to the sodawater fountain (154–55).

In this passage, Miss Cather deals with the thwarted impulses of the buried life. As in the early story, "A Sculptor's Funeral," we are not altogether convinced of the possibilities of these broken souls, even in the case of Miss Cather's hero, Claude. Once again Miss Cather's invective is more justified than her celebration.

Enid Royce, for instance, is an effective addition to Miss Cather's gallery of small-town prigs. Claude discovers Enid's true nature on the first night of their honeymoon when she pretends to be sick in order to avoid sex. He finds himself saddled with a smug, shallow, sexually frigid wife who is more passionate about prohibition meetings than about her husband. She even separates the farm rooster from his hens! Confronted by this situation Claude's (the unfortunate verbal echo "clod" was not Miss Cather's intention) only response is to have dreams that "would have frozen his young wife's blood with horror" (112). No doubt even the rooster could dream.

Eventually Enid goes off to China to take care of her ill missionary sister, and the novel suddenly becomes a war story as Claude embarks for Europe with the AEF to save agrarian France from the mechanized Hun. The war portion of the book is very bad. As Elizabeth Shepley Sergeant noted, "In her story there are a few smelly corpses, but no profanity, no sex, no rebellion, no chaos are even hinted at." Miss Cather's novel won the Pulitzer Prize because she wrote what people wanted to believe about the war.[21] The conclusion of the novel is that it is just as well Claude died in the war because life had become unbearably degenerate back home.

In *A Lost Lady* (1923), Miss Cather finally discovered a meaningful objective correlative to her mood of alienation and despair. The basic mode of her sensibility was elegiac, and this mode became increasingly dominant in her work. *O Pioneers!* may be an affirmation of pioneer creativeness, but in the last part of the novel, the mood darkens. The wild land is now tame, Alexandra has no more worlds to conquer. *My Ántonia* is frankly elegiac, a melancholy celebration of "the precious, the incommunicable past." [22] *One of Ours* is a sentimental funeral elegy dedicated to the supposed victim of a materialistic age—but the victim is less convincing than the villain. The heroine of *A Lost Lady* is also a victim, but her pathos is genuine; she is the single truly alive and interesting heroine in Willa Cather's writings, the only one who seems to merit such intense feeling of loss. Although Marian Forrester resembles Miss Cather's earlier heroines in representing a world, her world is a far different one from the raw struggle of the prairie. There were "two distinct social strata in the prairie states: the homesteaders and hard-workers who were there to make a living, and the bankers and gentlemen ranchers who came from the Atlantic seaboard to invest money and to 'develop our great West,' as they used to tell us." [23] Captain Forrester, a contractor, belongs to the latter class. Willa Cather explains that the railroad aristocracy used to travel over their lines with free passes; the Forresters are often visited because Mrs. Forrester is the perfect hostess. Miss Cather's description of her perfectly conveys her unique value:

She was always there, just outside the front door, to welcome their visitors, having been warned of their approach by the sound of hoofs and the rumble of wheels on the wooden bridge. If she happened to be in the kitchen, helping her Bohemian cook, she came out in her apron, waving a buttery iron spoon, or shook cherry-stained fingers at the new arrival. She never stopped to pin up a lock, she was attractive in deshabille and she knew it. She had been known to rush to the door in her dressing gown and her long black hair rippling over her shoulders, to welcome Cyrus Dalzell, president of the Colorado and Utah; and that great man had never felt more flattered. In his eyes, and in the eyes of the admiring middle-aged men who visited there, whatever Mrs. Forrester chose to do was "lady-like" because she did it. They could not imagine her in any dress or situation in which she would not be charming. Captain Forrester himself, a man of few words, told Judge Pomeroy that he had never seen her look more captivating than on the day she was chased by the new bull in the pasture. She had forgotten about the bull and gone into the meadow to gather wild flowers. He heard her scream, and as he ran puffing down the hill, she was scudding along the edge of the marshes like a hare, beside herself with laughter, and stubbornly clinging to the crimson parasol that had made all the trouble (12–13).

We remember Willa Cather's previous heroines as static figures against a backdrop; Mrs. Forrester is presented in images of motion. She has vividness and life, and she is one of the very few Cather characters, male or female, who is convincingly sexual.[24] It is this last quality that gives her a complexity denied to Alexandra, Thea, or Ántonia. For this charming woman is an adulteress. The narrator, Neil Herbert, who has accidentally discovered Mrs. Forrester's betrayal of her husband reflects, "Beautiful women, whose beauty meant more than it said . . . was their brilliancy always fed by something coarse and concealed? Was that their secret?" (87). Mrs. Forrester is characterized by "the magic of contradictions" (79). She is, in the perfect phrase of Elizabeth Shepley Sergeant, "a heroine who does not preserve the moralities, but clings to the amenities, and sometimes surprises us with the nobilities."[25] Mrs. Forrester is flawed but immensely valuable. Her downfall comes when her husband's loss of money and illness leave her unprotected. As the neighbors pry through her house on the pretext of a charity visit "Mrs. Forester drudged in the kitchen, slept half-dressed in one of the chambers upstairs, kept herself going on black coffee and brandy. All the bars were down" (138–39).

After the death of her husband, Mrs. Forrester is expropriated by Ivy Peters, a sadistic small-town oaf. Peters is meant to be the symbol of a new and unworthy generation, characterized by pettiness and meanness in contrast with the expansive vision of the pioneers. But surely this is fantasy. The railway aristocracy that Miss Cather glorifies was in reality one of the most blatantly corrupt forces in American life; it is an inadequate symbol of an ideal society.[26] Miss Cather's earlier novel of pioneering shows a prevailing mediocrity redeemed by a very few uniquely creative persons. Ivy Peters is also unsuccessful as an image of villainy. We believe in him neither as a character nor as a symbol. He reminds us not of Faulkner's archetypally evil characters, Popeye and Flem Snopes, but of Ayn Rand's straw man villains, unreal figures propped up as targets for the author's spleen. As a rather openly villainous type, Ivy Peters does not compare in reality to Miss Cather's earlier conformist villains.

Marian Forrester, however, is always convincing in both her glory and her degradation. Miss Cather catches her perfectly in her pathetic rationalization of the parties she has begun to hold for Ivy Peters and his coarse friends: "I am getting rested after a long strain. And while I wait, I'm finding new friends among the young men,—those of your age and a little younger. I've wanted for a long time to do something for the boys in this town, but my hands were full. I hate to see them growing up like savages, when all they need is a civilized house to come to, and a woman to give them a few hints" (155).

Ironically, one of Peter's friends is partially civilized and does respond to the magic of Mrs. Forrester's tarnished grace. It is the formerly boorish Ed Elliot who tells the narrator of the new life Mrs. Forrester found married to an Englishman in South America—a life characterized by an abundance of rouge, powder, and hair-dye but also by a pleasant if vulgar affluence. Neil asks if she is still living and Ed explains that

"Three years ago the post got a letter from the old Englishman with a draft for the future care of Captain Forrester's grave, 'in memory of my late wife, Marian Forrester Collins.'"

"So we may feel sure that she was well cared for, to the very end," said Neil. "Thank God for that."

"I knew you'd feel that way," said Ed Elliot, as a warm wave of feeling passed over his face. "I did" (174).

In *The Professor's House* (1925) Willa Cather returns to the big red rock, constructing an elaborate myth about the cliff village of the Blue Mesa (actually Mesa Verde, Colorado). The people on the mesa were self-sufficient, recreating in their secure isolation an aesthetic culture that is without inner conflict, untouched by acquisitiveness. Their principal enemies are the people on the plains who are philistines as well as savages and who eventually catch the cliff-dwellers away from their sanctuary and wipe them out. As John H. Randall points out, this interpretation of Mesa Verde is probably incorrect: its inhabitants were not self-sufficient, and they apparently migrated to the Southeast, settling along the Rio Grande.[27] What matters here is not Willa Cather's historical inaccuracy; as a novelist she has a perfect right to distort historical facts for the creation of a myth. It is the quality of the myth itself that is questionable. The myth is unsatisfactory, arbitrary, even sentimental. We may all feel the need to make momentary retreats from the confusion and anarchy of our everyday life into an orderly and simplified past. We may find in the past a source of values, an image of integrity, to aid us in the present. But it is well to recall, as

Frost does, in "Directive," that the past is "a time made simple by the loss/of detail." [28] The past itself was complex; it is we who simplify the past by our selective images of it. Moreover, the past, being safely dead, cannot force us to recognize our simplifications, whereas an overly simplified vision of the present results inevitably in some rude knocks. It is legitimate to seek images of value in the past; it is sentimental to contrast a falsely simplified past with a genuinely complicated present. Miss Cather's cliff paradise is impossible to believe:

> But Islands of the Blessed, bless you, son,
> I never came upon a blessed one.[29]

Yet worse, the Blue Mesa shares the fate of most paradises; it is not only unbelievable but boring. Its inhabitants were civilized and tradition-loving craftsmen free from internal conflict. No wonder they went down to the plains and got slaughtered; it is was something to do. In Miss Cather's later novels, she loves the past not so much for its pastness as for its deadness. The great still place that becomes a source for creative vitality to Thea Kronborg becomes a rationalization for a failure of vitality, a failure of nerve in these later novels.

Indeed, the major theme of *The Professor's House* is the death-wish of its protagonist, Professor St. Peter. The relation of this theme to the creative-acquisitive theme is that the motive behind St. Peter's death-wish appears to be his increasing alienation from an acquisitive culture. Louis Marsellus represents materialism and acquisitiveness but he is nowhere near the complete villain that Ivy Peters was. In fact, in some ways he is a more sympathetic character than St. Peter himself, for if St. Peter represents creation, he also represents death while Marsellus represents acquisitiveness but also life. In the final analysis, Miss Cather chooses the

Professor and death (though the Professor's half-hearted suicide attempt fails).

The alternatives are more nearly open than in any other Cather novel, for *The Professor's House* was the most complex book she ever wrote. The oppositions, to be sure, are as clearly established as usual but the relative value of the opposed positions are not clear at all. The characters are not her usual flat, altogether good or altogether bad figures but, with some exceptions, are interesting and rounded. St. Peter is the most convincing hero in Miss Cather's fiction although even he does not quite bear the emotional weight Miss Cather puts on him. Marsellus is a villain who has no intention or consciousness of acting villainously. He is brassy and insensitive rather than shrewd and vicious, and he has the easy generosity that Miss Cather usually allows only her heroes. His main sins are vulgarity and the fact that he lives by exploiting other people's ideas. If Mrs. St. Peter goes over to the enemy, Marsellus, it is because her son-in-law offers more of himself to her than the Professor. The Professor's position is not usurped; he abdicates. Marsellus, despite his faults, seems more decent than the Professor's other son-in-law, the surly and self-righteous McGregor. Nevertheless, as David Daiches notes, "the characters are all judged by their relation to the dead Tom Outland, and that is the principal reason why the McGregors emerge as in some undefined way superior to the Marselluses." [30]

It is on precisely this ground that *The Professor's House* falls short of complete success. Tom Outland is insufficiently real as a character and the values he presents are unconvincing. Outland binds the two plots of the book together; he is the discoverer of the Blue Mesa and the inventor of the engine that Louis Marsellus has economically exploited. The defects of the cliff-city as a symbol of the ideal society I have already discussed. Equally sentimental is Miss Cather's horror at the idea of exploiting a creative invention. Should the invention have been hidden in a cellar or perhaps destroyed after the sheer joy of creating it was over? Again Miss Cather's opposition to modern commercial culture seems merely sentimental and wilful, lacking in any real intellectual justification. Unlike the narrow and conformist villains of Miss Cather's earlier fiction, the objects of her rage now fail to properly justify the energy expended on them.

In my judgment, *A Lost Lady* is Willa Cather's finest novel. It should be remembered that, of the five novels she wrote between 1913 and 1923, only *One of Ours* is a complete artistic failure—an unusual record for an American novelist. After 1923 her career is not so impressive (see Chapter 8) although some critics greatly admire *The Professor's House, Death Comes for the Archbishop,* and *Shadows on the Rock.* Still Robert L. Gale's ranking of Willa Cather with Cooper, Hawthorne, Twain, James, and Faulkner seems excessive as does the general critical estimation of her writings.[31] The overrating of Miss Cather's writings does her no service since the general reader tends to over-react against an author whose writings do not live up to an inflated critical reputation. I suggest that of all Miss Cather's novels only *A Lost Lady* belongs in the same company with *The Great Gatsby, Babbitt, The Sun Also Rises, Studs Lonigan, Winesburg, Ohio, All the King's Men*—to pick a varied group. And, at that, I would rank it lowest on this list. (It is futile to rail against the practice of ranking authors since we all do it, and it is best to do it consciously and clearly. Willa Cather has been too often used by certain critics as the basis for attack on novelists who are, in reality, superior to her.)

The reasons that her novels fall short of excellence have been indicated in the course of this chapter. The causes might be generalized as a failure in characterization and a failure in intellect. Everyone knows that strong emotion is the first requirement of a novelist; we often disregard the equal necessity of a complex intellect. Willa Cather's emotions were strong and honest, but she was unable to work them out convincingly in a value scheme. Her central characters, with one exception, never justify the significance we are told they have. In her essay, "The Novel Démeublé," Miss Cather attacks the naturalistic novel. A careful reading of this essay will show that her attack is really directed against the central tradition of the novel: its interest in society and ideas. The essay is all too obviously a special pleading. Cather attacks qualities she does not herself possess and praises her limitations. The only kind of novel worth writing is the only kind she is able to write, and even she is at her best when she ranges a few enlightened and creative protagonists against a society of narrow-minded conformists.

Out of her best novels, Willa Cather distills some pure emotions. What we remember from a Cather novel is not plot or character but tone—a tone created from her personal need for austerity and simplicity coupled with generosity and openness; from a "vein of hardness, as of iron or flint, that runs through her world"; [32] from her rage at all narrowness and conformity; and from a mood of elegiac lament that recalls some of the earliest poetry in our language: "the days have departed, all the pomp of earth's kingdoms; kings, or emperors, or givers of gold, are not as of yore when they wrought among themselves greatest deeds of glory, and lived in most lordly splendour. This host has all fallen, the delights have departed; weaklings live on and possess this world, enjoy it by their toil." [33]

5. Brooks, Mencken, and the New Zona Gale

The period of the twenties is generally thought of as our great age of literary and cultural revolt. The popular image of the prewar decade, 1910–17, is stereotyped in mass culture as the last age of innocence, a time in which simplicity and moral idealism still reigned supreme in the small towns and Midwestern farmhouses (both technicolor) of a peaceful, serene, and happy nation. If some melancholy attaches to this appealing picture, it is a nostalgia for the irretrievably lost era before the complications of modern life began. But as Henry F. May points out, the period had an essential duplicity: "We can see the massive walls of nineteenth century America still apparently intact, and then turn our spotlight on many different kinds of people cheerfully laying dynamite in the hidden cracks." [1] The revolt against the genteel tradition and the second revolt from the village begins in this decade; in the course of the twenties the revolt became public, consolidated, established: an accomplished revolution.

The teens revolt, which Bernard Duffey has termed "the Liberation," was multifaceted but had a common principle in the demand for individual liberty, the search for self-fulfillment, the attack on genteel culture. [2] Some currents in the Liberation led towards symbolism, expatriation, and other of the varied literary and social phenomena we associate with

Fitzgerald, Hemingway and Cummings—those whom modern criticism exalts as the culture heroes of the twenties. My concern, however, is with the two dominant themes of the Liberation which appear, in one form or another, in all of the writers in this study: the discovery of the buried life and the attack on the herd mentality. The first of these themes was most thoroughly developed by Van Wyck Brooks, the second by H. L. Mencken. Brooks and Mencken are important not only for their direct influence on a good many writers but also as symbolic representatives of the pervasive intellectual ambience of the teens and early twenties.

The major concerns of the Progressive era, still underway in the teens, were political. Van Wyck Brooks, though vaguely socialistic, was representative of a new generation in his fascination with culture and his dismissal of politics as a relatively superficial phenomenon. Brooks and such allies as Waldo Frank and Randolph Bourne believed they had a major cultural mission to perform: the awakening of an emotionally repressed and intellectually sterile country. By their opposition to the prevailing cultural modes, they helped to define a new group that had only dimly begun to recognize its collective existence: the young intellectuals, estranged from their country by its unconcern with creative talent and its hostility to free self-expression. Cultural alienation, was, of course, nothing new in America; though they did not sufficiently realize it, the young intellectuals had much in common with the New England Transcendentalists. But since the Transcendentalists, there had been no large, consciously allied group of American intellectuals in such complete and explicit opposition to the "materialistic" values of their countrymen.

Van Wyck Brooks was the most persuasive voice of what was emerging as a self-conscious "younger generation." Brooks and his associates centered around the *Seven Arts* and the *Dial* saw cultural life in the terms of a simple, stark dichotomy: the eternal opposition of the creative impulse to the acquisitive impulse. All the forces in American life, Brooks believed, were bent toward the fostering of the acquisitive impulse and the suppression of the creative impulse.[3] American culture could not flower until the creation of an environment favorable to creative expression.

Brooks's first important book was *America's Coming of Age* (1915), "virtually the first book to voice the new age,"[4] as Carl Van Doren wrote. The basic thesis of the book was not new: American culture is dichotomized into two fragments with no middle ground. Tocqueville had noticed our cultural dichotomy in the early days of the republic, Emerson had tried to resolve it in "The American Scholar," and in 1911, George Santayana had brilliantly analyzed it in "The Genteel Tradition in American Philosophy." "This division may be found symbolized in American architecture: a neat reproduction of the colonial mansion—with some modern comforts introduced surreptitiously—stands behind the sky-scraper. The American Will inhabits the sky-scraper; the American Intellect inhabits the colonial mansion. The one is the sphere of the American man; the other, at least predominantly, of the American woman. The one is all aggressive enterprise; the other is all genteel tradition."[5]

The sources of the genteel tradition were Calvinistic religion, which had lost its agonized sense of sin, and transcendental philosophy, which had discarded its sense of the limits and mystery of knowledge. The genteel tradition thus retains only what is safe and complacent in the dual tradition from which it originated, having no use for Calvinistic self-inquisition or dark romantic doubt. The genteel tradition confirms rather than criticizes the dominant business culture; the two are related in a sort of unconscious conspiracy. The academic idealist defines "ideals" in such a way that they are safely detached from experience and neatly blocked from causing any difficulty in the "real world" of business. Such academic idealism is "simply a way of white-washing and adoring things as they are." [6] This tradition obviously has nothing to offer to a genuine artist. The best American writers have been outside the genteel tradition but were unable to develop any viable tradition to replace it. Santayana believes the lack of a valid spiritual tradition accounts for the existence of a certain American type: "those groping, nervous, half-educated, spiritually disinherited, passionately hungry individuals of which America is full." [7]

Van Wyck Brooks was less the analytical critic than the exemplary representative of the spiritual confusion that Santayana had so brilliantly defined. Brooks called for a resolution of the split between theory and practice but never practiced what he preached; he called for sharply defined issues but never defined his own terms; he called for context, fabric, and organic completeness, but his own thought was dichotomous, fragmentary and inchoate; he was a highbrow paleface who found himself pounding war drums of revolt. Perhaps because of his contradictions Brooks had an immense influence on the "younger generation" of his day. Santayana provided a cool analysis of the American cultural split; Brooks issued a stirring call to action. Exactly what Brooks was calling for was not entirely clear, but that, doubtless, was part of its appeal.

In *America's Coming of Age* (1915) and *Letters and Leadership* (1918), Brooks developed a metaphorical theory of American culture; whenever one looks for a definition in these brilliant and elusive writings, one finds either a metaphor or a personification. Pioneer and puritan, in Brooks's theory, are our cultural villains. [8] The pioneers were faced with a continent to subdue and needed all of their energy. The creative impulse is always at war with the acquisitive impulse; the nature of man is divided. The pioneer, then, had

to repress his creative impulse in order to turn all his re-
sources to practical ends. As for puritanism, it was

a complete philosophy for the pioneer, and, by making human
nature contemptible and putting to shame the charms of life, it
unleashed the acquisitive instincts of men, disembarrassing those
instincts by creating the belief that the life of the spirit is
altogether a secret life and the imagination ought never to
conflict with the law of the tribe. It was this that determined the
character of our old culture, which cleared the decks for practical
action by draining away all the irreconcilable elements of the
American nature into a transcendental upper sphere.[9]

But only spiritual life in touch with reality allows the free
growth of personality and the possibility of self-realization.
America sends up "the stench of atrophied personality." [10]

At this point we come across a central dilemma in
Brooks's writings. Brooks believes in an "organic" relation of
the individual to society: "The best and most disinterested
individual can only express the better intuitions and desires
of his age and place; there must be some sympathetic touch
between him and some visible or invisible host about him,
since the mind is a flower that has an organic connection
with the soil from which it springs." [11] America, however, is
"barren soil." [12] How, then, can the creative American express anything except barrenness? American experience,
Brooks believes, is unarticulated; we lack an ideal national
type to serve as the model for the growth of personality.
Thus "America is like a vast Sargasso Sea—a prodigious
welter of unconscious life, swept by ground-swells of half-
conscious emotion. . . . It is a welter of life which has not
been worked into an organism." [13]

If the culture is a mess and the individual can only express
the culture, there would seem to be no hope. But in *The
Literary Life in America* (1921) Brooks complained of the
"mass fatalism" and "pessimistic determinism" of American

writers; the writers seemed to feel victimized! [14] No wonder Edmund Wilson satirically imagined a young writer who, on reading *The Literary Life,* "broke down in a wild fit of weeping and cursed God for having made him an American." [15] Brooks treats the environment as if it absolutely determined the possibilities of writing and then attacks the writers for failing to overcome the environment.

Brooks never coped with his contradictions.[16] Thinking in metaphors and isolated impressions, his mind was inhospitable to qualification. Brooks, however, should be credited with the virtues of his impressionism, virtues especially evident in the section entitled "Our Poets" of *America's Coming of Age.* Who can doubt the accuracy of his characterization of Longfellow as "a sort of expurgated German student?" [17] The image of Hawthorne as "A phantom in a phantom world" [18] was seemingly confuted by Randall Stewart's supposedly definitive biography, *Nathaniel Hawthorne,* which presents Hawthorne as a solid, indeed dull, bourgeois. Vernon Loggins' book on the Hawthorne family, however, and F. C. Crews's psychoanalytic study of Hawthorne's fiction reconstruct a Hawthorne who is not unlike the one Brooks imagined. Best of all are Brooks's suggestive comments on Poe: "Nothing is more sinister about Poe . . . than his tacit acceptance of common morals. . . . Edison . . . resembles Poe as a purely inventive mathematical intellect, and with Edison, as with Poe, one feels that some electric fluid takes the place of blood." [19]

The defects of the impressionistic method show up more in what is, nevertheless, Brooks's most brilliant book, *The Ordeal of Mark Twain.* This book, published in 1920, *The Pilgrimage of Henry James* (1925), and *Emerson and Others* (1932) were the logical culmination of the themes of his early writings. All three were studies of the American writers' relation to his culture. Mark Twain succumbed to his environment; Henry James escaped but thereby lost touch with the organic roots of his experience; Emerson stayed and mastered the environment. The Emerson volume came last and really marks a shift in Brooks's point of view (as will be seen in Chapter 8). The *Pilgrimage* was probably, as F. W. Dupee notes, directed at the twenties expatriates [20] although Brooks himself had been one of the main contributors to the idea that true artists could not survive in America.

The idea behind *The Ordeal of Mark Twain* can be traced back as far as one of Brooks's earliest books, *The Malady of the Ideal* (1913): "Life, we feel, ought to be of such a character that every personality can be free to realize itself. And it is only by the study of personality that we can understand the obstructions that exist in the world and the method of removing them. The records of incomplete personalities are thus, in a sense, valuable—they are valuable as precepts." [21]

Mark Twain's life is valuable as a precept, a grim example of the deficiencies and thwarting effects of American culture. Although *The Ordeal of Mark Twain* is a morality tale, F. W. Dupee points out that the terms of Brooks's moralism were strikingly untraditional: "in deriving his ethical ideas from the new psychology of the Unconscious, he broke in part with the philosophy of traditional moral individualists. Like them he continued to conceive society by analogy with the structure of the human personality, but instead of picturing personality as a complex of higher and lower selves, as a Plato or Arnold—moralists even in their psychology—normally pictured it, Brooks saw it in the Freudian pattern of repression and sublimation." [22] This version of Freudianism was, in fact, the basic credo of the Liberation and carried over into the twenties. American culture was repressive; emotional life was buried and inarticulate in the absence of social forms that would allow the free development and expression of the impulses of the inner life.

Brooks, Randolph Bourne, and others of the Liberation

appear to a later eye somewhat sanguine in their Freudianism. Freud's pessimism and sense of moral ambivalence were filtered out. To Brooks and Bourne, spontaneous impulse was moral and healthy; free expression, the removal of restraint would result in a vast explosion of brotherly love, transforming society into a socialist Utopia. The idea that impulse could be violent and coprophiliac could be dismissed as a debased puritan notion; in itself, instinct was basically good though it could be corrupted by a repressive environment. In the thirties, Brooks was to express shock and disgust at fiction that displayed a dark and unsettling knowledge of the nature of the hidden self. He firmly believed in an unconscious that was, if allowed free expression, as high-minded as a Victorian essayist. The tone of the era is well conveyed in the unintentional comic pathos of Randolph Bourne's comment, "Perhaps no one can be really a good appreciating pagan who has not once been a bad puritan." [23] To this variety of pagan one could probably safely entrust one's daughter.

The Mark Twain that Brooks created in *The Ordeal* was the perfect exemplification of Brooks's psychological and cultural theories. Twain "repressed" not an Oedipus complex but rather his creative talent. The repressive forces were puritanism and pioneering, in accordance with the theory advanced in *Letters and Leadership*. Twain's environment was a "desert of human sand!—the barrenest spot in all Christendom, surely, for the seed of genius to fall in," [24] the "dry, old, barren, horizonless Middle West." [25] Twain's life served as an extended proof that "a vast unconscious conspiracy actuated all America against the creative spirit." [26] Brooks's basic thesis was that pioneering had a doubly damaging effect on the creative spirit: first, it had no use for painstaking craft but needed instead work that was quickly if sloppily performed; second, pioneering life was so grim that the pioneers could not face the reality of their situation and were forced to romanticize it. Pioneering militated against both the desire for perfection and the thirst for truth. Mark Twain's true vocation was to be a satirist, but he had to repress this vocation because a pioneer culture could not allow satire. Therefore, Twain turned to humor, which was approved by the pioneers because humor serves the psychic function of leading people, through laughter, to discount the discomforts and irritations they must suffer in a malign society rather than inspiring them to seek to change society for the better.

Ironically, Brooks's theory of humor is itself rather puritanical—which is not to say it is untrue. (Not only would it account for modern television "humor" but it is a plausible explanation of the anomalies of Twain's career as discussed in Chapter 3.) Brooks's case is badly damaged by his own lack of a sense of humor. He misunderstands obvious (and funny) Twain jokes as demonstrated in his attack on Twain's worship of successful men: "We know what [Twain] thought of Cecil Rhodes, yet 'I admire him,' he said, 'I frankly confess it; and when his time comes, I shall buy a piece of the rope for a keepsake.' " [27] Such a form of hero-worship would seem more comforting to the worshipper than to the hero. In attacking another of Twain's humorous passages, Brooks manages an unforgettable bit of critical bathos:

In "A Tramp Abroad" Mark Twain, at the opera in Mannheim, finds himself seated behind a young girl:
How pretty she was, and how sweet she was! I wished she could speak, but evidently she was absorbed in her own thought, her own young-girl dreams, and found a dearer pleasure in silence . . . For long hours I did mightily wish she would speak. And at last she did; the red lips parted, and out leaped her thought—and with such a guilelessness and pretty enthusiasm too: "Auntie, I just *know* I've got a hundred fleas on me!"
This bit of humor is certainly characteristic of its author. . . .

Mark Twain has, one observes, all the normal emotions of man confronted with a pretty girl: he has them so strongly indeed that he cannot keep his mind on the "business in hand," which happens to be the opera. He finds himself, actually, prevented as he is from expressing himself, in any direct way, [!] drifting into a rhapsody about her! What does he do then? He suddenly dashes a pailful of ice-water over this beautiful vision [!] of his . . . that young girl will no longer disturb the readers' thoughts! She has vanished as utterly as a butterfly under a barrel of quicklime. Beauty is undone and trampled in the dust, but the strong, silent business man is enabled to return to his labors with a soul purified of all troubling emotions.[28]

Despite its plentiful nonsense, *The Ordeal* was an influential book, a frightening depiction of the anticreative pressures in American life. Again, however, Brooks's message was ambiguous. His intention was to warn the young author of the dangers of compromise, of the necessity to maintain the integrity of artistic vision. But concurrently the book seemed to be another proof that the American writer did not have a chance. Moreover, in using Twain as an exemplum of failure, Brooks did not do justice to what was excellent and (even more important for the apprentice writer) usable in Twain's writing. Paul Rosenfeld accused Brooks of playing the district attorney against Twain, "stressing only the evidence favorable to the prosecution." [29]

Something had gone wrong with Brooks. In *Letters and Leadership,* Brooks had attacked the older generation of critics (More, Brownell, Babbitt) for failing to "spring loyally to the support of growing minds that bear the mark of sincerity and promise." [30] But in *The Literary Life* (1921), Brooks recognizes the creative talent burgeoning all around him only grudgingly, finding the new writers of use mainly as the source of pseudo-documentary evidence for his thesis of American sterility: "One has only to consider the writings of Messrs. Frost, Robinson and Masters, in whose presentation of our life, in the West as well as in the East, the individual as a spiritual unit invariably suffers defeat." [31] This statement is notable both for the irritatingly bland way in which Brooks slides out of taking these poets seriously as creative artists and for the complete misreading of Frost and Robinson. In his brilliant 1924 essay on Brooks, Rosenfeld saw that he was no longer in touch with his subject: "He is writing for all his apparent modernity . . . of the world of fifty years ago, under the impression it is the world of today; even then, not seeing it quite straight either." [32] As Rosenfeld notes, such critics as Waldo Frank had pushed further than Brooks in the paths that Brooks had earlier marked out. [33] Frank and others were providing the new writers with intelligent and sympathetic criticism while Brooks remained aloof and somewhat disapproving. In fact, Rosenfeld says, Brooks had come to be something suspiciously close to the unfriendly environment he constantly complained of. [34]

In the eclectic atmosphere of the teens and early twenties, Brooks and Mencken seemed allies in the war against puritanism, conformity, and provincialism. They were the voice of the freedom-loving "younger generation" as opposed to such older critics as More, Brownell, and Babbitt, who "were preaching discipline and restraint to a race already bound hand and foot." [35] Bernard Duffey acutely comments, "The Liberation . . . appeared most coherent as one kept its enemies in view." [36] As time went on, the immense difference between Brooks and Mencken became evident so that, by 1940, Mencken had lost all respect for Brooks and thought him "an extraordinarily hollow and silly fellow." [37]

This opinion was far in the future; in 1920, Mencken thought very well of Brooks. [38] In "Puritanism as a Literary Force," Mencken attacked American humor in much the same terms as Brooks. The humorists, Mencken said, joined the philistines in attacking and despising "beauty." And Philistinism and puritanism are the same thing; both are against art, "the first because it holds beauty to be a mean and stupid thing, and the second because it holds beauty to be distracting and corrupting." [39] Moreover, as Edward A. Martin shows in a very perceptive article, some of the impressionistic vignettes in Mencken's *Prejudices* evoke the loneliness and hopelessness of the buried life of small towns with a naturalistic pathos similar to that of E. W. Howe, Masters, and Anderson. [40] In a late essay, Mencken develops a notion of repression that reads almost like a parody of Brooks: "Every one of us has been under the steam roller; every one of us . . . conforms unwillingly and has the corpse of a good impulse belowstairs. . . . Psychoanalyze a Methodist bishop, and you'll probably find him stuffed with good impulses, all of them repressed . . . he may even, passing a public library, feel a sudden, goatish inclination to go in and read a good book." [41]

Brooks and Mencken may be read without noticing major differences between them, but the differences were there. Brooks, Randolph Bourne, and Waldo Frank wanted to somehow bridge the gaps in American life. To use Brooks's own organic metaphor, they wanted to cultivate the American soil in order to make possible the growth of enriched personalities. Seeing a conflict between the creative impulse and the acquisitive impulse, they sought to make the creative impulse prevail as a new collective national ideal. Mencken also saw a split in American life but in quite different terms. For Mencken, mankind was irremediably divided between the gifted, intelligent, individualistic, civilized minority and the mediocre, stupid, conformist herd. The division was absolute, and Mencken's aim was not the utopian project of bridging it but the more pragmatic one of protecting the minority from the assaults of their envious inferiors. Mencken distrusted all forms of social and intellectual collectivism.

Mencken, despite his criticism, was in the tradition of American humor. Santayana had noted that Western humor at least half escaped the genteel tradition. The humorists pointed to the contradiction between genteel ideas and brute fact, but having no real intellectual alternative to the genteel tradition, they interpreted the contradiction as a funny perversity of the facts. They accepted the genteel system but were subversively unable to take it seriously.[42] Menckens' advance on the humorous tradition was that he possessed an ideology, however dubious it may have been. Mencken's idea of a cultural elite was probably derived from an unquestioned conviction of his own superiority dating from early childhood, though he found intellectual support in Nietzsche and Shaw, the subjects of his early books. Frederick Hoffman notes that Mencken had no interest in the poetic and Dionysiac side of Nietzsche; to Mencken, Nietzsche's elite of supermen was merely a civilized leisure class amused at the antics of the boobs around it.[43]

In reality, Mencken's intellectual affinity was less with Nietzsche than with William Graham Sumner, who was, Mencken believed "one of the . . . most underestimated Americans of his generation."[44] Sumner's classic *Folkways* (1913) was an attempt to demonstrate that morals were really mores. A complex of mores shape the rituals that the members of a society unconsciously participate in. A society believes its mores or folkways to be per se right; indeed, folkways *define* what is right and are, therefore, invulnerable to moral criticism. Every society unquestioningly accepts its own historically shaped mores as valid and absolute standards; like the Caribs, they believe "We alone are people."[45] The folkways are learned and enforced mainly by suggestion. "What 'they say,' what 'everyone does,' and 'what everybody knows' are controlling suggestions." [46] Some few people are able to think critically and to resist suggestion, but the "masses" are the core of society and the masses live by tradition and habit, unable to think except in stock formulas: "what the masses do with thoughts is that they rub them down into counters." [47]

Freud's system of psychoanalysis never much interested Mencken, but he was fascinated by any sort of investigation into the herd mind and its folkways. [48] He and Nathan claimed that, in their exhaustive and exhausting list of stock American ideas in *The American Credo,* they were acting as "descriptive sociologists," [49] although their scientific impartiality may be somewhat doubted. The stated purpose of Mencken's collection of national idiocies, *Americana, 1925,* "is to make the enlightened minority of Americans familiar, by documentary evidence, with what is going on in the mind of the masses." [50] In *American Credo* as in his other quasi-sociological studies, Mencken's conclusion was that most Americans exemplify the mass mentality in their evasion of simple facts and their inability to think analytically. "Around scores of elementary platitudes there hangs a shuddering silence as complete as that which hedges in the sacred name of a Polynesian chief." [51] But Mencken's purpose was, of course, more militant than descriptive; he and his allies meant to blow the platitudes sky-high.

The need for such militancy was evident. The sap of revolt had been quietly rising in the teens to burst forth in the twenties. The forces of reaction had run almost exactly parallel, quietly increasing in pressure during the teens, exploding in an orgy of suppressiveness during World War I, and violently attempting to not only maintain their ground but go on to fresh conquests in the twenties. From our own perspective, the Reaction appears defensive and doomed to an inevitable defeat. We may feel even a slight irritation with the offensive vigor of Mencken's attack; why kick a dead horse so hard?

Something of this irritation may be detected in Philip Rahv's interpretation of Mencken as "the ideologue of enjoyment." [52] Mencken, Rahv says, overthrew a puritanical moralism that was out of key with the new economic era, an era of economic consummation as opposed to the past of painful accumulation. Mencken and other writers of the period "rose against conventions that society itself was beginning to abandon. They helped to 'liquidate' the lag between the enormous riches of the nation and its morality of abstention." [53] Rahv may be right, except for his implication that the battle was already over before it had begun. In fact, the very change in American mores provoked a furious but not yet desperate counterattack on the part of the puritans who for a time seemed to be winning all the battles even if eventually they lost the war.

Richard Hofstadter has described the emergence of a new American type in the teens and twenties: the 100 per cent mentality, "a mind totally committed to the full range of the dominant popular fatuities and determined that no one shall have the right to challenge them." [54] As an index to the strength of this reaction, it should be remembered that the Ku Klux Klan revived in 1915 and by 1923, its peak year, was a powerful political and social force in the United States. The period provides abundant historical evidence of Mencken's contention that the American "is beyond all things else a judge and a policeman." [55] A New York assistant district attorney proclaimed "the United States is one great society for the suppression of vice." [56] Billy Sunday hopefully announced, "America is not a country for dissenters to live in." [57] Mencken viewed the wave of moral persecution as a national "tendency to put moral considerations above all other considerations; and to define morality in the narrow

Puritan sense. The American, in other words, thinks that the sinner has no rights that anyone is bound to respect, and he is prone to mistake an unsupported charge of sinning, provided it be made violent enough, for actual proof and confession." [58]

The unifying theme of almost all of Mencken's writings was the defense of freedom in every sphere of American life, and his basic method of defense was to be as offensive as possible. Mencken used his comic style as a weapon against the flood of bigotry and banality that was poisoning American life. The Reaction was emotionally based on the fear of the white Anglo-Saxon protestant provincial ruling class that its status was no longer secure, that its powers to set social, literary, and moral norms was slipping away. [59] Mencken intuitively perceived this underlying fear and hit them where they lived. His attack was directed against the seemingly smug but secretly uneasy pride of the provincial American. His comic polemic becomes, in effect, a mirror image of the hysterical self-praise of the period. The teens and twenties were a period of racism; the embattled provincials identified their own threatened status with the cause of all civilization and saw the rise of the immigrants to positions of status and power as a threat to culture and decency. Mencken's response was that immigrants were, indeed, taking over for the simple reason that the Anglo-Saxons were too incompetent to manage their own country. In fact, he says, it is precisely in the most Anglo-Saxon areas of the country that civilization is at a low ebb:

> He runs the whole South—and in the whole South there are not as many first rate men as in many a single city of the mongrel North. Wherever he is still firmly in the saddle, there we look for such pathological phenomena as Fundamentalism, Prohibition and Ku Kluxery, and there they flourish. . . . One testimony will be sufficient: it comes from two enquirers who made an exhaustive survey of a region in southeastern Ohio,

where "the people are more purely Americans than in the rest of the state":

> There gross superstition exercises strong control over the thought and action of a large portion of the people. Syphilitic and other venereal diseases are common and increasing over whole counties, while in some communities nearly every family is afflicted with inherited or infectious disease. Many cases of incest are known; inbreeding is rife. Imbeciles, feeble-minded, and delinquents are numerous, politics is corrupt, and selling of votes is common, petty crimes abound, the schools have been badly managed and are poorly attended. Cases of rape, assault, and robbery are of almost weekly occurrence. . . .[60]

The burlesque of the attacks usually made on the immigrants is complete even to the use of sociological evidence. Mencken perceived that, despite the Anglo-Saxon's boast of his he-man toughness, "The normal American of the 'pure-blooded' majority goes to rest every night with an uneasy feeling that there is a burglar under the bed, and he gets up every morning with a sickening fear that his underwear has been stolen." [61]

Conventional thought set in opposition the malign immigrant and the ideal American who was not only Anglo-Saxon, white and Protestant but someone who either lived in or stemmed from a farm or small town. Mencken, in turn, conceived of the moralism and mass thought he attacked as essentially rural phenomena. In an introduction to a collection of Mencken's *Prejudices,* James T. Farrell notes "the superiority of the values of the city over those of the rural areas is crucial and central in these essays, as well as in much of Mencken's other writing. He saw issues of freedom of speech, scientific truth vs. superstition, and even the phenomenon of Prohibition as part of the conflict between city and country." [62]

Indeed, the passage of the Volstead Act in 1919 was

symbolic in the counteroffensive of small-town moralistic Protestantism against urban free thought and hedonism. In the words of Andrew Sinclair, the historian of American Prohibition, "Prohibition was the final victory of the defenders of the American past. On the rock of the Eighteenth Amendment, village America made its last stand." [63] The prohibitionist power base was rural, drawing more from the villages and small country towns than from the more isolated and less financially helpful farms.[64] The movement showed an obvious conjunction of evangelical Protestantism with small-town values: "The main supporters of prohibition were the Methodist, the Baptist, the Presbyterian and the Congregational churches, aided by the smaller Disciples of Christ, Christian Science, and Mormon religious groups. Four out of five of the members of these churches lived in small towns or in the countryside, for their converts had been made chiefly by missionary circuit riders." [65] The explicit ideology of the Prohibitionist movement was its defense of native, small-town, Protestant America against the encroachments of the city with its immigrants, Catholics, and saloons.[66]

Mencken's counterattack is at its most rhetorically vivacious in "The Husbandman." In keeping with his usual strategy of reducing his enemies to their lowest common denominator, Mencken blames all repressive legislation on the farmer—lovingly described as "a mundane laborer, scratching for the dollar, full of staphylococci, smelling heavily of sweat and dung" [67]—rather than on the more general rural power base, including the middle classes of the small towns and villages.

There, where the cows low through the still night, and the jug of péruna stands behind the stove, and bathing begins, as at Biarritz, with the vernal equinox—there is the reservoir of all the nonsensical legislation which now makes the United States a buffoon among the great nations. It was among country Methodists, practitioners of a theology degraded almost to the level of voodooism that Prohibition was invented. . . . What lies under it, and under all the other crazy enactments of the category, is no less than the yokel's congenital and incurable hatred of the city man—his simian rage against everyone who, as he sees it, is having a better time than he is.[68]

The Volstead Act exempts cider since the real impetus of the act is against not alcohol per se but urban and refined forms of it; the intent was to make the city man "drink such dreadful stuff as the farmer has always drunk." [69]

But the Volstead Act is only one among many instances of husbandmanly tyranny. Mencken theorizes that the Mann Act and a number of local ordinances against the use of automobiles for immoral purposes evidence a similar bias: "But there is nowhere a law forbidding the use of barns, cow-stables, hay-ricks and other such familiar rustic ateliers of sin. That is to say, there is nowhere a law forbidding yokels to drag virgins into infamy by the technic practised since Tertiary times on the farms; there are only laws forbidding city youths to do it according to the technic of the great municipalities." [70]

Even in the censorship of literature, Mencken notes, newspapers and cheap pornography are usually exempt because they can be understood and appreciated by the rural mind, whereas serious literature is a prime target. Finally, Mencken imagines the rural forces completely taking over and making civilization a felony in their barnyard utopia. "They have tried prayer and it has failed; now they turn to the secular arm. The dung-fork glitters in the sun as the host prepares to march. . . ." [71]

Mencken's burlesque exaggerations of American vices were the perfect counterpart to the chorus of self-praise that the Reaction promoted. Whatever was inflated and glorified —the small town, the farmer, the Anglo-Saxon—Mencken ridiculed in correspondingly extreme terms. If Mencken is unfair, there is no reason why he should not have been. The function of his humor was thoroughly pragmatic: he meant to support the morals of the civilized minority and to undermine the opposition. The Reaction, relying on stock thought and emotional invective, was untouched by the attacks of fair-minded intellectuals. Mencken realized that the provincials were, in general, unable to even understand fairness and objectivity, so he never bothered with either. In addition, his use of comic invective beat the provincials at their own game. The provincials found themselves not only denounced but ridiculed. Mencken had an almost uncanny talent for finding the tenderest areas of provincial pride and then setting a tack under the strategic position.

Mencken's mechanistic sociology was his chief weapon in constructing his dehumanized portrait of a mindless and mechanized booboisie. How real is Mencken's great American boob? Edmund Wilson notes that Mencken's boob is as ideal a monster as Swift's Yahoo,[72] and Lewis Kronenberger acutely comments that Mencken's "style has drawbacks . . . the greatest being that, as somebody said of Macauley's, it is a style in which it is impossible to tell the truth." [73] But Ernest Boyd says, "The fact is . . . that every point in his indictments is based upon some tangible fact of American life, however grotesque the hyperbole of his statement." [74] Mencken does distort the actualities of American life not only through polemical exaggeration but also by the behavioristic bias of his pseudo-sociology. Perhaps, however, the more mechanical aspects of American life are most clearly described through such a method. The method has a phenomenological justification. To the extent that people do, indeed, act mechanically, they can be described accurately in mechanical terms, but this behavioristic description should never, of course, be confused with the *total* truth.

Mencken's humor is in the Twain tradition; some of Twain's finest writing depicts the grotesque results of the operation of the social mechanisms of custom. Mencken tells us in his biography that his childhood discovery of *Huckleberry Finn* was "probably the most stupendous event of my whole life."[75] In his paragraph "Credo," Mencken proclaimed Twain as the greatest American writer and the father of our national literature.[76] Who more than Twain had shown the craven conformity and intellectual numbness of American life? If Brooks recognized Twain's failures, Mencken more clearly understood and appreciated his accomplishments. Mencken even fell into philosophical confusions similar to Twain's. Twain was, particularly in his later years, a dogmatic moralist who inconsistently believed in moral relativism and determinism. Mencken attacked the herd mind but nowhere clearly explained how the elite, the civilized minority, happened to become exempt from the mechanisms of custom and habits. Edmund Wilson comments, "We are not told what makes people gentlemen or what makes people boobs, or how it is that both these species happen to belong to the same human race, or of how it is that we often find them merging or becoming transformed into one another."[77]

Mecken's characteristic deficiencies are revealed in his admiration for James Branch Cabell's *Jurgen*. Cabell's "romanticism," Henry Steele Commager points out, is a variation of naturalism.[78] The idea behind *Jurgen* is that life is completely bleak and meaningless; romantic escapism should be indulged since it provides pleasure and is no more meretricious than anything else, but such romanticism must always be qualified by a tone of sophisticated irony that shows the author is quite conscious he is indulging himself in an illusion and that it all really comes to nothing in the long run. The romanticism, thus, depends on nihilism; it is a romanticism that is careful to always disbelieve in itself. The ironic thing about Cabell's irony, however, is that his "sophistication" now seems so dated and naïve. A Philistine at heart, Cabell was at ease in anti-Zion, smug in his smooth and self-congratulating disbeliefs and cynicisms. The shy pornography of Cabell's suggestive hints at sex (with much flourishing of phallic images: candles, a sword, a lance) that shocked the puritans and delighted Mencken now affect the reader as rather disgustingly coy, but Cabell was a genuine representative of one strain of twenties sensibility. The worst passages in Sinclair Lewis show a similar ironic romanticism, a pseudo-romanticism that might be defined as the attempt of these writers to eat their cake while simultaneously noting that it was made of papier-mâché.

Mencken's own collected opinions were accurately entitled *Prejudices,* for often enough, as we have seen, they were simply reversed images of the sacred cows of the booboisie. Mencken was never able to transcend his over-simplified dichotomies of conformist-individualist, herd-elite, puritanism-freedom. It is significant that after having done more than any other literary critic to free American writers from restraint, Mencken began to lose interest in literature once the freedom was achieved.[79] In 1926, he announced that, whereas he used to send his review copies of novels to the Y.M.C.A. when he was finished with them, he now, in recognition of a more than frank treatment of sex, sent them to a medical college.[80] Even as early as 1922, as Burton Rascoe pointed out in "Notes for a Literary Epitaph," many of the new writers had gone beyond the reach of Mencken's critical equipment.[81] Both his literary and cultural criticism from about 1926 on begin to have an air of premature obsolescence. By the thirties, Mencken's dichotomies no more than Brooks's seemed to apply to the new conditions of American life and the new problems resulting from them. If Brooks and Mencken seemed less relevant, perhaps the main reason was that their most usable ideas had been so thoroughly absorbed.

A new generation emerging in the teens and twenties found that the prevailing forms no longer answered, and they began to discover new nexuses of identity under the tutelage of Brooks, Mencken, and other rebels against the genteel tradition. An even more telling sign of a change in the *Zeitgeist* than the rise of a new generation is the conversion of one or another spokesman of the older viewpoints. Thus, it is significant that, among his group of village rebels, Carl Van Doren included Zona Gale, whose previous appearance in this study was as one of the most extreme of the village eulogists. It is not that Miss Gale was directly influenced by either Brooks or Mencken, but in 1918 and 1920, she wrote novels that were variants on, respectively, the buried life theme and the anticonformity theme. Miss Gale's changing idea of the village serves as an index to the increasingly irresistible pressures of rejection that built up in the teens and were released in the twenties.

Birth (1918) shows a view of the small town very near to the buried life tradition. The description of Barbara Ellsworth generalizes a village type that can be characterized mostly in terms of what environment has failed to provide:

> Village girls, ill-adjusted, wistful of the unknown, pretty— Barbara might have been any one of them. She had waked to a measure of consciousness, had gone on with little more. In some richer chamber of nature she might have risen to self-consciousness. But as life offered itself, she moved in little areas, and within her the struggling new functions, brain, spirit, lay budded but never called to bloom. The old inheritances, self-seeking, gregariousness, love of pleasure, passion, laughter, these she bore. She longed for "good times," for laughter. It seemed to be a physical thing which she desired, for talk as she understood it was hardly less muscular than laughter—a mere give and take of the discharge of nervous force.[82]

Having no mind of her own, Barbara's judgments are the mere reflex of the town's. Her God is "popularity," the idol of the young and spiritually immature.

Barbara marries Marshall Pitt who is even more radically deprived. Pitt comes from those vague lower depths of American life which by comparison make even village life seem rich in forms and manners. Because of Pitt's awkwardness and ignorance of social mores, Barbara loses her "popularity," the climax being her anguished reaction to being left out of a picnic. So far the story could almost occur in Friendship Village, except that no magical agency sets things right in the end, with Barbara discovering Pitt's true worth, Pitt's character becoming stronger in the worm-turned pattern, or some other sentimental resolution. Instead, Barbara runs off with a flashy circus man who abandons her when he finds she is married and has a baby. The best scene in the novel is the one in which the circus man finds he has picked up more than he bargained for as he enters the hotel room Barbara is waiting in:

> He fumbled for the gas, stood staring at her with delight. She was even prettier than he thought, he cried out. He drew out her hat-pins, laid her hat on the bed, and saw the baby.
> "Good God," said Bayard. "What's that?"
> Barbara answered: "He isn't the least trouble—I know you won't mind him."
> "Married?" said Bayard. "You're married?"
> Barbara stared at him. "Didn't you know that?" she said. "Why everybody knows it" (145).

The ignorance and stupidity of Miss Gale's characters offer nice comic possibilities; but Miss Gale plays for pathos, and it is here the book goes wrong, showing Miss Gale's inability to fully overcome the sentimental idealism of her earlier fiction. She tries to mitigate the harshness of her novel with vague idealistic undertones, hinting that there is a larger design behind the apparent chaos. Miss Gale's idealism is soft and its vagueness is suspect: either she does not know what she is talking about or she knows it is too nonsensical to be openly treated. Miss Gale cannot throw off the genteel tradition; she is dogged by an idealism and a watered-down optimism that she can give no proper warranty for in her novel, thus having to resort to rhetoric in attempts to show that her characters' lives are not so empty of meaning as they quite evidently are. The "idealism" shows in Miss Gale's assurances that Marshall Pitt, a nullity if there ever was one, is in truth a great soul. Pitt's virtue is unselfishness. Here Miss Gale's Victorianism shows like a slightly tattered slip. The virtuous character in Dickens is the one who never, never thinks of himself at all. Self, Self, Self is the enemy. Miss Gale's hero, like many of Dickens' abnegators, is unselfed rather than unselfish. One simply cannot create a character in such negative terms and then expect to generate much pathos.

The effectively pathetic character must have a convincing drive for life, a touch of the demonic perhaps, a soft flame the snuffing of which expresses the brutishness and waste of life. A mere loser, a void of potentiality, arouses a pity closely akin to disgust, like one's pity for a masochist. Such characters after all, deserve their troubles in a natural if not an ethical way: they are *suited* to their misfortunes. Thus, Miss Gale's pathos goes soft and rotten beside the successful naturalistic pathos of Masters and Anderson which will be examined in the next chapter.

Miss Lulu Bett (1920) is a slimmer book, and one more in tune with the twenties ethic of anticonformity and self-fulfillment. Miss Lulu is the poor relation and unofficial servant of Dwight Herbert Deacon, an insufferably complacent family tyrant, egotistical, cruel, and playful. Most of the novel is simply a record of the dullness of the provincial Deacon household:

"It's curious," Mr. Deacon observed, "how that clock loses. It must be fully quarter to." He consulted his watch. "It is quarter to!" he exclaimed with satisfaction. "I'm pretty good at guessing time." [83]

Dwight's constant little puns, jokes, and cute remarks are even worse. Eventually, Lulu rebels against a life of thankless and meaningless service and strikes out for her own happiness, a bit sorry, but not too much, at having to leave Dwight in a lurch. *Miss Lulu Bett,* then, is an opposite of *Friendship Village;* Miss Lulu breaks away from her family, shows no need of the community, rejects service to others as a "sell." As in the *Friendship Village* stories, however, the novel ends happily with the old formula of a marriage. The happy ending is not unrealistic and is called for by the minor comic tone of the novel. It is a pleasantly satisfying use of the worm turns convention. Still, the use of this convention shows a final scruple of optimism in Miss Gale that reveals her as something of a fellow traveler rather than a full-scale village rebel. Caught in a transitional period, Miss Gale never was altogether in phase with the emerging spirit, though dragged along without overmuch reluctance by the new current. The force of the current is shown by the reversals in patterns of feelings we find in Miss Gale's novels.

6. Masters and Anderson

A series of poems began appearing in Reedy's *Mirror* in 1914 which seemed a confirmation of Van Wyck Brooks's thesis of American repression. In 1918, Brooks used his characteristic plant imagery to show that in *Spoon River Anthology* Edgar Lee Masters

pictures a community of some thousands of souls every one of whom lives in a spiritual isolation as absolute as that of any lone farmer on the barren prairie, a community that has been utterly unable to spin any sort of spiritual fabric common to all. . . . And yet all the types that shed glory on human kind have existed in that, as in every community! . . . They have put forth one green shoot only to wither and decay because all the moisture has evaporated out of the atmosphere that envelops them. Poets, painters, philosophers, men of science and religion, are all to be found, stunted, starved, thwarted, embittered, prevented from taking even the first step in self-development in this amazing microcosm of our society.[1]

Waldo Frank, too, found the theme of buried life at the center of Master's poetry:

The simple device of the poet in letting the *buried* speak is one of those unwitting harmonies of form and spirit and classical instruction that proclaim the genius. The whole burden of Masters' song is of the burial of love and life beneath crass deposits of the American world. His community is common with all others in that love dwells in it, and aspiration and the need of beauty and the dream of human service. But all is thwarted. Love becomes lust and poison and despair: aspiration turns acid and devours: souls starve, women kill, dreams blight. The silence of convention, the scared cruelty of the driven herd, the Baal of success have done these things: have buried these loving men and women. Now they speak from the grave.[2]

Despite Frank's florid rhetoric, his passage is a precise and excellent impressionistic summary of the *Anthology*. It is not unfair, however, to question the typicality of Spoon River; is it even a representative small town, much less a microcosm of our society? From the publication of the poem to the present, defenders of the small town have complained that the source of the *Anthology* was Master's own twisted mind rather than any actual town. Philistine though the charge may be, it has a very small element of truth. Even the perceptive Frank believed that the *Anthology* reflected Masters' own spiritual deficiencies.[3]

Of course, the *Anthology* is literature, not sociology, a vision of a small town, not a factual report on one. Masters' own article on the *Anthology* shows that Spoon River was based on two Illinois towns, one of which represented to him all that was good in small-town life and the other all that was evil. Masters spent his childhood in Petersburg, a town in the Sangamon River country. Petersburg was idyllic, settled by Southerners uninfected by puritanism. Masters never knew better people than those he found in Petersburg; they account for some of the noblest portraits in the *Anthology*. Lewistown, in the Spoon River country, where Masters' family moved when he was eleven, was a complete contrast. There was continual political warfare in Lewistown between the conservative, prohibitionist, New England Calvinist element and the libertarian, democratic, Virginian group.[4] Masters, as he notes in his autobiography, was in the thick of this conflict since his father, four-time mayor of Lewistown, was the leader of the Democratic, anti-Prohibition forces in the town. Masters entirely sympathized with his father's battles against the "Lilliputian world"[5] of respectable Republicans. Lewistown is the source of most of Masters' portraits of the narrow, the mean, the hypocritical, the politically corrupt, and the emotionally sterile. Lewistown seemed to Masters a microcosm; it even illuminated the idyllic Petersburg by contrast. But the idea for *Spoon River Anthology* was not conceived until Masters attained yet a third perspective, that of Chicago. His law experience in Chicago convinced him that certain immutable types could be found anywhere: the city banker and the country banker were essentially the same. Lewistown could be a key that unlocked the world at large, and Masters saw the possibility of a book about a country town which would at the same time be a story of the world, "a universal depiction of human nature," rather than merely a neighborhood chronicle.[6]

Spoon River Anthology is balanced between two conceptions of human nature: (1) that certain essential types exist and (2) that human beings are the products of their environment. Samuel Gardner shows the manner in which the epitaphs summarize the entire life of the people of Spoon River:

> Now I, an under-tenant of the earth, can see
> That the branches of a tree
> Spread no wider than its roots.
> And how shall the soul of a man
> Be larger than the life he has lived?[7]

As in Dante's Hell[8] souls are frozen in their final essence, but while Dante presents his lost souls in terms of timeless moral laws, Masters' souls are the victims of the sterile environment that Brooks was contemporaneously excoriating. Dow Kritt responds to the comments of Samuel Gardner:

> Samuel is forever talking of his elm—
> But I did not need to die to learn about roots:
> I, who dug all the ditches about Spoon River.
> Look at my elm!
> Sprung from as good a seed as his,
> Sown at the same time,
> It is dying at the top:
> Not from lack of life, nor fungus,
> Nor destroying insect, as the sexton thinks.
> Look, Samuel, where the roots have struck rock,
> And can no further spread.
> And all the while the top of the tree
> Is tiring itself out, and dying,
> Trying to grow (241).

Political corruption, "the dreariness of village morality" (202), and the lack of community are the main thwarting forces. Serepta Mason complains:

> My life's blossom might have bloomed on all sides
> Save for a bitter wind which stunted my petals
> On the side of me which you in the village could see.
> From the dust I lift a voice of protest:
> My flowering side you never saw! (8)

Village judgments of people are one-sided, superficial, conventional, facile; the epitaphs set things right, allowing the victims to sum up a life of being misunderstood with a single passionate self-justification. They are able to compensate after death for the condition of life that Griffy the Cooper compares to a tub:

> You are submerged in the tub of yourself—
> Taboos and rules and appearances,
> Are the staves of your tub (67).

The despised reveal their inner goodness, the respectable their hidden evil. The deficiency of conventional moral values is clearly indicated as in the paired portrayals of Reverend Lemuel Wiley, whose epitaph celebrates his saving the Blisses from divorce, and of Mrs. Bliss's somewhat different viewpoint:

> Reverend Wiley advised me not to divorce him
> For the sake of the children.
> And Judge Somers advised him the same.
> So we stuck to the end of the path.
> But two of the children thought he was right,
> And two of the children thought I was right.
> And the two who sided with him blamed me,
> And the two who sided with me blamed him.
>
> . . . .
>
> Now every gardener knows that plants grown in
>   cellars
> Or under stones are twisted and yellow and weak.
>
> . . . .
>
> Yet preachers and judges advise the raising of souls
> Where there is no sunlight, but only twilight,
> No warmth, but only dampness and cold—
> Preachers and judges! (91)

The final note of wry contempt here is one of the recurrent tonal motifs of the *Anthology*.

Masters found complete expression in his epitaphs. They run through moods of pathos, idealism, and wry irony to sardonic jokes on his father's enemies:

A. D. Blood

> If you in the village think that my work was a good
>   one,
> Who closed the saloons and stopped all playing at
>   cards,
> And haled old Daisy Fraser before justice Arnett,
> In many a crusade to purge the people of sin;

Why do you let the milliner's daughter Dora,
And the worthless son of Benjamin Pantier
Nightly make my grave their unholy pillow? (69)

The true extent of Masters' self-revelation was not evident until the publication of his autobiography, *Across Spoon River*. Badly written, often strangely contorted in its grammar, this book is, nevertheless, one of the most expressive American autobiographies. Masters had a thoroughly personal knowledge of the intrafamilial warfare so brilliantly rendered in the *Anthology*. His parents mirrored the split in the town: the mother, a prohibitionist New Englander; the father of Southern ancestry and liberal convictions. Masters' mother "set out to break my father's will, and utterly failed all her life." [9] His parents, Masters notes without resentment, never cared much for him (86). As for his sister, he complains that she failed to inspire him, contrasting her, with sublimely unconscious egotism, very unfavorably with Dorothy Wordsworth! (20) In an unforgettable vignette, Masters tells of an interminable quarrel he had with his sister and mother, both of whom also wrote and tried to convince him that their writings were superior to his; meanwhile, "my father sat by wondering how he had ever got into such a mess" (134). The dominant metaphor of the book is poison; an embodiment of his own theory of human nature, Masters was both poisoned by his environment and "essentially" a poisoned man.

The source of this poisoning was not only his family life but his involved love affairs. The account of the affair with Anne is a tragicomedy of two mismatched village intellectuals. Masters tells us that in a previous, equally frustrated affair he had felt "cold poison" go through him, building up "antibodies" for the future; "it was an acid which had entered by spiritual veins with which I could subdue subsequent affections of the heart" (28–29). Despite this unhappy experience, Masters began his affair with the intellectual though physically crippled Anne, after deciding, "I should have a heart interest as Shelley and others had for inspiration to love poems and intellectual stimulus" (89). Anne was a remarkable person, having the same qualities of controlled passion and articulate agony as many of the heroes and heroines of Masters' epitaphs. The affair had educational qualities similar to those of Masters' family life; after a quarrel, Anne verbally tore him apart, knowing he wanted to free himself from her: "She could laugh even when bleeding to death; now she did not wince. She laughed at me. She laughed at my paper on Whitman, she laughed at my verses, at my pieces in the *News*. She played bright, poisonous lighting around me; and all the acid in me poured out in increased beats of the heart" (103). On another occasion, feeling him out about their relationship, Anne smiled and said " 'I can cut my heart right out and cast it here on the street.' She made a gesture of excising her heart" (111). It is no wonder that Masters suffered from dyspepsia; in describing a later and equally stormy affair, he tells us that his stomach nerves writhed and constricted like entangled snakes (307).

Masters' own experience taught him the dominant emotions of the *Anthology*. He is the master poet of frustration and spite; of dyspepsia, the snake within; of the poisoned and smothered life. Masters had noted that Theodore Dreiser's portrayal of ruthless womanizing capitalists was not so much an attack as a wish fulfillment. Masters quotes Goethe as his proof: "You are like that spirit which you comprehend . . ." (331). The quotation is the best possible summary of both the strengths and limitations of the *Anthology*. Masters bears out Brooks's early pessimism marvellously. Permanently crippled by his environment, Masters' great achievement was to render and record his poisoning and that of others. Of course, many epitaphs in the *Anthology* are idealistic, genuinely so, and these equally express Masters:

Emily Sparks

Where is my boy, my boy—
In what far part of the world?
The boy I loved best of all of the school?—
I, the teacher, the old maid, the virgin heart,
Who made them all my children.
Did I know my boy aright,
Thinking of him as spirit aflame,
Active, ever aspiring?

. . . .

My boy, wherever you are,
Work for your soul's sake,
That all the clay of you, all the dross of you,
May yield to the fire of you,
Till the fire is nothing but light! . . .
Nothing but light! (8)

The idealism is genuine but strained, intense but nebulous. In his idealism as in his bitterness, Masters perfectly expresses his own limitations and those of his village and his era. He is representative of a whole generation of thwarted idealists whose idealism never quite attained definition, idealists who are best remembered for their bitternesses.

The essential quality of *Spoon River Anthology* is a soured, sardonic, acrid, tangy bitterness that is coupled with a vague and intense idealism. These qualities express Masters and his environment. The very starved texture of his subjective life was the reflexive effect of the Spoon River country. To the charge that Masters' vision expressed his own twisted emotions rather than those of the small town, one can reply that it is precisely in Masters' starved emotions that the small town most shows. As with E. W. Howe, Masters' very deficiencies are the most revealing thing about him and about his world. Like many of the characters in his epitaphs Masters comes nearest to transcending his limits through the bitter honesty of his expression of them. In Dylan Thomas' excellent phrase, Masters "knew that people had poetry always, even if it wasn't always very good." [10]

Some of the finest epitaphs express just this quality of spiritual aspiration and homely honesty which is somehow misdirected or thwarted, not through stupidity, but rather through lack of knowledge and provincialism. Thus, the misapplied integrity and shrewdness of Wendell P. Bloyd's wonderfully comic provincial theology:

> They first charged me with disorderly conduct
> There being no statute on blasphemy.
> Later they locked me up as insane
> Where I was beaten to death by a Catholic guard.
> My offence was this:
> I said God lied to Adam, and destined him
> To lead the life of a fool,
> Ignorant that there is evil in the world as well as
> good.
> And when Adam outwitted God by eating the apple
> And saw through the lie,
> God drove him out of Eden to keep him from taking
> The fruit of immortal life.
> For Christ's sake, you sensible people,
> Here's what God Himself says about it in the book of
> Genesis!
> "And the Lord God said, behold the man
> Is become as one of us" (a little envy, you see),
> "To know good and evil" (The all-is-good lie exposed):
> "And now lest he put forth his hand and take
> Also of the tree of life and eat, and live forever;
> Therefore the Lord God sent Him forth from the
> Garden of Eden."
> (The reason I believe God crucified His Own Son
> To get out of the wretched tangle is, because it
> sounds just like Him) (81–82).

In many epitaphs, characters similarly both reveal and transcend their limitations by forcing an insight into expression
in an analogy drawn from the limits of occupation. Sexsmith
the Dentist sums up the curious connection between puritanical reforms and the economic advantage of the reformers—

> Do you think that Daisy Fraser [the town prostitute]
> Had been put out and driven out
> If the canning works had never needed
> Her little house and lot? (168)—

with a metaphor drawn from his trade:

> Why a moral truth is a hollow tooth
> Which must be propped with gold (168).

In fact, the dominant effect of the epitaphs is that most
characters have found some one essential truth that is expressed with a tart finality. Even some of the villains come
off pretty well in the integrity of their cold self-sufficiency:

> Thomas Rhodes
>
> Very well, you liberals,
> And navigators into realms intellectual,
> You sailors through heights imaginative,
> Blown about by erratic currents, tumbling into air
>   pockets,
>   .   .   .   .
> You found with all your boasted wisdom
> How hard at the last it is
> To keep the soul from splitting into cellular atoms
> While we, seekers of earth's treasures,
> Getters and hoarders of gold,
> Are self-contained, compact, harmonized,
> Even to the end (109).

Spoon River Anthology to some extent bears out Rhodes's
defiance; the most concrete and effective epitaphs reflect cyni-
cism or defeat.

In the "Epilogue," to be sure, Masters attempts to transcend the petty despairs and conflicts of the Spoon Riverites *sub specie aeternitatis* in an allegorical checkers (not chess!) game between Beelzebub and God, the main theme being that the fevers of the will always twist and pervert the aims of the soul. The cloudy epilogue, with its clumsy imitation of Goethe and Shelley, is a complete failure as a unifying and transcendent frame. The book is really held together from within by the tone of irony and naturalistic pathos. This second is not only the dominant tone of much modern literature but an emotion natural to the country itself, a country isolation that gave Masters "soul fatigue": "There was a loneliness in this town and the surrounding country which could not be borne many years longer. It was this loneliness and an introspection produced by the country that gave me melancholy" (79). Not until he escaped to Chicago was he cured of the "pathos of the country" (404). It is this pathos that pervades the *Anthology* and is its most local yet most universal quality. The real frame of the book is not the pretentious cosmic drama of the ending but the homely, sad, flat, beautiful lyric that is its beginning:

Where are Ella, Kate, Mag, Lizzie and Edith,
The tender heart, the simple soul, the loud, the proud,
       the happy one?
All, all are sleeping on the hill (1).

Sherwood Anderson wrote the first of the stories that became *Winesburg, Ohio* six months after he had read *Spoon River Anthology*.[11] In a letter of 1918, Anderson intuitively noted, "I get the notion fixed in my mind that his [Masters'] successes have been founded on hatred. A burning arose in him and galvanized his lackadaisical talent into something real and sharp. Then the fire went away and left the man empty."[12] Nevertheless, the *Anthology* was a central influence on *Winesburg, Ohio*. Masters showed the possibility of building a book around isolated characters who were unified by their reflection of the spiritual quality of the town, by the common theme of the buried life, and by the tone of naturalistic pathos qualified by irony. To this scheme, Anderson added the linking character of George Willard, serving as a further unifying device. But the major difference between the books is that while Masters' characters hide their feelings, Anderson's inarticulate characters hardly know what their feelings are.

The theme of inexpressibility is central to Anderson's first novel, *Windy McPherson's Son*. Like all Anderson novels, *Windy* is structural and stylistic chaos. It contains, however, one excellent and characteristically Andersonian scene: the one in which Windy McPherson, leading the Fourth of July parade, confidently puts his bugle to his lips and produces a "dismal squawk" that touches off roars of laughter in the crowd. Although Windy lied his way to his uncomfortable eminence as bugler, he is, nonetheless, amazed at his failure:

Windy looked about him with troubled eyes. It is doubtful if he had ever had a bugle to his lips until that moment, but he was filled with wonder and astonishment that the reveille did not roll forth. He had heard the thing a thousand times and had it clearly in his mind; with all his heart he wanted it to roll forth, and could picture the street ringing with it and the applause of the people; the thing he felt, was in him, and it was only a fatal blunder in nature that it did not come out at the flaring end of his bugle.[13]

The psychological tragicomedy generated out of the chasm between fantasy and reality, impulse and expression, feeling and communication, desire and potency was to become the central theme of Anderson's writings.

Even more than *Story of a Country Town* or the *Anthology*, Anderson's best writings may be classified as masterpieces of, to use Northrop Frye's definition, low mimetic tragedy, the modern naturalistic tragedy of ordinary people, a form characterized by the prevalence of pathos and irony. Pathos, Frye notes, is the result of the isolation of the individual from the group, the shattering of the individual consciousness on the conflict between inner imaginative subjective reality and outer socially defined reality. In contrast to the self-assertion of the high mimetic tragic hero, the low mimetic victim is all the more effectively pathetic for his inarticulateness.[14] *Winesburg, Ohio*, even more than the passage quoted from *Windy*, perfectly embodies these qualities. The dominant modes are pathos and irony, the second being used as a control on the first, preventing the descent into sentimentality and bathos. Most of the central characters feel excluded from the community. They are bearers of some deep emotive insight that they are almost completely incapable of articulating in word or in act. The tragedy in *Winesburg* is neither esoteric nor archaic; it is a realistic and contemporary tragedy of an inchoate society's failure to provide forms and patterns for the life of the heart.

The literary parent of American naturalistic pathos was Theodore Dreiser, to whom both Masters and Anderson acknowledged considerable debt. In Dreiser is found the characteristic blend of qualities that constitute the essence of naturalistic pathos: pathos and irony, the combination of a bleak atheism with a quasi-mystical sense of melancholy awe at the strangeness and distance of nature (naturalism, paradoxically, reinvigorated the religious sense of nature's "otherness"), and the valorization of sex as the symbolic focus of all human longing. Like Dreiser, Masters and Anderson saw puritanism as the enemy, the creator of artificial barriers to self-realization, but in his concern with the buried life, Anderson shows correspondences even more with Brooks than with Dreiser.

Popular American literature sentimentalized the small town and celebrated the standard virtues, ignoring the tragic potential in American life and reinforcing an aggressive and exclusionary morality based on the idols of the tribe. Anderson's rebellion took the form of dipping below the complacent surface: "There was all of this starved side of American small town life. Perhaps I was even vain enough to think that these stories would, in the end, have the effect of breaking down a little the curious separateness of so much life, these walls we build up about us. I thought of our puritanism. It seemed to lead so inevitably to our hypocrisy." [15]

The similarity in thought to Brooks is evident. Anderson, Jarvis Thurston points out, did not know Brooks's work at the time he wrote *Winesburg,* but he soon found a confirmation, an abstract equivalent of his book in *America's Coming of Age.*[16] Anderson hoped Brooks might find some realization of his hopes for a national awakening in *Winesburg.*[17] Many years later, writing Paul Rosenfeld his gratitude for Rosenfeld's laudatory article in *Port of New York,* Anderson commented, "One of the most lovely things in it is your recognition of my immense debt to the man Brooks." [18]

Despite Brooks's distressing coolness toward *Winesburg,* it expressed much of his own view of America, as Brooks's allies, Frank and Rosenfeld, clearly saw. Frank's best study of Anderson was written for *Story* after Anderson's death. In a Brooksian cultural interpretation, Frank saw Anderson's village as "the deliquescence of an Agrarian culture." [19] The villagers live in the aftermath of a religious, sacramental English agrarian culture that had begun to decline even before the crossing of the Atlantic. If the agrarian culture has declined, its sense of life as a mystery and a mission surviving only as "a beat and refrain in the blood," no new cultural form has replaced it. In the nebulous and smothered emotion of village life, nothing remained "but the memory of dynamic yearning." [20] An earlier but parallel analysis by Paul Rosenfeld pointed to the lack of a common cultural tradition to provide a medium for relation.[21]

Of course, Winesburg society is not atomized in the modern manner of those megalopolises where the pervasive contact between people is an unavoidable rubbing together in mutual irritation. The stories give brief glimpses of hay-rides, county fairs; Winesburg is slow-paced, pre-industrial. Nevertheless, it is, in Paul Rosenfeld's phrase, a "noncommunity." [22] Superficial, friendly relations are possible, but deep feeling lacks forms to enable its articulation. Moreover, Anderson, who was still supporting himself by writing advertising copy, had learned to mistrust abstractions and assertions. Feeling, he learned, could be conveyed only tentatively through seemingly offhand hints and unpretentious symbolism. Anderson's instinct was correct in so far as his own writings go; his attempts at abstract formula in "Tandy" lead to bathos.

The characters in *Winesburg* are divided between the grotesques, twisted by their inner intensities, and the clods, who appear to have a "normal" absence of disturbing subjectivity.[23] Anderson's delicate celebration of the twisted sweetness of the grotesques escapes sentimentality through style: irony and the avoidance of abstraction. Sometimes the irony goes all the way into straight comedy, a quality in Anderson too little recognized. In "Paper Pills," Anderson has a passage of psychological comedy that perfectly employs the devices of anticipation, building up, anticlimactic reversal of expectations, and a doubly ironic reversal in which one expectation is fulfilled but in an unexpected and ridiculous manner. The passage is about a young heiress and her suitors:

Except two they were all alike. . . . The two who were different were much unlike each other. One of them, a slender young man with white hands, the son of a jeweller in Winesburg, talked continually of virginity. . . . The other, a black-haired boy with large ears, said nothing at all but always managed to get her into the darkness where he began to kiss her.

For a time the tall dark girl thought she would marry the jeweller's son. For hours she sat in silence listening as he talked to her and then she began to be afraid of something. Beneath the talk of virginity she began to think there was a lust greater than in all the others. At times it seemed to her that as he talked he was holding her body in his hands. She imagined him turning it slowly about in the white hands and staring at it. At night she dreamed that he had bitten into her body and that his jaws were dripping. She had the dream three times, then she became in the family way to the one who said nothing at all but who in the moment of his passion actually did bite her shoulder so that for days the marks of his teeth showed.[24]

In "A Man of Ideas," grotesqueness is again used for comedy rather than pathos. Joe Welling, the compulsive declaimer of eccentric ideas, is saved by his apparent deformity. He has taken the risk of courting Sarah King whose father, Tom, and brother Edward are the most dangerous and sinister men in Winesburg. They come to visit Welling, but the tension is dispelled when Welling becomes gripped by one of his obsessive ideas, sweeping his unwilling visitors before him. As Joe rolls on with his exposition "Tom King laughed good-naturedly, and the shivery, nervous laugh of Edward King rang through the house" (121). Finally, with complete self-assurance, Joe Welling cries, "Say, I wish Sarah was here. . . . Let's go up to your house. I want to tell her of this" (121). In the final scene, Anderson shows Welling scurrying down the street with the emotionally disarmed Kings who are by this time entirely absorbed, bemused, and fascinated.

For all of Anderson's comic talent, the dominant emotion of *Winesburg* is pathos. The characters are continually seeking to reach out, to break through the walls of emotional repression, to express their inner voices to another human being. These attempts are always abortive, always failures, for these people are unable to define or explain their inner longings, however deeply felt. Their gestures toward sympathy usually take a sexual form that is both expression and betrayal of their primal impulse. Expression because sexuality is part of their impulse, betrayal because it obscures the underlying need for wordless understanding, unselfish love. It is so in the story of Louise Bentley who never forgives her husband's failure to understand "the vague and intangible hunger" that was the real cause of her sexual surrender. Fornication, deceptively definable and blatantly material, obscures the total psychological configuration of sexual experience with a false mask of concreteness. The early attacks on Winesburg as a "sex book" showed exactly this misunderstanding, the puritans ironically revealing their confusion of sex with fornication, their repressive fear of the subjective life. Anderson's stories are not about fornication but about longing.

As Irving Howe rightly says, *Winesburg* cannot be read as social fiction for no such town could exist.[25] D. H. Lawrence acutely noted that the book was "like a nightmare one can hardly recall distinctly."[26] The book is essentially an abstract, even cubistic[27] representation of the buried life, the seed fallen on barren ground, this last a central symbol in *Winesburg*. In Howe's excellent analysis of the structure of *Winesburg*, he notes the prevalence of broken rhythms, aborted communication, suppressed feeling, misunderstood gestures. The grotesques are traumatized, frozen into stiff postures of defence. The choreography of many of the stories is the movement of the grotesque toward the central figure of George Willard and the consequent failure of understanding.[28] But in spite of his inability to aid the grotesques, George Willard, symbolically representative of Anderson himself, transcends the dichotomy of grotesque dreamer and Philistine clod.

"Sophistication" is the unifying story of *Winesburg*.[29] It takes place in the fall, in a warm twilight as a light wind blows, littering the ground with dry, brown leaves. Amid these archetypal symbols of death and naturalistic drift, George Willard comes to his maturity:

There is a time in the life of every boy when he for the first time takes the backward view of life. Perhaps that is the moment when he crosses the line to manhood. . . . Ghosts of old things creep into his consciousness; the voices outside of himself whisper a message concerning the limitations of life. . . . If he be an imaginative boy a door is torn open and for the first time he looks out upon the world, seeing, as though they marched in procession before him, the countless figures of men who before his time have come out of nothingness into the world, lived their lives and again disappeared into nothingness. The sadness of sophistication has come to the boy. With a little gasp he sees himself as merely a leaf blown by the wind through the streets of his village (286–87).

This is essentially a transcendental although thoroughly naturalistic revelation. The grotesques are trapped within the unbreakable walls of morbid self-consciousness. No matter what their ages, they are eternally imprisoned in the agonies of adolescence. George Willard transcends self-consciousness and self-pity though an epiphany of the universal pathos of the passage of time; with elegaic sensibility, he perceives the tears of things and realizes his place as a remote atom in an overwhelming universe and his connection with all men in the democratic brotherhood of death. This liberating insight, inexpressible through abstraction in its blend of joy and sadness, demands someone to share it in wordless communion: "Already he hears death calling. With all his heart he wants to come close to some other human, touch someone with his hands, be touched by the hand of another. If he prefers that the other be a woman, that is because he believes that a woman will be gentle, that she will understand. He wants, most of all, understanding" (287).

George Willard and Helen White sit alone together in an old grandstand, momentarily withdrawn from the stream and bustle of the village. The two, in identical mood, feel the presence of the ghosts of the past and share the mixed joy and sorrow in the perception of the universal journey from life into death:

> He had reverence for Helen. He wanted to love and be loved by her, but he did not want at the moment to be confused by her womanhood. In the darkness he took hold of her hand and when she crept close put a hand on her shoulder. A wind began to blow and he shivered. . . . In that high place in the darkness the two oddly sensitive human atoms held each other tightly and waited. In the mind of each was the same thought. "I have come to this lonely place and here is this other," was the substance of the thing felt (296).

Having attained a perspective outside himself unlike any of the grotesques, George is able to do that rare and momentary thing: break through to the world and to another human being. In contrast to the stories of Louise Bentley and Elizabeth Willard ("Mother"), the diffuse impulse to communion is not confused and destroyed by narrow limitation to direct sex. Both George and Helen feel "chastened and purified" by their shared and unspoken mood.

A disciple of Kenneth Burke's might even interpret the story as a perfect transposition of the classic tragic mode into modern naturalistic pathos with a naturalistic "recognition" and "discovery" (of time and death) and a naturalistic "transcendence" and "catharsis" through the realization of the individual's participation in the universal fate.

In the final chapter, "Departure," the season is spring and the time is morning. The very realization of impending death has freed George into a maturity and sophistication that cannot ever be the lot of the lost but not dishonored grotesques. "Sophistication" shows the completed rhythm, the natural cycle of evening and fall, that counterpoints and places the broken rhythms of the grotesques. Having seen the beauty of fall and death, George is free to attain his brief moment of spring and life; but his most mature realization and his richest memory is of the uncelebrated beauty of the failures, the broken lives of the grotesques.

Part of the interest in the writings of both E. W. Howe and Edgar Lee Masters is the unconscious revelation of their own spiritual barrenness as reflected in the lean quality of their visions. Anderson's *Winesburg,* in contrast, completely renders the buried life, never succumbing to the inarticulate deprivations it evokes. Sadly, Anderson's career hit its peak with *Winesburg;* he never wrote a book of comparable excellence. There are stories, to be sure, like "The Egg," which are as fine as anything in *Winesburg,* but Anderson badly damaged his future reputation with a succession of grossly banal novels (see Chapter 10) and with the development of an irritatingly smug persona of *naif* primitivism. As a writer of short stories, Anderson continued to show sporadic bursts of talent, but as the mystagogue of cornfields, he became insufferable.

The fact that the persona was actually a mask for Anderson's uncertainty concerning his role as a writer is made clear in his letters to Van Wyck Brooks, particularly those bearing on Brooks's projected study of Twain. Identifying with Twain, Anderson felt a personal threat in Brooks's analysis. Anderson seized the expedient of blaming Twain's Eastern friends and his Eastern wife for all that went wrong with him, ironically anticipating the alibi his own Chicago friends later used to exculpate Anderson's failures—that the Eastern group of Frank, Rosenfeld, and others played up to Anderson's role of Midwest mystic and confirmed him in it. In Anderson's admission that he loved Twain for "his very failure," [30] it is hard to escape the suspicion that he is indulging in a bit of curiously premature special pleading: if a Twain failed, how extraordinary would be even the partial success of an Anderson! Both the identification with Twain and the limitations of the naïve persona become startlingly evident at moments: "I've a notion that after Twain passed under the influence of Howells and others of the East, *he*

*began to think of himself as a writer and lost something of
his innocence."* [31] But Anderson's anxiety over Brooks's destruction of Twain also led him to some acute perceptions.
Brooks was drifting toward his own highbrow classification
through his inability to tolerate imperfections.[32] He resented
the artist in Twain and adopted the viewpoint of a judge
trying a criminal—an accusation Brooks later admitted to.[33]
Finally, to Paul Rosenfeld, Anderson observed that, although
Brooks was not born in New England, "spiritually he belongs there and has in his make-up the beauty and the cold
inner fright of the New Englander," [34] a brilliant, not un-
charitable characterization. As Edmund Wilson noted, the
Brooks-Anderson letters echo the imperfect understanding
between Emerson and Whitman,[35] an earlier confrontation
between the theoretical cultural prophet and the all too
concrete disciple.

Ironically, Brooks failed to adequately recognize the real
validation of his own criticism. *Winesburg,* more than any of
the other American books, *shows* the waste and suffering of a
society that cannot comprehend or honor the subjective. If
Brooks continues to be read, it will be as a critical aid to the
study of writers like Anderson, for *America's Coming of Age*
states the values and insights that lie beneath *Winesburg* like
the hidden part of the iceberg. (Again, although Anderson
had not read Brooks before publishing *Winesburg,* Brooks
sums up the motives and frustrations of Anderson's generation.) Loneliness and isolation have, as everyone knows,
been the central themes of American fiction. But Anderson,
concurrently with Brooks's theoretical investigations, got at
the roots of the common anguish in a way no predecessor had
and became the inescapable influence on successive fictive
variations on the most American of themes. Anderson, the
disciple Brooks rejected, was the writer who made such
Brooksian themes as the buried life and the noncommunity
fictionally available in a way that Brooks himself, limited by
some final historically obsolete scruple, could not.

7. Sinclair Lewis: Caricaturist of the Village Mind

Masters and Anderson more ignored than attacked the myth of the small town in their tragicomedies of the buried life, whereas Sinclair Lewis' *Main Street* was a 1920 sensation largely because of its explicit polemic against the myth and its presentation of a counterimage. With *Main Street,* the revolt from the village became official, public, almost institutional. *Main Street* was not only a sociological novel but a sociological event.

Many critics see *Main Street* and Lewis' other novels only as sociological and historical events: superficial and intrinsically valueless reflections of a widespread discontent with old values. Lewis is attacked for the very faults his fiction satirizes: the banality and Babbittry that he does, in truth, partially share with his characters. Lewis lacks very obviously the psychological penetration and the subjective sensibility that modern criticism does well to value. His characters are, it is true, all surface, no depth, but Lewis' talent lies precisely in the incisiveness and suggestiveness of his delineations of the social surface, his unmasking of the dominant middle class. As a sociological satirist, Lewis deserves critical attention and respect.

Lewis' best novels are sociological in content and, to a large extent, in form. Mark Schorer notes, "With Lewis, the subject, the social section, always came first; systematic research, sometimes conducted by research assistants and carrying Lewis himself into 'the field' like any cultural anthropologist, followed; the story came last, devised to carry home and usually limping under the burden of data." [1] Lewis conceived of novels in sociological terms. *Main Street* is a fictional study of the small town, *Babbitt* is a study of the "businessman," later novels deal with a social worker (*Ann Vickers*), with organized "philanthropy" (*Gideon Planish*), and the "race problem" (*Kingsblood Royal*). The structure of his novels is often sociological. The first seven chapters of *Babbitt*, for instance, are based on the businessman's day—a standard sociological method—followed by twenty-seven chapters built around sociological topics that reflect various aspects of bourgeois manners and mores. Finally, the intended and actual importance of *Main Street* and *Babbitt* is as cultural critiques.

Lewis even makes half-hearted efforts toward the fairness and objectivity that sociologists strive for, but Lewis is not fair and not objective; like Mencken he uses sociology as a satirical weapon. In one sense, Gopher Prairie and Babbitt are sociological ideal types. The most general and essential qualities of small towns and of businessmen are abstracted and then put together in the concrete image of the ideal type: Gopher Prairie is the typical town; Babbitt, the archetypal businessman. But the image is stacked, and tendentious; the portraits are caricatures.

Caricature, in Ernst Kris's interpretation, is a form of symbolic aggression: the enemy, generally some frustrating force too powerful to be defeated in the realm of actuality, is symbolically brought low through ridicule.[2] The technique of both literary and pictorial caricature is to exaggerate a salient and revealing surface quality that unifies all the diverse aspects of a face or literary characterization into a single expression of greed, fatuousness, malice, or whatever. The paradox of satire is that the emphasis on surface serves to unmask some underlying and essential quality of character. Satire thus both reveals and distorts through the process of abstraction. A powerful caricature can mold the perception of actual people so that a really quite complex individual may be stereotyped in our vision as, say, a mere "Babbitt" because Lewis has trained us to note only the Babbitt-traits.

Lewis' caricatures, as defined by Arnold Hauser, are in the European cultural tradition of unmasking. Hauser shows that "unmasking" is the basic technique used by hostile critics of bourgeois values. Such varied figures as Ibsen, Nietzsche, Freud, and Marx have in common their exposure of psychological, economic, and sociological realities that are disguised by bourgeois rationalizations. Unmasking is a device, ironically, developed by the middle class and now turned against it; the origin of unmasking was the Enlightenment's attack on religious and feudal mystifications. In modern fiction, Shaw, a thoroughly bourgeois antibourgeois, was the great unmasker with his comic demonstrations that life is generally seen through a veil of ideological conditioning. Having no sense of reality, his characters are capable of denying the most obvious and clearly demonstrated truths if they inconveniently collide with a prejudice.[3] Mencken and Lewis are very much in this tradition, although without the genius of their European predecessors or, for that matter, of the one great American unmasker, Mark Twain.

Main Street is a sociological caricature unmasking the small town. The idea of writing a novel about the "village virus" of dullness had occurred to Lewis as early as 1905.[4] A fresh impetus was his 1916 visit to Sauk Center with his attractive, moderately snobbish young wife. Through his wife's eyes, Lewis attained a fresh outlook. He could now see his home town from the sociological perspective, the perspective of an investigator who views his own culture not as an unquestionably natural given but as a set of social and economic conventions that the investigator must newly define and explain because the popular and accepted explanations of them are mere rationalizations.

In sociological manner, Lewis attacks false stereotypes of the small town. The stereotype of the hick town populated by comic farmers with whiskers is, Lewis notes, forty years out of date. The 1920 small town differs from the city mostly in negative terms: it has the same standardized products but with less a variety, the same social and political orthodoxies but with less dissent. The more popular stereotype is that "the American village remains the one sure abode of friendship, honesty, and clean sweet marriageable girls." [5] To this favorable stereotype, Lewis opposes his caricature: Gopher Prairie, a sketch unifying the physiognomy of the town into a single expression of mechanical and fatuous dullness.

The ideas behind Lewis' image come from several sources. Like Van Wyck Brooks, Lewis was what might be termed an aesthetic socialist in the tradition of Ruskin and Morris. The physical ugliness of the village, from this point of view, reflects its dearth of spiritual values. Church, school, and post office are all shabby, but the bank is an "ionic temple of marble. Pure, exquisite, solitary" (37). Lewis overrates bank architecture, but the spiritual stature of finance as contrasted to church and state is clearly established. As an aesthetic socialist, Lewis blames the ugliness of the town on its lack of a guiding and unifying spiritual ideal—the *sine qua non* of all great architecture in the view of the Victorian culture critics. In Brooksian fashion, Lewis blames the hangover of pioneer values for the "planlessness, the flimsy temporariness of the buildings" (37). The town is a frontier outpost that has lost its vigor and its contact with nature without gaining culture.

Main Street also has the Brooksian buried life, though treated with gross and clumsy clichés. The Vida Sherwin of

Main Street is an unintentional parody of Masters and Anderson: "She lived an engrossed useful life, and seemed as cool and simple as an apple. But secretly she was creeping among fears, longing, and guilt. She knew what it was, but she dared not name it. She hated even the sound of the word "sex." When she dreamed of being a woman of the harem, with great white warm limbs, she awoke to shudder, defenseless in the dusk of her room. She prayed to Jesus, always to the son of God . . ." (251).

Lewis did not have to have read Brooks to pick up such ideas. They were in the air though Brooks was their most influential exponent. Such is the case with Thorstein Veblen, as well, but it is hard to believe Lewis' later claim that he had never read Veblen.[6] *The Job,* an earlier novel, seems to reflect Veblen, as do *Main Street* and *Babbitt.* At any rate, Lewis' characters read Veblen: Carol Kennicott and Miles Bjornstam are Veblen readers (117, 263). When Carol decides that the most properly subversive thing she could do would be "asking people to define their jobs" (441), she is talking Veblen's language. Much of Veblen's writings consist of vituperative redefinitions of economic functions which unmask the merchant class as exploitative and parasitic. Lewis makes it clear that Gopher Prairie lives off the farmers whom the town despises, overcharges, and cheats.

The central influence on *Main Street,* as later on *Babbitt* and *Elmer Gantry,* was H. L. Mencken. For what most bothers Carol is not the ugliness of the town, not its injustice, but the soul-destroying intellectual conformity that leads to a pervasive and inescapable dullness.

Percy Boynton has commented that the reader has difficulty remembering individual characters by the end of the book.[7] The characters are indistinguishable because, though some are kinder or better-natured, they all think in the same clichés. The sociology of the book is Mencken's and Sumner's: the group mind thinks in stock formulas and is controlled by group conventions. The dominant metaphor of the book is the machine. The villagers sit "in rocking chairs . . . listening to mechanical music, saying mechanical things about the excellence of Ford Automobiles" (265). When a standard prejudice is mouthed, the townspeople nod "solemnly and in tune, like a shop window of flexible toys, comic mandarins and judges and ducks and clowns, set quivering by a breeze from the open door" (50).

The townspeople completely lack the sympathetic and the critical imagination. They are as unable to conceive of the possibility of anyone outside their own class having a mind or emotions as they are to conceive of the possibility that any value of the in-group might be wrong. They are in mental prisons, able to see the world only through the narrow slits of self-interest and accepted ideas. In such a world, critical thought cannot exist, and conversation consists either of the ritual chanting of orthodoxies or of gossip about personalities. As for personality, the villagers discuss it at the lowest level of superficiality. Someone's personality is forever fixed and tagged by some ancient joke or scandal about him or by some peculiarity of manner or physique.

This anatomy of provincialism still holds fairly true: provincial people are closed-minded and unable to cope with objective thought. Worse yet, they really believe in the mythology of the small town: that it is decent, moral, democratic, honest, God's own country, etc. This is what most irritates Lewis' heroine, Carol Kennicott. The villagers have faith in their superiority to the undemocratic East, but in reality the town is a "sterile oligarchy" (267). The final straw for Carol is the town's boosting campaign: "she could, she asserted, endure a shabby but modest town; the town shabby but egomaniac she could not endure" (417). Like most satirists Lewis was less irritated by the dreariness of his targets than by their complacent pride in their dreariness. His satire is an attack on the pride of what seemed to be a village civilization newly inflated to a world power:

> Doubtless all small towns, in all countries, in all ages, Carol admitted, have a tendency to be not only dull, but mean, bitter, infested with curiosity. . . .
> But a village in a country which is taking pains to become altogether standardized and pure, which aspires to succeed Victorian England as the chief mediocrity of the world, is no longer merely provincial, no longer downy and restful in its leaf-shadowed innocence. It is a force seeking to dominate the earth. . . .
> And such a society, such a nation is determined by the Gopher Prairies. The greatest manufacturer is but a busier Sam Clark, and all the rotund senators and presidents are village lawyers and bankers grown nine feet tall (266–67).

The United States in 1914 was a debtor nation; in 1920, it was a creditor nation and the major economic power in the world.[8] Although revisionist historians suggest that the image of the "irresponsible twenties" is simplistic and inaccurate, few would deny that the United States found itself in a position of world power that it was intellectually and emotionally unprepared for.[9] If provincialism still ruled in the twenties, the small towns did not. In 1920, more people lived in towns or cities of over 2,500 than in villages of fewer than that number.[10] The nation had become more urban than rural. Since this increase in cities was caused mostly by a movement from the farms and small towns, a large proportion of the city population retained rural attitudes and loyalties.[11] In both cities and towns, in fact, provincialism was intensified by the very threats to it.

Further complicating the situation was the political use of the small town myth. American business and industry was revolutionizing the country: telephones, automobiles, and radios brought the towns closer to the cities, ending their relative isolation.[12] Moreover, despite a temporary postwar recession, an economic boom developed which, though it skipped whole regions and economic groups, did bring a genuine new affluence that drastically changed social and moral patterns.[13] Thus, if one force had to be named which was doing the most to break up the old rural scheme of values and attitudes, which was most effective in destroying the prestige and power of the villages, it would have to be American business.[14] Yet, paradoxically, it was business and its political front man, the Republican administration, that most invoked the mythology of the small town and most anathematized its enemies. As late as 1928, Herbert Hoover, an international financier, was offering as one of his quaifications for the presidency of the United States the fact that he was "a boy from a country village."[15]

One explanation is that business wanted to avoid governmental power and interference. The myth of a simple, uncomplicated America was an effective way to justify a government that, for the most part, tried its best not to govern. The myth pictured an ideal decentralized independent rural America that had no need for a large and centralized government.[16] Meanwhile, business itelf, monolithic and pervasive, could do most of the governing.[17] Many people, businessmen as well as others, felt a genuine nostalgia for lost simplicity.[18] People want to have their cake and eat it too. Americans of the twenties wanted to enjoy the fruits of economic dynamism without losing the comfort of old stabilities.[19] This resulted in something like a bootleg mentality. An urbanite might enjoy all the pleasures of the city in practice while maintaining the values of the village (which the village itself often honored mostly in the breach) in theory.

Lewis, then, exaggerates the actual power of the American small town but not its mythic significance. He attacks widespread American provincialism at its symbolic source. The popularity of *Main Street* is not hard to account for; the myth it deflates was—like all combinations of pride, hypocrisy, smugness, and meanness—ripe for unmasking and a vast amount of irritation was released by the public exposure of what everyone really knew.

Lewis' anatomy of provincialism is accurate but it is also old hat. No one is likely to be surprised by anything in *Main Street*. Lewis has become so assimilated as to become almost obsolescent. This could not happen to an author who *renders* human experience, but *Main Street* is largely editorial; we are told about, rather than shown, the town. Its gossips and dullards never come to life even in their deadness so that the weakest passages in the novel are those in which Lewis has dialogue or action. Even at the level of abstract editorializing, Lewis' ideas are trite and obvious. His exposure of small towns never cuts to the bone as Mark Twain's often does. There is a more intense vision of human meanness in two or three passages of "The Man That Corrupted Hadleyburg" than in all of Lewis' overstuffed novel.

Lewis' banal style is another element contributing to the loss of favor his writings have suffered. He should, however, be granted the virtues of his vices: his personal superficiality is mirrored in his style, but so is his intense nervous vitality; his writing is thin but electric.

Even 1920 readers were irritated by Carol Kennicott, though many thought Lewis intended her to seem ridiculous. Some modern readers like to suppose, conversely, that Lewis has no idea of his heroine's defects; Lewis is properly shown up by such a reading. In fact, not only Lewis but Carol herself is aware of her faults. The pattern of the book is made up of her self-assertions followed by her self-doubtings. She thoroughly realizes the absurdity of many of her ideas, and Lewis' irony can hardly be doubted in his descriptions of her belief in a "rather vaguely conceived sweetness and light" (2) or of her desire to "conquer the world—almost entirely for the world's own good" (3). Nevertheless, Lewis does overrate his heroine and in some ways he is reflected in her. He overrates her, however, not through failing to realize her silliness but because of his indulgence toward it. He did not expect as much from a heroine as most readers do. (Perhaps the reader's irritation is slightly priggish, for that matter.) Some critics seemed to feel that Carol should be content with Gopher Prairie simply because she herself was no genius but that is to miss the point of the book. Carol does not condemn the ignorance of Gopher Prairie so much as its complacency in ignorance nor its stupidity so much as its resistance to knowledge. Carol has the one quality Lewis most admires: she wants to know, she stays loose, she refuses to renounce her freedom to criticize and to wonder. This is what gives her a life in the novel which the other characters, fixed in their provincial orthodoxies, lack.

Freedom is, in fact, the main theme of Lewis' novels. At the beginning of *Main Street,* we find Carol in an attitude of "suspended freedom" (1). Since freedom was the one and only thing that Lewis really believed in, freedom can only exist in suspension; an absolute conviction enslaves. When someone asked Lewis if Carol were a self-portrait, he replied: "Yes . . . Carol is 'Red' Lewis: always groping for something she isn't capable of attaining, always dissatisfied, always restlessly straining to see what lies just over the horizon, intolerant of her surroundings, yet lacking any clearly defined vision of what she really wants to do or be." [20] This commitment to a rootless and indefinable freedom is the key to Lewis' writings and career, the essential quality responsible for his success and failure. Lewis is nervous and alive, a man on the move, but he never gets anywhere. He is free to go but where to?

As far as the theme of freedom goes, *Babbitt* is a mere rewriting of *Main Street* though far superior in technique. In *Babbitt,* the protagonist is at the center of the world Lewis is attacking rather than on the periphery, illustrating the absurdities that Carol merely editorializes. Carol sees Gopher

Prairie from the outside whereas Babbitt is the archetype of Zenith.

Zenith is something more than Gopher Prairie. As Lewis' unpublished introduction to *Babbitt* makes clear, Zenith is meant to represent the typical, small, boom city, a relatively unexploited literary subject: "Unfortunately American literature has discerned as types of community only the larger or older cities—as New York, San Francisco, Richmond—and the villages, with nothing between. Yet there is a sort of community in between, an enormously important type—the city of a few hundred thousand, the metropolis that yet is a village, the world-center that is yet ruled by cautious villagers." [21]

Zenith is between the large city and the small village in more aspects than merely size. Gopher Prairie aspires to reach the heights of Zenith, but in all too many ways Zenith is merely a monstrously enlarged Gopher Prairie. Zenith is an anomaly: physically it is a city, but spiritually it is still a small town: "Villages—overgrown towns—three-quarters of a million people still dressing, eating, building houses, attending church, to make an impression on their neighbors, quite as they did back on Main Street, in villages of two thousand. And yet not villages at all, the observer uneasily sees, as he beholds factories with ten thousand workmen, with machines more miraculous than the loaves and fishes, with twice the power and ten times the skill of a romantic grand duchy." [22] This along with the usual freedom-conformity conflict is the essential theme of *Babbitt:* the anomalous relationship of the American businessman with his small-town mass mind to the vastly powerful urban-industrial complex that he rules without understanding. It is a fictional variation on the themes of Thorstein Veblen's *The Theory of Business Enterprise* and a fictional anticipation of Ortega y Gasset's *The Revolt of the Masses.*

Lewis' image of the businessman and his relation to his

culture begins in the early pages of *Babbitt* with a Veblen-like comparison of industrial power and the businessmen who take credit for it. Zenith at dawn is described in a passage emphasizing what Lewis believes to be the beauty and majesty of industrial power. The essential joke in the book is established with the description of the man who lives in "a city built—it seemed—for giants":

There was nothing of the giant in the aspect of the man who was beginning to awaken on the sleeping-porch of a Dutch Colonial house in that residential district of Zenith known as Floral Heights.

His name was George F. Babbitt. He was forty-six years old, now, in April, 1920, and he made nothing in particular, neither butter nor shoes, nor poetry, but he was nimble in the calling of selling houses for more than people could afford to pay.

His large head was pink, his brown hair thin and dry. His face was babyish in slumber. . . . He was not fat but he was exceedingly well fed; his cheeks were pods, and the unroughened hand which lay helpless upon the khaki-colored blanket was slightly puffy.[23]

The businessman as baby is the dominant image that runs throughout *Babbitt*. The name itself suggests part of the image: Babbitt = baby, babble. Moreover, in addition to the details given in the quoted passage which establish the image of a baby—the pink head, the baby plumpness, the helpless hand—there are the later touches of Babbitt's "baby-blue pajamas" (4), his childishly petulant face (5), and "the sleeveless dimity B. V. D. undershirt, in which he resembled a small boy humorlessly wearing a cheesecloth tabard at a civic pageant" (8). In this last image, Babbitt is less the baby than the pre-adolescent, but nowhere in the book does he seem to have wandered very far from the border of puberty. Even his wife is an indulgent mother, "as sexless as an anemic nun" (7). She calls him "Georgie boy" (4).

Babbitt does have sexual fantasies about a "fairy child,"

but if the fairy child sometimes seems to be a dream substitute for a flapper, at other times she is a childish playmate and sometimes, like Myra Babbitt, a mother: "He wanted the fairy girl—in the flesh. If there had been a woman whom he loved he would have fled to her, humbled his forehead on her knees" (273). Even the fantasies expressive of Babbitt's "buried life" are adolescent.

Babbitt's world, like that of any small boy, is ruled by rituals of speech and behavior. The more commonplace the action, the more of a ritual it becomes. Even having the car filled with gasoline is a "rite" (28). Driving the car is both a rite and a game: "Babbitt . . . devoted himself to the game of beating trolley cars to the corner: a spurt, a tail-chase, nervous speeding between the huge yellow side of the trolley and the jagged row of parked motors, shooting past just as the trolley stopped—a rare game and valiant" (30).

Babbitt's relation then to the complex technological world around him is that of a baby surrounded by shiny toys. His small-town mind is quite as incapable of understanding the scientific principles underlying his world as Theron Ware's was to cope with the new theology. Babbitt's car, for instance, is a private fighter plane, a virility-substitute. Babbitt lives in a world of meaningless gadgetry, a world typified by the worship rather than the understanding of machinery: "He had enormous and poetic admiration, though very little understanding, of all mechanical devices. They were his symbols of truth and beauty. Regarding each new intricate mechanism —metal lathe, twojet carburetor, machine gun, oxyacetylene welder—he learned one good realistic-sounding phrase and used it over and over with a delightful feeling of being technical and initiated" (68).

The purposes of all this technology are trivial. In a strange reversal of Kant, machines rather than people are regarded as ends in themselves, as with the electric cigar lighter that

Babbitt buys: "It was a pretty thing, a nickeled cylinder with an almost silvery socket, to be attached to the dashboard of his car. It was not only, as the placard on the counter observed, 'a dandy little refinement, lending the last touch of class to a gentleman's auto,' but a priceless time-saver. By freeing him from halting the car to light a match, it would in a month or two easily save ten minutes" (54). The lighter is similar to Babbitt's own business function: he too is expensive, decorative, and modern but not very useful. As the small-towners of *Main Street* have a parasitic relationship with the farmers, so is Babbitt a mere parasite of modern industry.

The bathroom is the supreme architectural accomplishment of Babbitt's culture. At the end of his working day, we see Babbitt, "plump, smooth, pink," reverting unashamedly to babyhood in the bathtub: "He patted the water, and the reflected light capsized and leaped and volleyed. He was content and childish. He played. He shaved a swath down the calf of one plump leg" (94–95). The porcelain tub, the nickel taps, and the tiled walls of Babbitt's bathroom symbolize a civilization that is typified by all that is antiseptic, cellophane-wrapped, and standardized: a civilization separated from nature and inimical to human nature. The modern temple is the Roman Imperial washroom at the Zenith Athletic Club, a "Neronian washroom, where a line of men bent over the bowls inset along a prodigious slab of marble as in religious prostration before their own images in the massy mirror" (58–59).

The main difference between Zenith and Gopher Prairie, and between Babbitt and Doctor Kennicott, is just this predominance of the machine and the hygenic. Zenith is cleaner and—on the surface—more lively and dynamic than Gopher Prairie. Babbitt and his friends, for that matter, thoroughly appreciate their advantages:

Chum Frink had recently been on a lecture tour among the small towns, and he chuckled, "Awful good to get back to civilization! I certainly been seeing some hick towns! I mean— Course the folks there are the best on earth, but gee whiz, those Main Street burgs are slow, and you fellows can't hardly appreciate what it means to be here with a bunch of live ones!"

"You bet!" exulted Orville Jones. "They're the best folks on earth, those small-town folks, but oh, mama! What conversation! Why, say, they can't talk about anything but the weather and the nee-oo Ford, by heckalorum!"

"That's right. They all talk about just the same things," said Eddie Swanson.

"Don't they though! They just say the same things over and over," said Vergil Gunch (117).

Babbitt congratulates himself on his own initiative for having got out of his own home town of Catawba and having come to the city, but Vergil Gunch offers a defense of the town: "But, by golly, there's this you got to say for 'em: Every small American town is trying to get population and modern ideals. And darn if a lot of 'em don't put it across! . . . you don't want to just look at what these small towns are, you want to look at what they're aiming to become, and they all got an ambition that in the long run is going to make 'em the finest spots on earth—they all want to be just like Zenith!" (119)

Which is exactly what Babbitt is all about: Zenith is merely a Gopher Prairie enlarged, mechanized, and cleaned up; Babbitt and his friends merely small-towners who are better dressed, closer shaved, slicker, and running on faster though equally mechanical rhythms. These men have graduated to the machine age only in the most superficial manner; their relation to the machine is merely that of superstitious worship and mindless, uncomprehending imitation. Essentially they are small-towners, mass minds, babies lost in a world of machines.

The world of Lewis' novel is machine made. It is characterized by images of glittering surfaces, meaningless hustle and bustle, inescapable noise, and standardized people. At times, Babbitt himself seems merely a mechanical cog in this world-machine, as, indeed, he imagines himself: "He felt superior and powerful, like a shuttle of polished steel darting in a vast machine" (53). Babbitt's very name has a mechanistic as well as babyish association: babbitt metal is an antifriction alloy used for bearings. Yet Babbitt, other-directed though he is, does not always avoid friction nor is he forever content as a cog in a machine. Babbitt is humanized not only by his childishness but also by a pathetic attempt at rebellion. Although incapable of impersonal critical thought, he is able to attain to a glimpse of his own situation: "He beheld, and half admitted that he beheld, his way of life as incredibly mechanical. Mechanical business—a brisk selling of badly built houses. Mechanical religion—a dry, hard church, shut off from the real life of the streets, inhumanly respectable as a top-hat. Mechanical golf and dinner-parties and bridge and conversation. Save with Paul Riesling, mechanical friendships—back slapping and jocular, never daring to essay the test of quietness" (234). When his one real friend, Paul Riesling, is jailed for attempting to kill his wife, Babbitt's rebellion against "a life of barren heartiness" (342) comes out into the open. His buried emotional life attempts to assert itself.

A very unsatisfactory and abortive rebellion it is. Babbitt manages to make a brief escape to the Maine woods in an attempt to find solace in nature, in the manner of Thoreau, who was a central influence on Lewis' writing.[24] Thoreau's influence shows in Babbitt's curious choice of the Maine woods as a refuge rather than the nearer wilds of Minnesota or Michigan; in Babbitt's realization that he is living "a life of barren heartiness" with its echo of "lives of quiet desperation"; and in the pervasive presence of a set of values in opposition to those of Babbitt's world—an organic, natural, inward existence, fronting the essential truths of life. Far from becoming transformed into a Midwestern Thoreau, Babbitt turns out to be a babe in the woods. He conceives of nature in terms of the childish adventure story and the motion picture: "Moccasins—sixgun—frontier town—gamblers —sleep under the stars—be a regular man" (295). Babbitt, corrupted by his culture, lacks the inner quietude, the ability to absorb experience without its being thrust upon him. Thoreau was able to discover nature by freeing his mind from the petty encumbrances of a busy and unimportant civilization. Babbitt, however, as a victim of the machine age "could never run away from Zenith and family and office, because in his own brain he bore the office and the family and every street and disquiet and illusion of Zenith" (301). If Thomas Wolfe could not go home again, Babbitt could never leave.

At home in Zenith, Babbitt's ineffectual rebellion continues. He becomes a liberal for a while on no better grounds than a conversation with a lawyer. He has an affair. But these efforts are merely impotent attempts to escape the vague dissatisfaction that haunts him throughout the novel. He has dim intimations of what he wants to escape from but no idea of what he wants to escape to. He cannot escape from his world of standardized and mechanical thought for he has nothing with which to replace it. In fact, he has no real alternative, for he is trapped not by outer circumstances so much as his own conditioned and inert mind.

Eventually, the near-fatal illness of Babbitt's wife allows him, rather gratefully, to return to the comfortable world of stereotypes and expected responses, free from the insupportable requirements of freedom. Accompanying his wife to the hospital, he burns his hand on the radiator. His wife immediately assumes her accustomed role and he his: "So as they drove up to St. Mary's hospital, with the nurses already

laying out the instruments for an operation to save h
was she who consoled him and kissed the place to ....
well, and though he tried to be gruff and mature, he yielded
to her and was glad to be babied" (387).

Still Babbitt does not wholly succumb. He keeps the spark
of freedom alive by defending his son's elopement with a girl
who is the embodiment of Babbitt's own wished-for fairy
child. It is no accident that this ending is an almost exact
repetition of *Main Street:* the unequipped rebel finally suc-
cumbs but with an inner defiance and hopes for a younger
generation. Both novels begin well but begin to get a bit dull
when it becomes apparent that neither the characters nor the
plot is really going anywhere and that both are condemned
to circle back to their starting point, with nothing gained and
much energy lost. Lewis' own dilemma is exactly mirrored.
Although his life was, in a sense, a continual flight from
Sauk Center, he was never able to transcend the limiting
dichotomies bequeathed him by his background. He has only
two basic characters: the conformist and the nonconformist,
the latter symbiotically dependent on the former since his
only energy is in rejection. Even this rejection cannot become
an absolute and transcendent gesture since total rejection
would demand a reflexive conviction—and Lewis has none to
offer.

It is questionable as to whether the actual limitations of
freedom in American society are as strong as Lewis represents
them to be in his novels. Genuinely critical thought may run
into obstacles anywhere, but Lewis exaggerates the strength
of the obstacles and the weakness of the rebels. Lewis himself, after all, was a successful rebel; he made rebellion pay to
the extent that he even became honored in his own country,
Sauk Center's "favorite son." But such success is denied his
main characters as if to indicate his own apparent freedom
was illusory. Lewis would likely defend himself on realistic
grounds. When Floyd Dell complained that *Main Street* was

too one-sided, not fairly representing the presence and strength of nonconformist elements, Lewis replied that Gopher Prairie was a much smaller town than the more mixed Port Royal of Dell's *Moon-Calf*.[25] Similarly, a real estate man might find it difficult to be unorthodox, whereas a lawyer (like the liberal Senaca Doane, a minor character in *Babbitt*) has more leeway. The truth is that Lewis simply cannot imagine freedom within the social structure of America.

Moreover, Lewis cannot make up his mind about another of the major conflicts that runs through the novel, that of the mechanization of life. On the one hand, Babbitt and his cohorts are judged for having failed to measure up to the romantic possibilities of an industrial-technological world. They are in the wrong for not being adequately attuned to the machine world they live in. They are small-towners and provincials in their inability to truly comprehend the rich possibilities of a technological world. On the other hand, one of the key indictments against the Babbitt-world, just as against the Main Street world, is its mechanism, and Lewis indicts this in the traditional organic *vs.* mechanical formula of the Victorian culture critics (not to mention Van Wyck Brooks). Here the complaint is that the small-town mind is *too* mechanistic, too willing to submit to merely mechanical rhythms. If Lewis had any notion of how to reconcile these contradictions, it is not apparent in *Babbitt*.

8. Elmer Gantry and That Old Time Religion

In theocratic New England, morality was quite unambiguously legislated, but as the theocracy lost its political control (though retaining much of its influence), more subtle measures of social control were adopted. Perry Miller shows that a key document in this transition was Cotton Mather's *Bonifacius* or *Essays to Do Good* (1710) with its reformulation of puritan strategies. Miller notes, "Behind the reformulation was still a hope that control might be achieved, but not now by legislation or by compulsion: the new energies would be moral example and the unofficial mobilization of pious conformity." [1] Mather's advice to the elect was that "if any in the neighborhood are taking to bad courses—lovingly and faithfully admonish them." [2]

In the teens and twenties, such sects as the Baptists and Methodists were still enthusiastically following Mather's advice, sometimes without heeding his adverbial qualifications. And occasionally, as in the case of Prohibition, not to mention innumerable petty blue laws, they managed to translate morality back into legislation. The virulence and ugliness of the religious reaction marked a change in the course of American Protestantism. Modernism and the social gospel had seemed triumphant in the progressive era and were, of course, still operative in the teens and twenties. By the middle teens the churches were following the well-to-do to the suburbs and discovering that continued financial support was contingent upon the scuttling of the social gospel.[3] Many preachers preached a mean a priori moralism that seemed to condone and even encourage business chicanery and self-righteous cruelty while vigorously condemning sex and alcohol. Or rather, with the bootleg hypocrisy of the era, what was condemned was getting caught, on the one hand, and the even worse offense of verbally attacking the moral formulae, on the other.

The worst of the religion of the twenties (and the worst is what I am mainly concerned with here) was summed up in Billy Sunday as an individual and in the Ku Klux Klan as a group. Sunday's major popularity was in the late teens rather than the twenties, but there is no better example of the kind of preacher that *Elmer Gantry* unmasked; Sunday was undoubtedly one of Lewis' several models for his hero. William G. McLoughlin's excellent biography, *Billy Sunday Was His Real Name,* shows why. Sunday, born in Ames, Iowa, boasted he was "a rube of the rubes." He dressed in businessman's clothes, used business methods, even got sermon ideas from advertisements. Although he would rip off his coat in the pulpit, the emotionalism of his meetings was carefully contrived. The crowd was manipulated into a calculated mass response. Sunday was a "fighting saint" who attacked such immoralities as smoking, drinking, dancing, and reading novels. Sunday was opposed to social legislation since poverty, in his view, was the result of immorality, rather than the cause. However, he recommended such moral reforms as a law forbidding dancing except between husband and wife. A one-time professional baseball player, Sunday denied that a Christian must be a "sort of dishrag proposition, a wishy-washy sissified sort of galoot that lets everybody make a doormat of him." Rather, the Christian was a fighter, and his enemy was anyone who was "immoral," theologically unorthodox, or "un-American"—to sum it all up, a nonconformist of any sort.[4] In short, Sunday was an Elmer Gantry, the only difference being that he really believed in and more or less practiced his preachings.

H. L. Mencken may have exaggerated when he remarked that the Klan was the secular arm of the Methodist church,[5] but David M. Chalmers' history of the Klan establishes the quite genuine connection between the Klan and the more puritanical Protestant sects.[6] When the Klan was establishing itself in a new area, its first move was to try to win over the local Baptist and Methodist ministers, who all too often responded with eagerness, seeing the Klan as a heaven-sent answer to their slipping prestige and waning power over community mores. Many ministers were in perfect accord with Klan values, since their own "call" was sometimes one of stupidity and opportunism, dishonor and dishonesty.

The moralistic Protestant not too infrequently felt the lure of what he most condemned. In fact, the excess of moralism in the twenties may be attributed mainly to two causes: first, the reaction to the prevailing hedonism; second, the projection of secret and guilt-laden inner desires. No other explanation seems to explain the phenomenon of the Georgia superintendent of a Baptist Sunday school and moderator of twenty Baptist churches who was discovered to have held the head and directed the flogging of a (white) woman for "immorality and failure to go to church." [7] Of course, such behavior was exceptional, but the blend in it of self-righteousness, pruriency, and sexual sadism was not. Comically enough, the Klan was discredited partly because its two major leaders were, at various times, indicted for violation of the Mann Act. As Chalmers notes, one cause for Klan influence was that it provided approved outlets for the repressed sexuality of the moralistic Protestant.[8]

For all its genuine offensiveness, the religious reaction was a primarily defensive phenomenon. As Chalmers notes, even the ultra-militant Klan conceived of itself in defensive terms:

"The world . . . endangered was that of the American village whose formal mores, and often actual values, were those
preached from the Protestant pulpits. The Klan, as the aggressive self-constituted instrument of Protestant evangelism,
was concerned with much more than defense against the
immigrant and Rome. It placed special emphasis on morality,
which meant opposition to the increasingly rapid erosion of
small-town, heartland America." [9] Similarly, William E. Leuchtenburg notes: "The Klan centered in the small towns and
recruited the poorer and less educated. It drew its chief support from the sense of desperation experienced by Protestant
townsmen of native stock in these years, when they felt
themselves eclipsed by the rise of the city, engaged in a battle
which their failing birth rates doomed them to lose." [10]

The Scopes trial in 1925 was as dramatic a symbol of the
religious reaction as Billy Sunday or the Klan. The Volstead
Act meant more to its proponents than the repeal of alcohol.
As a symbolic gesture, it was the repeal of cities, immigrants,
automobiles, and all other forces making for a new society
and a revised moral code.[11] Similarly, the Tennessee antievo-
lution statute was a symbolic attack not simply on Tennessee
teachers of Darwinism but on the complexities of urban
modern thought itself, with its denial of the religious and
moral certainties of the provincial mind.[12]

To H. L. Mencken, nothing was more predictable of the
rural mind than that it would attempt to repeal scientific
thought. The war between city and country was to Mencken
simply another variation of the old war between science (i.e.,
truth) and religion (i.e., superstition). In a glossary to
Americana, 1925, prepared ostensibly for the use of foreign
readers, Mencken defines the Bible Belt as "that portion of
the United States in which the people believe in the literal
accuracy of Genesis. It includes the whole country, save for

only areas of ten mile radius around the cities of 100,000 population." [13]

Nothing delighted Mencken more than to battle for the cause of science. In behalf of science and sanitation, Mencken had waged war, in his "Free Lance" column of the *Baltimore Sun,* for an improved water filtration system, choosing the following strategy described by his biographer, William Manchester: "Two leagues were formed, the National and the American with standings determined by the number of typhoid cases in a given city. Baltimore led its league all season, copped the world series, and then in an International World Series swamped Constantinople." The strategy worked, endearing Mencken to the medical faculty of Baltimore.[14]

Mencken was, in fact, an arrant science-worshipper, but what impressed him most was not humanitarian accomplishments or technological triumphs but the scientific discovery of truth. In Mencken's 1922 *Prejudices,* he characterizes the "scientist" as a man whose main purpose is not to save life or to cure disease; the scientist knows his discoveries may do as much harm as good. His real motive is simply curiosity. "And yet," adds Mencken, "he is one of the greatest and noblest of men." [15] That is because, to Mencken, the scientist represents free thought. The scientist has no ulterior motives, no preconceived dogmas to defend in the face of objective truth.

If science was the positive element in Mencken's philosophy, religion was the negative. For a time, Charles H. Grasty, the owner of the *Sun,* kept Mencken off the subject of the clergy, but the clergy made the tactical error of taking the offensive, attacking Mencken's column from their pulpits, and Mencken was unleashed. Manchester reports: "For weeks, with the aid of a clipping service, he had been collecting news stories of ministers accused of various crimes throughout the country. These he printed, with ripe insinuation, as the hubbub grew. At length, as the storm surged toward a climax, he scored an astonishing victory with the help of his old friends at police headquarters. A Methodist clergyman, head of the local vice crusade and an attacker of 'The Free Lance,' was seized at the local Y.M.C.A., closeted with a naked boy scout." [16]

Mencken's most effective sortie in the war between science and religion was his raid into Tennessee to cover the Scopes trial which is memorably reported in "The Hills of Zion" *Prejudices: Fifth Series*. This brilliant essay begins with Mencken's impressions of the town of Dayton. Expecting to find dully pious folk, he discovers townsmen who, though they literally believed the Bible, were not averse to the charms of pretty girls and whose "faces were far too florid to belong to teetotalers." [17] He then discovers that Dayton is the local metropolis; "That is to say, it was to Rhea county what Atlanta was to Georgia or Paris to France" (77). But all is not lost.

Mencken and the other reporters take a trip into the hills to spy on a backwoods meeting that promises to be more representative of country religion than worldly Dayton. Circumspection is necessary in order not to frighten the mountaineers:

. . . we parked our car in a little woodpath a mile or two beyond the tiny village of Morgantown, and made the rest of the approach on foot, deployed like skirmishers. Far off in a dark, romantic glade a flickering light was visible, and out of the silence came the rumble of exhortation. We could distinguish the figure of the preacher only as a moving mote in the light; it was like looking down the tube of a dark-field microscope. Slowly and cautiously we crossed what seemed to be a pasture, and then we crouched down along the edge of a cornfield, and stealthily edged further and further. The light now grew larger and we could begin to make out what was going on. We went ahead on all fours like snakes in the grass (79).

There follows a description of the preacher and his discourse. After the preacher has denounced books and education, a strange rite begins. A young girl is led out, and the preacher explains that she has asked for prayers. She throws herself on the penitent's bench, and the mob gathers about her and prays. Prayer leads to excitement and excitement to frenzy:

A comic scene? Somehow, no. The poor half-wits were too horribly in earnest. It was like peeping through a knothole at the writhings of people in pain. From the squirming and jabbering mass a young woman gradually detached herself. . . . Presently her whole body began to be convulsed—great throes that began at the shoulders and ended at the hips. She would leap to her feet, thrust her arms in the air, and then hurl herself upon the heap. Her praying flattened out into mere caterwauling, like that of a Tom cat on a petting party. I describe the thing discreetly and as a strict behaviourist. The lady's subjective sensations I leave to infidel pathologists, privy to the works of Ellis, Freud, and Moll. Whatever they were, they were obviously not painful, for they were accompanied by vast heavings and gurglings of a joyful even ecstatic nature. . . . By this time the performers were quite oblivious to the profane universe and so it was safe to go still closer. We left our hiding and came up to the little circle of light. We slipped into the vacant seats on one of the rickety benches. The heap of mourners was directly before us. They bounced into us as they cavorted. The smell that they radiated, sweating there in that obscene heap, half suffocated us (83–84).

Finally, Mencken says, the reporters tired of the "show" (85) and returned to Dayton: "Dayton was having a roaring time. It was better than the circus. But the note of devotion was simply not there; the Daytonians, after listening for a while would slip away to Robinson's drug-store to regale themselves with Coca-Cola, or to the lobby of the Aqua Hotel, where the learned Raulston sat in state, judicially picking his teeth. The real religion was not present. It began at the bridge over the town creek, where the road makes off for the hills" (86).

The point of view in Mencken's essay is as revealing as the description, although in a quite different way. Mencken and the other urban reporters stealthily approach as if they were skirmishers. What they are is apparently a reconnaisance unit sent out by the city to explore the dangerous, enemy world of the country. Mencken's attitude toward the enemy is curious. Having them at a perfect disadvantage by his position of unwatched watcher, he can afford to be patronizing rather than violently denunciatory. Such language as "half-wits" lends a more than aesthetic distance to the scene, but it is mild compared to Mencken's usual store of epitaphs for all those unfortunate enough to be living outside the charmed circle of the city. Of course, the scene speaks for itself in the judgment of country religion; mere denunciation would seem an anticlimax to the sheer impact of the description. Mencken's note here is more qualified than usual. The spectacle seems less comic than pathetic to him. The weakness of his position is that the voyeuristic image of looking through a knothole at people in pain conveys a curious impression; it calls to mind the pleasure trips to Bedlam that the English gentry used to make. Even more curious is the image conveyed by the reporter sitting down on a bench to watch the "show"; it is like a circus even down to the smell of the animals. At times, Mencken seems to take his own overuse of animal imagery so seriously as to really consider country people as a separate and lower species. When the cavorting worshippers bounce into the reporters there is no real contact.

The trick in the point of view, however, the trick that effectively dehumanizes the hill people Mencken describes, is the mixture of the spectacle perspective with a scientific perspective—the preacher is seen as if through a microscope and the religious orgy is described from the point of view of a strict behaviorist. Mencken is partly the scientific observer, partly the circus spectator. He is his own scientific hero, motivated by simple curiosity, but in reality, the "scientific" viewpoint he adopts is anything but objective. It is rather a device of comic rhetoric, used as a *reductio ad absurdum* of religion, presumably represented in its undisguised essence by the obscene spectacle described. Mencken is, of course, being cute when he claims to describe the scene discreetly and as a strict behaviorist. Knowledge of the subjective sensations of the participants in the orgy would actually make the scene *less* gross because it would to some degree humanize the emotions involved. Yet it must be granted that the behaviorist strategy is not inappropriate to describe responses that are for the most part mechanical.

Sinclair Lewis, fully as much as Mencken, was a propaganda agent in the war between science and religion and in much the same terms as Mencken. To Lewis, as to Mencken, the scientist is the exemplar of completely free thought. Thus, the real theme of Lewis' novel about a scientist, *Arrowsmith,* is simply another variation on Lewis' eternal theme of freedom. Arrowsmith's banal "prayer of the scientist" is an assertion of faith in the free mind's pursuit of truth: "God give me unclouded eyes and freedom from haste. God give me a quiet and relentless anger against all pretense and all pretentious work and all work left slack and unfinished. God give me a restlessness whereby I may never sleep nor accept praise till my observed results equal my calculated results or in pious glee I discover and assault my error. God give me strength not to trust in God." [18] In the end, Lewis' scientific hero casts off his family in order to keep the faith: the pattern is that of the saint.

If the scientist, in Lewis' scale of values, is a saint, the minister would have to be the chief of sinners. As much as the scientist represents free thought, the minister represents dogma; the scientist's aim is discovery, the minister's justification; the scientist's universe is open, the minister's closed, determined, long ago explained. The logical opposite to Arrowsmith, the pure scientist, is Gantry, the fundamentalist preacher.

Elmer Gantry unmasks the hypocrisy and inner corruption of moralistic fundamentalist Protestantism. Is *Elmer Gantry* fair? Most of the reviewers did not think so. Lewis does include some decent ministers in the book, but they are overshadowed by the corrupt, the hypocritical, and the vicious. It is, of course, a mistake to read *Gantry* as a realistic novel. Essentially, the book is a lengthily elaborated nasty joke on the worst aspects of the religious reaction described above. It would be ridiculous to complain that such a book is unfair. Satire is usually repulsive and ineffective when it kicks people who are down, but it is salutary and vigorous when it attacks the smug and self-righteous, and it is all the better for the exaggerations, deliberate distortions, and calculated meanness that the target has asked for. The Gantry aspect of American religion was not open to rational persuasion. In its disrespect for rational thought, it was the ultimate exemplar of the small-town mind. The only place it was vulnerable was, so to speak, below the belt. Since the revenge is purely symbolic and mental, the more complete and elaborate the punishment, the better.

Lewis' punishment of moralistic Protestantism is to inflict the ineffable Elmer Gantry on it as its representative and then to build the thematic unity of the book around two prolonged jokes on religion: to characterize a preacher of the doctrines of the immortal soul and divine love entirely in terms of (1) conditional response and (2) ungovernable lust. As we first see Elmer Gantry, he is a natural man: a drunken, pugnacious, lustful slob, a star football player thoroughly out of place in the milksop atmosphere of a Baptist college. His involvement with religion comes about through

a misunderstanding. Elmer stumbles into a street meeting
where his sappy, evangelistic classmate, Eddie Fislinger, is
being baited by a husky atheist. Elmer slugs the atheist
purely for the fun of it, but his motives are misinterpreted:
"Eddie Fislinger bleated to his mates: 'Oh, fellows, Elm
Gantry! Saved!' " [19] In fact, Elmer is lost.

After saving Eddie, Elmer is expected to give testimony, so
he pops out with the appropriate stock response that although he has been a sinner, he knows that only religion
gives anyone the hope of ever leading a decent life. Lewis'
point is, of course, that religion corrupts. Elmer is "converted" from an honest animal into a hypocritical animal; he
becomes a rat as well as a hog. But, and this too is part of the
joke, it is not really his fault. He has no intellectual weapons
with which to resist conversion. Elmer is all right as long as
he is under the wing of his sardonic village atheist roommate,
Jim Lefferts, but he has not enough of a mind to hold out on
his own. Once detached from Lefferts' atheist conditioning,
he is easy game.

An earlier and deeper mental conditioning than any that
Jim Lefferts is able to supply works against Elmer. The
church was the major conditioning factor of his childhood.
He had "got everything from the church and Sunday School,
except, perhaps, any longing whatever for decency and kindness and reason" (28). Weakened by this early religious
conditioning, Elmer is officially converted at a climactic
meeting of Annual Prayer Week. The entire emotional
weight of the mob is directed at him, and he loses his
unfaith:

An instant he saw Jim Lefferts, and heard him insist: "Why,
sure, course they believe it. They hypnotize themselves. But don't
let 'em hypnotize you!"

He saw Jim's eyes, that for him alone belied their bright
harshness and became lonely, asking for comradeship. He strug-
gled; with all the blubbering confusion of a small boy set on by

his elders, frightened and overwhelmed, he longed to be honest, to be true to Jim—to be true to himself and his own good honest sins and whatever penalties they might carry. Then the visions were driven away by voices that closed over him like a surf above an exhausted swimmer. Volitionless, marvelling at the sight of himself as a pinioned giant, he was being urged forward, forced forward, his mother on one arm and Judson on the other, a rhapsodic mob following. . . .

He had but little to do with what he said. The willing was not his but the mob's; the phrases were not his but those of the emotional preachers and hysterical worshipers whom he had heard since babyhood (47–48).

Elmer's "soul" is "saved" through a mechanical conditioning process.

Lewis' use of behavioral and social psychology as a comic rhetorical weapon uncovers a curious paradox in his and Mencken's belief in "free thought." Science is the image of free thought, but what science discovers are the laws that bind humanity. Gottlieb, from whom Arrowsmith learns the religion of science (the name itself being an obvious, seriously intended pun), was based mostly on Jacques Loeb, best known for his theories of biological mechanism. Mencken, Lewis, and other "freethinkers" use such materialistic and deterministic theories to attack the "idealism" that moralizers and theists professed. (The Ku Klux Klan, after all, believed in "idealism.") Thus in the opposed rhetorics of narrow theists and freethinkers, "idealism" was used to mask, materialism to unmask. Lewis, in a small way, is in the tradition of Voltaire and Swift.

Elmer's next problem after his conversion is the sermon he is expected to deliver as the formal seal of faith. Naturally, he is at a loss until Jim Lefferts disgustedly throws him a book by the famous agnostic, Robert G. Ingersoll. Elmer chances upon the passage that becomes the keynote in his career: "Love is the only bow on life's dark cloud. It is the morning and the Evening Star. It shines upon the cradle of the babe, and sheds its radiance upon the quiet tomb. It is the mother of art, inspirer of the poet, patriot and philosopher. . . . It fills the world with melody, for Music is the voice of Love. . . . It is the perfume of the wondrous flower—the heart—and without that sacred passion, that divine swoon, we are less than beasts; but with it, earth is heaven and we are gods" (57).[20] This sermon runs as a leitmotiv through the course of the novel. Elmer's sermon notes on a later occasion read:

> Love!
> Rainbow
> AM & PM star
> from cradle to tomb
> inspires art etc. music voice of love
> slam atheists etc. who not appreciate love (143)

Elmer's appreciation of love is the second major joke of the novel. Preaching at various times for the two most puritanical of major Protestant sects, the Baptists and the Methodists, Elmer is a compulsive lecher—for this reason the tone of the novel with its traveling salesman coarseness and animal imagery, the joke being on the actual pruriency that underlay extremist morality. The Lulu Baines episode is a variation on some thousands of farmer's daughter jokes. Later, Elmer rapes his wife on their wedding night in a grotesque parody of that sacred passion without which we are less than beasts: "Between his long embraces, though his anger at her limpness was growing, he sought to encourage her by shouting, 'Come on now, Clee, show some spunk' " (293).

The climax of Elmer's affair with the female evangelist, Sharon Falconer, "the first authentic passion of his life" (162) is an outrageous parody in which Sharon invokes the whole pantheon of fertility goddesses before they proceed to fornicate.[21] Sharon's evangelical meetings are shrewdly calculated brain-washing sessions in which even the hymn singing is used "to lead the audience to a state of mind where they would do as they were told" (197). Sharon's popularity as a revivalist is based mainly upon sex appeal, though Lewis describes the antics of evangelist and audience as a strict behaviorist, merely suggesting rather than analyzing or rendering the complexities of the union of sexual and religious emotions.

Elmer's passion for Sharon is the nearest thing to a spiritual emotion in the novel, but eventually even this feeling is outweighed by Elmer's naturalistic impulse to self-preservation. When Sharon resists his effort to save her from the tabernacle fire, he cuts and runs. Finding the choir jammed against the rear exit, a door that opens inward, Elmer again becomes pure id: "In howling panic, Elmer sprang among them, knocked them aside, struck down a girl who stood in his way, yanked open the door, and got through it . . . the last, the only one, to get through it" (225).

After Sharon's death, Gantry takes up the confidence game of New Thought for a while, but this turns out to be a blind alley. Breaking into the Methodist establishment he rises steadily to power. The central joke of the novel is compounded when Elmer becomes a popular antivice crusader, meanwhile carrying on a bit of private vice with the remet Lulu Baines. Elmer's dream of glory is to combine all of the various moralistic pressure groups into one united organization. Elmer as the head of this immense lobby would be "able to dictate what a whole nation should wear and eat and say and think" (410).

Our last view of Elmer is at the peak of his career, leading his New York City congregation in prayer:

He turned to include the choir, and for the first time he saw that there was a new singer, a girl with charming ankles and lively eyes, with whom he would certainly have to become well acquainted. But the thought was so swift that it did not interrupt the paean of his prayer:

"Let me count this day, Lord, as the beginning of a new and more vigorous life, as the beginning of a crusade for a complete morality and the domination of the Christian church through all the land. Dear Lord, thy work is but begun! We shall yet make these United States a moral nation!" (432)

There is a weakness in *Elmer Gantry,* but it is in the characterization of Frank Shallard, not of Gantry. Frank Shallard is an honest God-seeker who gradually loses faith in Christianity and becomes a sort of evangelical atheist. Shallard is the typical Lewis hero, the quester, ever in search of some ungraspable truth, but he is not really the hero of the novel, only a counterpoise to Gantry; Shallard's defeats and eventual mutilation are concomitant with Gantry's triumph. Both *Main Street* and *Babbitt* end in defeat, but in neither was the defeat so unqualified and bitter as in *Elmer Gantry.* Since Lewis' truth-seekers are always, to some degree, reflections of himself, *Gantry* would seem to be his darkest, most pessimistic novel. Such is not our impression of it. Shallard is too weak and too silly a character to engage the reader's sympathies. What are we to think when he scores the following great intellectual point against Christianity: "Did he ever —think of it, God himself, taking on human form to help the earth—did he ever suggest sanitation, which would have saved millions from plagues?" (377)

Even the name gives pause: Shallard-Shallow. The intended pathos of Shallard's martyrdom fails to come off, partly because of the reader's lack of sympathy, partly because the style goes bad as it invariably does in Lewis' attempts to describe violence, death, or, indeed, any serious and profound situation or emotion. The intended contrast between Shallard and Gantry breaks down, and Gantry carries off all the honors.

As Shallard himself puts it, "My God, Gantry, what a perfect specimen you are!" (105) Sharon Falconer would agree: "Do you know, I like you! You're so completely brazen, so completely unscrupulous, and so beatifically ignorant" (165). Gantry has the virtue of completeness, and he also has the demonic virtues: the vitality of the grasping id, a sweaty animal energy. Lewis always transferred his own nervous force into one of his central characters. In *Elmer Gantry,* Lewis' intellectual sympathies are all with Shallard, the uncommitted character in search of freedom, but his emotional sympathies are with Gantry, who is endowed with the galvanic electricity that keeps a Lewis hero (or heroine) bouncing through adversity. (Perhaps there is even an underground sympathy with Elmer's lechery; Mark Schorer's account of Lewis' life during the writing of *Gantry* would suggest as much.) At any rate, wrong though it may be, the reader is unable to feel genuine dissatisfaction with Gantry's eventual victory. He is, after all, the real hero of Lewis' Pavlovian beast-fable.

9. Stribling and Wolfe

In 1920, H. L. Mencken wrote an essay on the South with the unforgettable title of "The Sahara of the Bozart." Mencken compared the South to the Gobi desert, to Asia Minor, Poland, Serbia, Esthonia, and Lapland. The South's cultural deficiencies were summarized in an apt quote from J. Gordon Coogler, the Georgia bard:

> Alas, for the South! Her books have grown fewer—
> She was never much given to literature.[1]

The only author worthy of approval in this "gargantuan paradise of the fourth-rate" (138) was James Branch Cabell.

With his novel tactic of adopting and reversing the opposition's premise, Mencken gave a racial explanation for Southern inferiority. The bloodlines of the South, he said, were not Anglo-Saxon but Celtic mixed with Negro. For that matter, after generations of being fertilized by the upper classes, the Negroes had better "blood" than the poor whites. The South was racially degenerate and intellectually barren, a region in need of fundamental criticism but unable to tolerate even moderate departures from its rigid set of political, social, and religious orthodoxies. Moreover, the only major cultural change in the South was for the worse: the emergence of a Southern Babbittry, a commercial middle-class "of third-rate Southerners inoculated with all the worst traits of the Yankee sharper" (153–54).

Ironically, Mencken was writing on the very eve of the "Southern Renaissance" of literature. But though Mencken approved much of the new Southern writing, he disliked the two Southern writers who most contributed to the belated Southern revolt from the village. Mencken's review of T. S. Stribling's *Teeftallow* found the novel truthful but humorless.[2] In a 1931 letter to Alfred A. Knopf, Mencken stated flatly that Thomas Wolfe could not write.[3] Certainly this was a sad reception for writers so much in accord with Mencken's own view of the South.

T. S. Stribling's novels are sociological anticonformist satire in the manner of Mencken and Lewis and quite different from the later mythic-conservative Southern tradition associated with the Fugitives, who saw the South as concrete and human in contrast to the abstract industrial North. In one of Stribling's books, a Southern girl, while talking to a Southern politician about the conflict between the South and the North, asks him for "some more differences that make us seem grand and them seem mean and little."[4] Could this be a dig at *I'll Take My Stand* by "Twelve Southerners"? Stribling's South, whether ante- or post-bellum, always comes off badly in comparison with the North, and its main defect is precisely what the Fugitive myth held the South to be free from (except by the accident of infection from the North): dehumanizing abstraction.

Teeftallow (1926) is set in the hill country of Wayne County in south-central Tennessee (rather transparently disguised in the novel as "Lane County") and dedicated "to the Hill People, the Last Theocracy." Stribling's thesis is that cultural and historical conditions have led to the dominance of a basic personality trait in the South: the prejudiced mind, which is impermeable to either logic or experience and lives by an abstract code. As Stribling editorializes in another novel: "We have all heard about the 'Southern code' and it sounds very romantic and chivalric when a person is up North, but to get a close-up of a code in operation is something else again. I say that any man who habitually acts by a code becomes *ipso facto* a moral automaton . . . a code means a person is going to perform certain actions under certain circumstances without regard to motivation. A code throws away individual judgment and the possibility of mercy and mechanizes human relationships." [5]

Most of Stribling's characters are moral automatons, ethno- and egocentric sleepwalkers, whose thoughts are passive recapitulations of social orthodoxies. Stribling gets at "something grotesquely stolid and cruel in village existence —the 'nice' folk, the church members; there was a mechanical, unimaginative quality to their functioning that inflicted ghastly wounds of which they knew nothing." [6] Poverty of imagination is the dominant village quality. Village religion condemns all forms of artistic, cultural, and emotional expression except those provided by religion itself. The gratifications of fundamentalist religious orgies are debased and illusionary: "It would be difficult to put into words what the protracted meeting meant to Mr. Perry Northcutt. He did not smoke, drink, or curse. His wife was fat and obstinate. He compressed his whole emotional outlet into an annual protracted meeting. . . . He prayed almost incessantly. He fasted two whole days. At the end of the second day, while praying in his home, he felt God stroke his thin hair and say 'My son, your faith shall be rewarded by the greatest revival Irontown has ever known' " (138–39).

Stribling's "hero," Abner Teeftallow, wants to participate in the excitement of a lynching but is held back by his tender-minded girl friend, Nessie Sutton. Both, however, are affected by the charged emotional atmosphere and without prior intention, Abner seduces the girl. His first feeling after he leaves her room is regret for having missed the ceremony. Yet Abner is presented as a relatively sympathetic character, with no innate cruelty. It is simply that a lynching is, along with a revival, about the only thing the hill culture offers in the way of an organized emotional experience. The imagination responds to lynchings since it is offered no competitive appeals.

After Abner has had to leave town with his construction crew (he is a teamster), Nessie's "sin" becomes known. The respectable town women automatically convert the energy of their own repressions and frustrations into moralistic aggression against the convenient transgressor. Miss Scovell, bothered by a "life-long sense of wrong," is outraged when Abner returns, willing to marry Nessie: "She could but sense, not analyze, the logic of these facts—if an illicit love finally could be rewarded . . . then her own solitary inhibited life had been in vain. The punishment of evil-doers was a sort of negative dividend that fell due on Miss Scovell's negative investment in morality" (242).

Nessie, as it happens, has escaped the town after hearing she was to be run out by the "whitecaps," but the mob that intended to chastise Nessie stumbles across Abner and beats him brutally—but only after one of its masked leaders recites a Southern litany:

"A woman is the noblest handiwork of God, Abner Teeftallow. Her station is above man and next to the angels. Beauty adorns her head, tenderness reigns in her heart, and innocence dwells in her soul. If your vile flesh were fed to the dogs, would that atone for the degradation of one of the handmaids of the most high?"

The teamster grew more frightened than ever at this rhetoric, for the deep voice was intoning what may be called the Southern oratorical view of woman. It was what Southern speechmakers always say of women in the abstract, and somehow Southern men believe these dithyrambs, although not one of them ever knew an actual woman who approached such a seraphic being. Still, that never shakes the Southern credo. The country stands in the droll position of worshipping women, but entreating their women rather hardly (250).

Stribling's trilogy, *The Forge* (1931), *The Store* (1932), and *The Unfinished Cathedral* (1934), carry on his analysis of the prejudiced mind. The trilogy pursues the fortunes of the Vaiden family from the Civil War on into the twenties. The setting is Florence, Alabama, and the country thereabouts. The most interesting theme of the trilogy is the insulation of the Southern white from the Negro he exploits. As in *Teeftallow,* the characters differ mainly in the degree of their solipsism. Almost all of them confuse reality with the cultural stereotypes their false consciousness projects, mistake mores for morals, and are incapable of sympathetic imagination.

In *The Forge,* Miltiades Vaiden's fiancée, Drusilla, elopes with another man the night before the marriage was to take place. Meanwhile, the Vaiden's slave, Gracie, is anguished at the discovery that her husband, belonging to a storekeeper nearby, has been sold down the river. Miltiades, finding Gracie alone in the barn, rapes her as a surrogate for Drusilla. This is not even an act of conscious cruelty. Miltiades has no idea that Gracie feels human emotions; Negroes are not popularly supposed to have such feelings. He quite genuinely supposes that the rape makes no difference to Gracie. In fact, Miltiades is thinking only of himself and Drusilla; Gracie never enters his mind, and his only afterthought about the rape is that it is "a saturnine jest at Drusilla's expense." [7] Though Stribling does not mention it, a standard motif of Southern folklore used to be the white boy's feverish dash to the Negro whorehouse after an evening spent in the tantalizing and unfulfilled courtship of a Southern belle. Negroes exist as blank surfaces capable of reflecting various white projections.

Unknowingly, Miltiades has compounded incest with rape since Gracie is his half-sister. Gracie eventually escapes to the Union Army and becomes the mistress of Beekman, a Northern officer. Miltiades, a proper Southern gentleman, feels contempt for Beekman's open avowal of his relationship with a Negro woman. In *The Store,* Drusilla's daughter, Sydna (Alberta Sydna after the Confederate general), a proper Southern lady, asks Miltiades about Gracie's son. Miltiades mistakenly informs her that the father was Beekman. Sydna smugly responds, "I can't possibly understand the taste of Yankees." [8] Southerners must manipulate their imaginations in such a way as to properly rationalize their relations to Negroes out of real existence.

Jerry Catlin, Miltiades' hobbledehoy nephew, is another illustration. A typical Stribling character, he combines a deep and tender self-pity with complete unconcern for others. Jerry is sitting in a kitchen surrounded by food when a Negro shows up begging charity. The Negro explains that he had been working for the Handbacks, Miltiades' great enemies, and was thrown off his land after he prevented Handback from shooting Miltiades in a brawl. Now he and his family are destitute and need food. Jerry refuses the request thinking with a beatified disregard for reality, "They'll do anything in the world to get a white person's sympathy and take advantage of it" (264). Later in the novel, Miltiades' Negro tenant has a wagon stolen from him by a poor white. Miltiades automatically assumes that the Negro's reluctance to recover the wagon is as an illustration of the abstract truth: Negro cowardice. As a white Southerner, he knows that the poor white could attack and kill the Negro boy with impunity and that conversely the Negro might well be lynched for an overly successful self-defense. It never occurs to Miltiades to wonder how brave he himself might be in similar circumstances.

In *The Unfinished Cathedral,* one of the characters curses the fact that most people do not "bloom out into what they really were instead of having to seep into forms already prepared for them like pseudomorphic rock." [9] But Marsan Vaiden, Miltiades' daughter, does break through, sending a telegram to a Northern Negro organization about the local rigged trial planned for some Negro boys accused of rape. (Stribling draws on the Scottsboro boys.) One of the nice ironies of the novel is the conversation between Marsan and a high school girl friend about Marsan's pregnancy. Marsan's mother supposes that her daughter will be a social pariah and that Marsan's friend is visiting her only because she does not yet know the awful truth: " 'Listen to that . . . just listen to those innocent children. . . .' She was speaking of laughter from Sarah May Tergune and Marsan which came upstairs from below. 'It doesn't seem possible that one of those innocent girls could ever know—what life is.' " Meanwhile, Marsan and her friend, who knows more about the circumstances of the pregnancy than the mother, are in the midst of an animated if somewhat uninformed discussion of hormones. The younger generation is neither rebellious nor even self-consciously skeptical, but it is enough in touch with reality, enough affected by new social tendencies, to feel a constant slight amazement with the antiquated delusions of adult society.

Stribling's value is in such observations. He does much to explain the Southern cast of mind that makes the current "closed society" of Mississippi so difficult to comprehend. The closed society is simply the result of a major challenge to the prejudiced mind, a personality type that, by definition, is capable of looking straight at a fact and denying its existence. How, then, does Stribling's fiction differ from straight sociology? [10] It is in the *demonstration* of prejudiced thinking, showing how a particular person *can* think in this manner. Most sociology tells us that people have certain misconceptions; this is not the same as giving us an image of such people and of their false consciousness.

But sociological fiction has a built-in trap. From the sociological point of view, a writer who has no explicit concern with society may be more revealing than an explicitly sociological novelist. Too often the sociological novelist is limited by and to his thesis. The critic looking for a pattern or idea to abstract finds the sociological novelist has beat him to it: the fiction itself is abstract and overexplained. Robert Penn Warren complains that Stribling's characters "retain the taint of illustration: they are too mathematically exact, and, in consequence, predictable." [11] But, then, Stribling's main judgment against his characters is that they *are* automatic, that they generally *do* act predictably.

The ironic dilemma of the sociological novelist is that he is confined by the limitations of his subject. His plot is usually as automatic as his characters; if they lack imagination, so, too often, does he. Lewis very nearly overcame this dilemma in *Babbitt* and *Elmer Gantry*. Though the plots of both novels are crude and clumsy, Lewis unified each novel by a live central image: Babbitt, the baby; Gantry, the wolf in shepherd's clothing. Stribling's characters are more realistic but less interesting. With even less unity than Lewis, Stribling is even more prolix. His trilogy totals 1479 pages, an unjustifiable length. There is a thematic plot, though it only surfaces from time to time: the white Vaidens' repeated failures of responsibility to their unacknowledged Negro relatives. The plot is really mythical in substance which is why it never comes off; Stribling's style cannot bear the weight of myth. The extent of his failure is evident by comparison with the incest section of Faulkner's *The Bear* in which the same theme is successfully handled.

Moreover, even on sociological grounds, Stribling can be faulted. His characters, with rare exceptions, seem unrealistic in their nearly unanimous inability to think and in their incapacity for doubt or guilt. The built-in distortion in the writings of Stribling, as in those of Mencken and Lewis, is not that people are not like this, but that so many people are so consistently mindless so much of the time. If any real person could have been expected to be an almost perfect prototype of the prejudiced mind portrayed by the anticonformists, one would expect it to be John Washington Butler, the author of the Tennessee anti-evolution bill that led to the Scopes trial. But this is an instance of our own stereotyping. Ray Ginger portrays Butler thus:

Butler was no vindictive, pleasure-hating, puritanical fanatic. In maturity he looked back with pride to his youthful skill at baseball. He loved music, and his three sons had a band. His religion looked toward love rather than toward retribution. Clerk of his own congregation and clerk of the district session of the Primitive Baptists, he had chosen this sect over the more popular Missionary Baptists because of a doctrinal issue: "Now *I* don't believe, and *no* Primitive Baptist believes that God would condemn a man just because he never heard of the gospel." [12]

To compound seeming inconsistency, Butler told reporters that he had read Darwin and would not object to his children doing the same.[13] During the trial, Butler was upset by the judge's decision to exclude scientific evidence, believing that it was unfair to the defense and that it would have been an educational experience.[14] Other fundamentalists may have more perfectly accorded with the stereotype, but it seems evident that there are more skew people in reality than in the writings of the anticonformists. Stribling's novels are half-truths, but within their limits, they are valuable comments on Southern society. As much as Stribling leaves out, no Southern novelist more completely unmasked the mental machinery of prejudice.

Thomas Wolfe's notorious weaknesses are at the opposite extreme of Stribling's. Wolfe did not leave out enough; what exists of form in his novels almost disappears beneath a sludge of headlong rhetoric and irrelevant incident. If Stribling too much subjects his characters to a thesis, Wolfe appears to have no thesis, no theme, no controlling idea of any sort but solely a large and irrepressible vocabulary. Wolfe's word-hoard was something of a Pandora's box; once opened almost everything flew out except one poor shade caught halfway out by the descending lid: the pale wraith of structure. Nevertheless, there are themes to his novels although they are always weakened by Wolfe's compulsive inclusiveness. In fact, it is Wolfe who really works out the two major themes of the revolt from the village to their logical conclusion and, at his best, transcends them. Wolfe is the poet of the buried life, the unmasker of economic sham, and the creator of a fictive town of a textural density and a concrete actuality unrivalled by any American writer.

Most of Wolfe's best writing came from his life-long quarrel with his home town. Though not a lover's quarrel, there was more than ambivalence in Wolfe's hate. Wolfe's aggression towards Asheville is always, when he writes well, transformed into its opposite: an elegiac gesture of frustrate and doubting love, of irremediable loss. Wolfe discovered he could not go home again but exile was the source of his creativity.

It took, of course, some time for Wolfe to become fully aware of the necessity of Asheville. An amusingly vigorous borrowing of the Lewis-Mencken point of view is apparent in the letters he was writing to his mother in the early twenties:

I will step on toes, I will not hesitate to say what I think of those people who shout "Progress, Progress, Progress"—when what they mean is more Ford automobiles, more Rotary Clubs, more Baptist Ladies Social Unions. I will say that "Greater Asheville" does not necessarily mean "100000 by 1930," that we

are not necessarily 4 times as civilized as our grandfathers because we go four times as fast in automobiles. . . . What I shall
try to get into their dusty little pint-measure minds is that a full
belly, a good automobile, paved streets, and so on, do not make
them one whit better or finer,—that there is beauty in this world,
—beauty even in this wilderness of ugliness and provincialism
that is at present our country. . . . In the name of God, let us
learn to be men, not monkeys.[15]

Wolfe saw his relation to Asheville in somewhat exalted
terms: "Tell the Philistines that Samson bids them 'go to
H————.' "[16] In 1923, George Pierce Baker's Harvard 47
Workshop Group produced a Wolfe play dedicated to just
that proposition. *Welcome to Our City* attacks the new Asheville of the real estate boom. Wolfe attacked the usual target
of the materialistic boosting businessman in the usual way.
Occasionally, however, there are some quite genuine touches
of the new commercial South. In the most successful scene,
two young Southerners parody the historical novel's treatment of the Civil War:

Lee: Any late dispatches from the front, Captain?
"Bull": Yes, General, a young lady has been captured in the
bushes near headquarters.
Lee (muttering): Strange! In the bushes you say? Was she
alone?
"Bull": Absolutely alone, General. We suspect her of being
Ophelia Saltonstall, the notorious Yankee spy.
Lee: Did she look disheveled? Did she have any grass on the
back of her back? Was there any hay or confetti on her person?
"Bull": I cannot tell, General—she refuses to talk with
officers. She prefers the privates.[17]

This nicely catches the satirical spirit of the college sopho-
more.

The play as a whole is less successful. Wolfe overdoes the
unmasking of a North Carolina governor whose imposing
public image is shown to depend on a toupee, false teeth,

false shoe soles and leather arches, shoulder pads, shoulder braces, abdomen supporters, and three suits of underwear. The racial conflict around which the play revolves loses dramatic effectiveness because of Wolfe's muddled point of view. Almost every character in the play is undercut but not from any consistent set of Wolfe's own values. Wolfe uses irony self-indulgently in an attempt to hide his own indecision. At this point in his career, he seems to offer his "honest indignation" at everyone else as a substitute for any values or viewpoint of his own. Of course, like any twenties writer, he was certain that he was for art and freedom and against materialism.

This viewpoint is the *ostensible* theme of *Look Homeward, Angel,* but here Wolfe came into his own. The poorest sections of *Look Homeward* embody the theme of the sensitive young artist in a Philistine society. Wolfe's subtitle, *A Story of the Buried Life,* was meant to refer to the autobiographical hero's drive to protect and understand his own secret life, but the execution does not correspond with the intention. In fact, Eugene is the least interesting, least valid character in the novel. The effectively rendered "buried life" in Wolfe's novel is that of the family and the town. The mood of the best sections of the novel is not defiance but bittersweet elegy.

Louis Budd's exceptionally fine article, "The Grotesques of Anderson and Wolfe," shows the tonal and thematic influence of Anderson's *Winesburg* on Wolfe's first novel. Both treat the theme of isolation, loneliness, and buried life; in both "the theme of life's frightening meaninglessness was linked with a tender belief in life's magic that in Anderson and Wolfe amounted to a crude religiosity." [18]

The tone and themes Budd analyzes are but another variant of the naturalistic pathos to be found in E. W. Howe and, more fully expressed, in Dreiser, Masters, and Anderson. The spirit of self-righteous personal revenge with which

Wolfe began his novel is gradually eclipsed by a growing sense of the universal pathos of humanity lost in time. The weakness of the book was Wolfe's failure to realize the inconsistency of the often maudlin subjective rhetoric with brilliantly objective scenes that speak quite adequately for themselves. Self-pity and self-righteousness spoil the novel; objective pathos enriches it.

The depiction of the Gant family is a case in point. The rhetorical voice is usually moralistic and condemnatory; only Ben and Eugene (naturally) escape censure. The actual rendering of the family, however, is from a quite different perspective. The Gants, including Ben, suffer from a radical inability to communicate with one another. Unable to articulate the language of the heart, they employ such comic-pathetic substitutes as W. O. Gant's formal invective, Helen's ritual of complaint, and Eliza's provincial formulas and predictable rhythms. But the surface Gant is an illusion beneath which each Gant conceals his own form of vitality. Luke lives in a world of sentimental clichés, "large, crude and gaudily painted, labelled 'Father,' 'Mother,' 'Home,' 'Family,' 'Generosity,' 'Honor,' 'Unselfishness,' made of sugar and molasses and gummed gelatinously with tear-shaped syrup." [19] Luke's egotism and need for affection lead him to project himself as big-hearted and unselfish. In order to win the approval he hungers for, Luke is a complete conformist to the banal pretenses of the village. Underlying these appearances is a "demonic exuberance" (253), a subliminal comic intelligence that shatters the restraints of convention, quite apart from Luke's conscious intentions.

Thus, listening to an old lady of the church, who with all her power of persuasion and earnestness was unfolding the dogmas of Presbyterianism to him, he would lean forward in an attitude of exaggerated respectfulness and attention, one broad hand clenched about his knee, while he murmured gentle agreement to what she said:

"Yes? . . . Ye-e-es? . . . Ye-e-e-e-es? . . . . Is that right?
. . . Yes? . . ."

Suddenly the demonic force would burst in him. Inanely tickled at the cadences of his agreement, the earnest placidity and oblivion of the old woman, the extravagant pretense of the whole situation, his face flooded with wild exultancy, he would croon in a fat luscious bawdily suggestive voice:

"Y-ah-s? . . . Y-a-h-s? . . . Y-ah-s? . . ." and when at length too late she became aware of this drowning flood of demonic nonsense, and paused, turning an abrupt startled face to him, he would burst into a wild "whah-whah-whah-whah" of laughter, beyond all reason, with strange throat noises, tickling her roughly in the ribs (253–54).

Similarly, Eliza, Helen, and W. O. Gant have a vitality that renders each a unique and memorable character. Even the quiet Ben has his leitmotiv, the gesture to his ever-present silent demon, that is his response to all fakery and pretense: "a brief nod upwards and to the side of the companion to whom he communicated all his contemptuous observations —his dark satiric angel: 'Oh, my God! Listen to that won't you'" (124). The Gants express their essential selves only in such semiarticulate gestures.

Similarly, the tone of the best passages about the town are not savagely satirical but indulgently comic, with an almost nostalgic complexity. No American novel conveys the texture of small-town life with more fidelity, with less resort to half-truth, distortion, or exaggeration. The atmosphere of small-town adultery is brilliantly evoked in the description of Mrs. Selborne, a summer boarder at Eliza's Dixieland:

She was one of several handsome and bacchic daughters of a depleted South Carolinian of good family: she married at sixteen a red heavy man who came and went from her incomparable table, eating rapidly and heartily, muttering, when passed, a few shy sullen words, and departing to the closed leather-and-horse smell of his little office in the livery-stable he owned. She had two children by him, both girls: she moved with wasted stealth all around the quiet slander of a South Carolina mill-town, committing adultery with a mill-owner, a banker, and a lumber man, walking circumspectly with her tender blonde smile by day past all the sly smiles of town and trade, knowing that the earth was mined below her feet, and that her name, with clerk and merchant, was a sign for secret laughter. The natives, the men in particular, treated her with even more elaborate respect than a woman is usually given in a Southern town, but their eyes, behind the courteous unctions of their masks, were shiny with invitation (148).

The portrait is less satirical than celebratory. More satirical but equally good-natured is Wolfe's description of the effect of Mrs. Thelma Jarvis' sensual amble on two upright Altamont citizens:

Mr. Paul Goodson, of the Dependable Life, closed his long grinning dish-face abruptly, and ceased talking. He doffed his hat without effusiveness as did his companion, Coston Smathers, the furniture man (you furnish the girl, we furnish the house). They were both Baptists.

Mrs. Thelma Jarvis turned her warm ivory stare upon them, parted her full small mouth in a remote smile, and passed, ambulant. When she had gone they turned to each other, grinning quietly. We'll be waiting at the river. Swiftly they glanced about them. No one had seen (344–45).

The usual critical complaints against Wolfe are that he is (1) merely autobiographical, (2) merely rhetorical, and (3) formless. These criticisms are true but only partially so. Eugene Gant is an embarrassing character; Wolfe is rhetorical and his rhetoric is bad; not one novel of Wolfe's is completely controlled in form. On the other hand, Eugene Gant is overshadowed by other thoroughly real characters, the Gant family and Altamont are completely revealed in perfectly objective and evocative description, and certain episodes in *Look Homeward, Angel* achieve a limited but definite form. Certainly, Wolfe is a failure if the only criterion of excellence is the well-made novel, flawless in construction from beginning to end. But there are fewer such novels than many critics admit; most classic American novels have major defects of structure, though this fact has been somewhat obscured by the tendency of critics to ingeniously overread books they like. At any rate, the only true criterion for excellence is, as Henry James knew, the *interest* a book has. One of the innumerable sources of fictional interest is the shock of recognition a reader feels as he encounters an accurately perceived reality, an observed and recorded segment of the texture of life given its full comic or pathetic value. Enough such passages may give certain books more interest to a reader than a relatively well-made novel full of lifeless characters, such as countless forgotten writers have produced.

This is not to deny that Wolfe did a good job of hiding his best writing under the mountainous deposits of his worst, nor do a few good passages excuse an over-all failure of coherency. The case for Wolfe must rest on his creation of a richly textured fictive world, albeit one too often intruded upon by the heavy tread of pseudo-poetic rhetoric. In some sections of *Look Homeward, Angel,* Wolfe manages to escape rhetoric (and Eugene Gant, too) almost altogether in an objective showing forth of his world.

One such section is Wolfe's characterization of the gradual awakening of the town, Altamont, on an April morning. The life of Altamont is represented as it awakens in "sharp, broken fragments" (169). Ben Gant arises before dawn to go to his work; newspaperboy Number 3 is accused of trading newspapers for sexual favors; Tom Cline drives Engine 36 up the Saluda slope. The progress of the people is enclosed and paced by the progress of the morning. Wolfe's description of the gradual spreading of the morning light acts as a leitmotiv throughout, generally coming at the beginning or end of one of the fragments of human activity that he records.

The scene is thus grounded in a structure of natural and human time. It is also defined in space as Wolfe's focus moves through and outside town from the Uneeda Lunch No. 3 to Judge Webster Tayloe's domain at Lunn's Cove. The context is further enriched with imagery running from the smell of nicotine to the sound of Number 3's newspaper thwacking against May Corpening's red shack porch to the coolness of the pearl-gray dawn and even the taste of Tom Cline's thick sandwich of cold, buttered fried meat.

With Ben Gant's entrance into the Uneeda Lunch No. 3, Wolfe introduces the characters of the scene and proceeds to reveal their interrelationships through conversation and description. Ben finds Doctor McGuire drunkenly trying to spear kidney beans as Doctor Coker sardonically looks on. Ben, Coker, and McGuire mask their underlying friendship with sarcasms and light malice. Their tone changes as Doctor Spaugh comes in. Spaugh is not disliked, but it is evident that the mountaineer turned socialite doctor is not quite in with the group. The response to Spaugh's pretentious complaints about his elegant new dancing shoes is less than sympathetic: " 'Patent Leather pumps!' " said McGuire. 'Hurt his feet. By God, Coker, the first time he came to town ten years ago he'd never been curried above the knees. They had to throw him down to put shoes on him' " (174). Later in the scene, Spaugh makes a covert social bid by offering his room at the hotel for McGuire to wash up in. The offer is turned down.

The undertaker, Horse Hines, comes in for rougher treatment. The others feel a hostility toward him that is only barely covered over with the mask of humor. Finally the undertaker is irritated into a defense:

"The sacred rites of closing the eyes, of composing the limbs, and of preparing for burial the lifeless repository of the departed soul is our holy mission; it is for us, the living, to pour balm upon the broken heart of grief, to soothe the widow's ache, to brush away the orphan's tears; it is for us, the living, to highly resolve that—"

"Government of the people, for the people, and by the people," said Hugh McGuire.

"Yes, Horse," said Coker, "you are right. I'm touched. And what's more we do it all for nothing. At least I never charge for soothing the widow's ache."

"What about embalming the broken heart of Grief?" asked McGuire.

"I said *balm*," Horse Hines remarked coldly.

"Say, Horse," said Harry Tugman, who had listened with great interest, "didn't you make a speech with all that in it last summer at the Undertaker's Convention?"

"What's true then is true now," said Horse Hines bitterly, as he left the place (175).

The passage is a flawless mimesis of small-town badinage, of the fellowship and aggressions of a subliminal *Gemeinschaft*. But though the type of conversation is perfectly familiar, there are no wearisome clichés—except those of Horse Hines. The very familiarity of the scene in life becomes part of its freshness in literature.

The scene is held together not only by the nuances of personal relations and the clumsy jokes of tired men but by an enveloping mood; throughout the scene runs the pathos of McGuire's alcoholism and the prevalence of death and decay:

McGuire, drunkenly lost in revery, stared witlessly down at his bean plate and sighed.

"Come on, you damned fool," said Coker, getting up, "you've got to operate in forty-five minutes."

"Oh, for God's sake," said Ben lifting his head from the stained mug, "who's the victim? I'll send flowers." ". . . all of us, sooner or later," McGuire mumbled puffily through his puff lips. "Rich and poor alike. Here today and gone tomorrow. Doesn't matter . . . doesn't matter at all" (173).

Here, in place of a merely rhetorical wail of "O lost," is a revelation of an actual "lostness" that permeates the scene and the characters. The characters are lost in time. The progress of morning not only paces and structurally divides the chapter, it also becomes part of the texture and atmosphere, part of the theme and meaning. In contrast with human time—men wasting away to the final destination of the sickbed and the funeral parlor—is the time of nature: "The town emerged from the lilac darkness with a washed renascent cleanliness. All the world seemed as young as spring" (179). This coming after Coker's comment to the coughing McGuire. " 'You're drowning in your own secretions,' " said Coker, with his yellow grin. 'Like old lady Sladen.' " (171) The irony is less literary than natural; it is the irony of man's place in nature.

Through the juxtaposition of natural and human time, Wolfe shows the lostness of his characters, this lostness being the common human condition that supplies a ground for their diverse personalities. Wolfe achieves in this part of his novel an organic unity, a fusing into oneness of the dichotomies of structure and texture, individual character and the human condition, the commonplace and the wondrous. Even personality, which Wolfe too often treated as a locked-in and utterly incommunicable essence, is seen in this chapter as interpenetrating the atmosphere of the scene: " 'Oh listen to this!' Ben said, laughing irritably and bending his peaked face in the coffee mug. His bitter savor filled the place with life, with tenderness, with beauty" (172). The chapter is grounded in a density of atmosphere: the freshness of the morning, the savor of personalities, and the less indefinite auras of McGuire's whiskey breath and, later, Eliza Gant's medicine—glycerine and mentholatum.

The final fusion of the chapter is between Wolfe's sensibility and the people and things about which he is writing. Consciousness blends with material, subject with object, until the author is lost sight of, completely absorbed in his creation. Creation, in fact, seems almost a misnomer; Wolfe reveals rather than creates. Nowhere in any of Wolfe's writing is his annoying and embarrassing ego more absent, and nowhere is his writing more lucid, more authentic.

The chapter closes on exactly the right note as the mimesis of Altamont, the representation of its inner life, ends with the culmination of some movements and the beginning of others:

> At this moment Number 3, having finished his route, stepped softly on to the slime-scummed porch of the house on Valley Street, rapped gently at the door, and opened it quietly, groping his way through black miasmic air to the bed in which May Corpening lay. She muttered as if drugged as he touched her, turned toward him, and sleepily awakened, drew him down to her with heavied and sensual caress, yoked under her big coppery arms. Tom Cline clumped greasily up the steps of his residence on Bartlett Street, swinging his tin pail; Ben returned to the paper office with Harry Tugman; and Eugene, in the back room on Woodson Street, waking suddenly to Gant's powerful command from the foot of the stairs, turned his face full into a momentary vision of roseflushed blue sky and tender blossoms that drifted slowly earthward (189–90).

Wolfe defines "wonder" as "the union of the ordinary and the miraculous" (476). When Wolfe orates on the beauty and wonder of life, he manages to be both hysterical and dull at the same time. Wolfe's romanticism becomes viable when it is employed as a way of *seeing* or principle of vision. Romance, George Santayana notes, "involves a certain sense of homelessness in a chaotic world, and at the same time a sense of meaning and beauty there." In romance is "the magic of strangeness and distance, and the profound absurdity of things." [20] This perfectly defines the romantic strain that is an essential element in the naturalistic pathos of Dreiser, Anderson, Masters, and Wolfe. In the best of *Look*

Homeward, Angel, Wolfe manages to release himself from personal grievance and obsessive self-love, and he is able to look at his town *sub specie aeternitatis,* seeing the sadness of its beauty and the beauty of its sadness.

The revolt from the village ends with Wolfe, an appropriate culmination. For in *Look Homeward, Angel,* Wolfe evoked the buried life with a greater fidelity of texture than Anderson or Masters, and in *You Can't Go Home Again,* he wrote a near definitive unmasking of a business civilization. The unmasking, however, is more grotesque than satiric. For *You Can't Go Home Again* is a novel of the thirties. Business had collapsed, and business values no longer prevailed although many businessmen continued to believe in their own propaganda. Effective satire is always against the inflated, and the business balloon had already been pricked.

Thus Wolfe's unmasking is conducted in a spirit of reassessment. *You Can't Go Home Again* is Wolfe's second best novel. It lacks his first and best novel's richness of character and texture. None of the characters, not even Mr. and Mrs. Jack, have the abundant vitality and credibility of half a dozen characters in the earlier book. But this later volume, one of two quarried by Edward Aswell from Wolfe's gigantic posthumous manuscripts (the other is *The Web and the Rock*), goes well beyond any other of Wolfe's works in its judgment on society.

The Altamont of *Look Homeward, Angel* disproves Wolfe's strictures about it. Wolfe was trying to apply the standard Mencken-Lewis critique and the old sensitive-artist *vs.* Philistine formula, but the town emerges rich, strange, anything but dull. In *You Can't Go Home Again,* Wolfe goes all the way back to themes and devices used in *Welcome to Our City* but with a transmutation of key devices from indignant, "smart," uncentered satire to a sober, grim unmasking based not on Wolfe's personal vindictiveness but on the self-evident collapse of the reigning values. Business had, in effect, unmasked itself; the writer merely had to hold the mirror up to nature.

The unmaskings in *You Can't Go Home Again* lack subtlety, for subtlety was superfluous. Moreover, Wolfe's talent, at its best, worked with natural symbols, those that most obviously expressed the case. So with his unmaskings: the symbols are direct and literal. The best satirical scene in *Look Homeward, Angel* is the gruesome comedy of Horse Hines's undertaking parlor as he "prepares" Ben's body:

> Horse Hines looked raptly at the cold strange face.
> "A fine boy," he murmured as his fish-eye fell tenderly on his work. "And I have tried to do him justice."
> They were silent for the moment, looking.
> "You've d-d-done a fine job," said the sailor. [Luke] "I've got to hand it to you. What do you say, 'Gene?"
> "Yes," said Eugene, in a small choking voice. "Yes."
> "He's a b-b-b-bit p-p-p-pale, don't you think?" the sailor stammered, barely conscious of what he was saying.
> "Just a moment!" said Horse Hines quickly, lifting a finger. Briskly he took a stick of rouge from his pocket, stepped forward, and deftly, swiftly sketched upon the dead gray cheeks a ghastly rose-hued mockery of life and health.
> "There!" he said with deep satisfaction; and rouge stick in hand, head critically cocked, like a painter before his canvas, he stepped back into the terrible staring prison of their horror.
> "There are artists, boys, in every profession," Horse Hines continued in a moment, with quiet pride, "and though I do say it myself, Luke, I'm proud of my work on this job. Look at him!" he exclaimed with sudden energy, and a bit of color in his gray face. "Did you ever see anything more natural in your life?"
> Eugene turned upon the man a grim and purple stare, noting with pity, with a sort of tenderness, as the dogs of laughter tugged at his straining throat, the earnestness and pride in the long horse-face.
> "Look at it!" said Horse Hines again in low wonder. "I'll never beat that again! Not if I live to be a million! That's art, boys" (571).

The scene symbolizes what is editorialized later in the novel. The buried life is the result of secret fear, the American fear of facing the ultimates: sickness, horror, death. All is glozed over, disguised, cheapened. Eugene "was terrified before the loud good health of America, which is really a sickness because no man will admit his sores" (586).

Similarly, direct and naïve symbolism is used in *You Can't Go Home Again*. The book literally unmasks. George Webber, the autobiographical hero, is returning home in the Libya Hill Pullman car for his aunt's funeral. The mayor and leading town businessmen have been excitedly discussing the real estate boom, even urging George to buy, but

As George went into the washroom, suddenly he came upon the mayor cleaning his false teeth in the basin. The man's plump face, which George had always known in the guise of cheerful, hearty, amiability, was all caved in. Hearing a sound behind him, the mayor turned upon the newcomer. For a moment there was nothing but nameless fright in his weak brown eyes. He mumbled frantically, incoherently, holding his false teeth in his trembling fingers. Like a man who did not know what he was doing, he brandished them in a grotesque yet terrible gesture indicative of—God knows what!—but despair and terror were both in it. Then he put the teeth into his mouth again, smiled feebly, and muttered apologetically, with some counterfeit of his usual geniality:

"Ho, ho!—well son! You caught me that time, all right!" [21]

The scene is a literal unmasking, a device borrowed from *Welcome to Our City* but here used with a new seriousness, not to merely expose a fake, but to reveal the hidden terror of the official representative of Libya Hill, still determinedly masking his knowledge of the town's imminent financial collapse.

The mayor's opposite in Wolfe's symbolic structure is Judge Rumford Bland, a blind seer and an open sinner. A rarity in Wolfe's writings, this character is pure invention, not based on any real person. Perhaps this is why Wolfe's attempt to humanize Judge Bland by "explaining" that his evilness is the result of a goodness that the town can find no use for (*corruptio optimi,* etc.) is such a failure. Bland works in the novel as a symbolic character, a given; the attempt at explanation merely weakens a weirdly suggestive characterization. This one flaw aside, detail of description adds to the total effect the characterization creates:

> There was something genuinely old and corrupt at the sources of his life and spirit. . . . It was palpable in the touch of his thin, frail hand when he greeted you, it was present in the deadly weariness of his tone of voice, in the dead-white texture of his emaciated face, in his lank and lusterless auburn hair, and, most of all, in his sunken mouth, around which there hovered constantly the ghost of a smile. It could only be called the ghost of a smile. . . . When one looked closely it was gone. But one knew that it was always there—lewd, evil, mocking, horribly corrupt, and suggesting a limitless vitality akin to the humor of death, which welled up from some secret spring in his dark soul (77).

In *Look Homeward, Angel,* Wolfe shows that health is really illness. In the character of Judge Bland, he shows, complementarily, an illness that is, in some ways, health. Though blind from syphilis, Bland sees through the townspeople. Openly acknowledging the loathesome source of his blindness, Bland mocks the hidden illnesses of his conventional and apparently healthy neighbors. Bland is the great unmasker, exposing the "stark underlying terror" (84) of Libya Hill. Leaving the devastated travelers after his cold denunciation of their corruptions and hypocrisies, his last words are "I'll be seeing you" (88).

What Bland sees is the spiritual death of his townsmen; " 'Let the dead bury their dead,' " he tells George, " 'Come sit among the blind' " (81). But Bland himself is the very effigy of death, and in a curious and not entirely explicable way, he stands for as well as exposes the town. Wolfe manages this effect through a web of symbolic suggestion that does not entirely yield to paraphrase. It is as though Bland has almost deliberately transformed himself into a symbol and parody of the town, a self-constituted exaggeration, embarrassment, and exposure of Libya Hill. His business—lending money to Negroes at extortionate rates of interest—is, in effect, a *reductio ad absurdum* of the exploitative element in any business. As the Judge puts it, " 'Oh—' with a deprecating nod—'a little nigger squeezing here and there, a comfortable income out of Niggertown, a few illegal lendings, a comfortable practice in small usury—yet my wants were few, my tastes were very simple. I was always satisfied with, say, a modest five per cent a week. So I am not in the big money. . .' " (87).

The Judge's filthy store, filled with broken-down Negro furniture seized for "unpaid" debts, has something of the symbolic quality of the junk shop in *Bleak House*. As in Dickens, the symbol is rendered by indefinably suggestive concrete detail: "Above the shambles of the nigger junk, upon the second floor, were Judge Bland's offices. A wooden stairway, worn by the tread of clay-booted time, and a hand rail, loose as an old tooth, smooth besweated by the touch of many a black palm, led up to a dark hallway. Here, in Stygian gloom, one heard the punctual monotone of a single and regularly repeated small drop of water dripping somewhere in the rear, and caught the overpowering smell of the tin urinal" (75–76). In literature, symbolic opposites always attract, so it is fitting that, in a later chapter, it is Bland who discovers the suicided Mayor lying grotesquely beneath the urinal. As the Judge notes, "there was no accounting for tastes—but if a man wanted to do it, that was probably as good a place as any" (368).

The later episodes of the novel—Mrs. Jack's party, the portrait of Lloyd McHarg, the trip to Germany—are not relevant to the revolt from the village except as they reflect the theme of every Wolfe novel: homelessness. "Home" is the ever-recurrent, always resonant complex word in the vocabulary of Wolfe's emotions. All of his writings reflect the search, doomed from the beginning to failure, for "the great forgotten language, the lost lane-end in to heaven, a stone, a leaf, an unfound door." [22] "Home," then, as in the vocabulary of the existentialists, means the transcendent sphere of vaguely intuited but unattainable reality, a sphere of human communion beyond the limits of malice, ambiguity, and error. These absolutes can be sometimes approached in dim gropings and expressed in fugitive gestures, but they can never be fully possessed, for the human condition is to be caught in a world that is relative, chaotic, incomplete, graspable only in isolated insights, small achievements of form against a background of overarching chaos. The transcendent home, whose existence Wolfe learned from romantic poetry and his own emotions, is unreachable; it serves mainly as the ideal by which the real is measured and found to be chaotic and partial.

But "home" is also the chaos itself. What we love, what we must love is what is close at hand, natural to us, conditions that chaos fills as does its opposite, order. So Wolfe's subject is really the celebration of lostness. Like Cather and Anderson, his form is elegy, the form that imaginatively orders the chaos of time past. *You Can't Go Home Again* unmasks but also mourns the lost town, the lost talent (Lloyd McHarg), the lost second homeland of the soul (Germany). *Look Homeward, Angel* is one of the great American elegies, and the elegy is one of our most prolific forms; but in all of Wolfe's novels, elegy is qualified with satire. Indeed, the satire is a condition of the elegy, serving to keep things straight. The satire reminds us that "home," here the real home, therefore the chaotic home, is loved *because* it is lost. If it were not lost, it would be impossible to love. The priority involved in elegy must be emphasized: the elegist values the past because it *was* his past, it was the scene of his most intense emotions; it is not valued because of any imagined social, economic, or political advantage that it possessed. Wolfe's most valuable insight is that you can't go home again "to your childhood . . . back home to the old forms and systems of things which once seemed everlasting but which are changing all the time—back home to the escapes of time and memory" (706). The principle of the elegy from Walt Whitman to Wallace Stevens is that "Death is the mother of beauty." It is our best piety to love, respect, and mourn the past but always with a touch of satire or a measure of distance. It is right to mourn the dead; perverse to wish for their return.

Finally, Wolfe realized that "home," the small-town home associated with childhood, could not be gone back to because home itself changed, refusing to oblige nostalgia by retaining in some sort of historical amber the exact face and tempo of the childhood world. Like many towns, Libya Hill was a mirror of, rather than a refuge from, the national speculative hysteria. The town had transformed itself in a decade from Gopher Prairie to Zenith and, before the collapse, had visions of Atlanta. For that matter, even though Wolfe expressed regret, he realized what had happened; he knew that the towns were in time, part of the historical process, and that they represented no haven.

10. The Thirties and After

The revolt from the village that began so bravely in 1915 fizzled out rather dismally in the thirties. Business values, a main target of twenties satire, had suffered the same fate as the main stocks; they survived but in a thoroughly deflated form. Also undercut were self-proclaimed guardians of public morality; people worried less about their neighbor's faulty mores than about their own economic survival. A symbol of the times might be seen in the permutations of Akron, Ohio, an industrial city mainly populated by transplanted Southern mountaineers. In the twenties, Akron was a strong Ku Klux Klan town; by the late thirties it was dominated by the C.I.O.[1]

The exuberant satire of the twenties became superfluous, dying from lack of opposition, and yielded to the grim ironies of Dos Passos and Ruth McKenney (*Industrial Valley*). Successive literary eras are almost always intolerably smug about their supposed moral superiority to the period just ended, and the thirties was no exception. Twenties satire, despite its unmasking of the businessman, began to appear frivolous and negative to a decade that was increasingly demanding viable alternatives rather than "mere" criticism. It is easy to be unfair to thirties intellectuals who were, in fact, quite right in spotting a certain emptiness in the twenties writers whom they now began to attack. Nevertheless, the thirties demand for high seriousness and more or less prefabricated radical ideas seems priggish and stodgy from a later perspective, though no more priggish and stodgy, perhaps, than many of the forties and fifties critiques of the thirties.

The immoderation of such cultural warfare is probably necessary; the gesture of total rejection clears the ground for a necessary reconstruction of cultural attitudes. The viewpoints and issues of the twenties were simply no longer relevant. The rebels seemed irrelevant in their attempt to reform a middle class that, many of the new radicals fondly believed, was finished, about to go down for good. Moreover, by 1930, it was evident that the village rebels had written themselves out, that their best work was in the past, and that many of them were nostalgically retreating to the bourgeois values that they had helped, in their best work, to discredit and destroy. Of course, none of them had completely changed. Their characteristic ambivalences were reversed; now they praised with considerable doubt and qualification where before they had attacked with certain half-admitted reservations. Nevertheless, if the later writings did represent a genuine potentiality that was in these writers from the beginning, the new emphasis also resulted in a loss of the bite that had made them important cultural critics. Although their later writings show occasional examples of wit and charm, they no longer came to grips with significant cultural issues. At their worst, these writers now seemed to affirm some of the same values that they had spent their best energies attacking.

Thus, Mencken, Lewis, Cather, and Brooks all lost direction in the late twenties and early thirties. Mencken retreated to an archaic conservatism, Lewis to a glorification of banality, Cather and Brooks to an artificial past. As for Masters, *Spoon River Anthology* is, except for his autobiography, his only book of any real importance, and even the autobiography is of value mainly as an extended footnote to *Spoon River Anthology*. The southern village rebels were exceptions to this general record of decline, partly because they were younger and began later. (Though Wolfe's best novel was his first.) It might help to place the village rebels by remembering that Mencken was born in 1880, Lewis in 1885, Cather in 1876, Brooks in 1886, and Masters in 1869. By 1930, all of these writers were well into middle age.

On no writer did the air of critical obsolescence settle more quickly and completely than on Mencken. For that matter, Mencken's influence, like that of Lewis and Anderson, had begun to decline even in the mid-twenties. Ernest Boyd's 1925 book on Mencken has more the tone of a general assessment of a completed corpus than that of a preliminary critique of a still-developing writer. Boyd's judgment was substantially correct; most, though not all, of Mencken's writings after 1925 were just more of the same. Nevertheless, Mencken remained relatively popular until the thirties, at which time his innate conservatism began to offend and alienate some of the readers who had formerly delighted in his irreverent iconoclasm. For Mencken's conservatism, although never disguised, had been less apparent in the twenties when he seemed to be one with the liberals in a common opposition to moral and civil intolerance. In the thirties, Mencken's conservatism became more and more salient in direct ratio to the triumphs of the liberals. He now turned his invective on the New Deal liberals, seeing them as a new variant of the "reformers" he had always despised. Mencken's opinions began to seem curiously abstract and unreal, out of touch with the concrete problems of the time. His invective against "Roosevelt Minor" lacked the bite of his attacks on such earlier foes as Bryan, Coolidge, and Hoover, partly because, for the first time, he was facing an opponent whose sense of humor and verbal facility were more than equal to his own. At a press conference, Roosevelt pointedly read a brilliant indictment of the reactionary press which, shamed and enraged, Mencken recognized as his own 1924 essay.[2] Mencken's satire, a weapon well adapted to batter the obvious idiocies committed by the Protestant ministry and the Ku Klux Klan, was too broad and blunt to even nick the liberals—whose characteristic idiocies were more subtle, less definable.

The best work of Mencken's later years were the books on American language and the three volumes of reminiscence, both rather patriotic projects. In fact, Mencken's memoirs completely bear out Ernest Boyd's contention that for all Mencken's fulminations against bourgeois provincialism, he was essentially a provincial bourgeois.[3] *Happy Days,* the first volume, opens with Mencken's ringing affirmation that he is now and always has been a dues-paying member of the bourgeoisie.[4] The book is a mellow and charming celebration of a bourgeois, provincial, but nonstandardized Baltimore, a beer-and-oyster-tinged paradise, as it seems in Mencken's evocation. Altogether the book is a cheerful justification of a tolerant, easy-going, good-humored, old-time, middle-class form of existence. It becomes obvious that Mencken's was a lover's quarrel with America. Most of the conventional values of middle-class America he never ceased believing in— with the significant exception of democracy.

Mencken's class loyalties help explain his conservative reaction in the thirties. With the worst of the middle class in power in the twenties and the radicals completely powerless, the middle class needed self-criticism. The alignment of poetic *vs.* practical, of tolerant *vs.* moralistic, was as valid and authentic in the twenties as that of capital *vs.* labor, privileged *vs.* proletariat, was in the thirties. (Of course, the *fake* poetic was as popular in the twenties as the *fake* proletariat in the thirties). In the thirties, the issues changed, the whole *idea* of a middle class was under attack, and some of its twenties critics began to defend what they previously had attacked. The thirties confirmed what many had begun to suspect even in the twenties: for all of their attacks on the middle class, some of the village rebels were congenital and incurable bourgeois. Of Lewis and Mencken it might be said that they had a home in bourgeois banality, that it was their fated subject and the boundary of their talents.

By 1930, Sinclair Lewis was finished as a serious novelist. His later novels are distinguished only by their somewhat differing degrees of dullness and shoddiness. In 1932, even Mencken had decided, as he commented to Philip Goodman, "Red was hopeless. . . . It takes more than one generation to breed out the stigmata of Sauk Center." [5] Lewis' last good novel, Dodsworth (1929) seems to mark a complete shift —a shift that was absurdly mistimed. As Mark Schorer observes, Lewis "turned back to a reassertion of those very middle-class, middle-brow and Middle Western values that the decade of the Twenties seemed to have destroyed forever, and that it had most emphatically modified at least; and with these values, he, who would henceforth seem to be the most old-fashioned of modern American novelists, would henceforth abide." [6] But Schorer notes that Lewis' change was not so extreme as it appeared; Lewis was merely returning to the themes and attitudes of his early, pre-*Main Street* fiction.[7]

There is a strange continuity in Lewis' fiction from his first novel to his last. His structure is usually a quest romance, the main theme an ambivalence between opposed cultural attitudes (East *vs.* West, Europe *vs.* America, the civilized snob *vs.* the vulgar good fellow, etc.). Almost all of the novels reflect Lewis' belief that the commonplace is intrinsically romantic. Another recurrent element is that in most of Lewis' novels the heroine is based on Lewis' wife or companion of the time. Most of the early heroines, Carol Kennicott, chief among them, are based on Grace Hegger Lewis. As the Lewises progressed toward divorce, female characters much like Carol appear as near-villains: Joyce Lanyon in *Arrow-*

smith and Fran Dodsworth in *Dodsworth*. Lewis' second wife, the journalist Dorothy Thompson, is dimly reflected in the social-worker heroine of *Ann Vickers*. Marcella Powers, the companion of his later years, is the source of Jinny Marshland in *Cass Timberlane*.[8]

A fine example of the style and substance of these early works is the following sentence from *The Trail of the Hawk* (1915), whose hero is a Swedish-American aviator named Carl Ericson: "'Carl's flying was as sordidly real as laying brick for a one-story laundry in a mill-town. Therefore, being real, it was romantic and miraculous.'"[9] All one can say of such a sentence is that the idea expressed was true—until it was expressed in just *those* words.

Even Lewis' three best novels, *Main Street, Babbitt,* and *Elmer Gantry* contain the quest, the ambivalence, and the romanticism of the commonplace. The superiority of these novels is that the satire overshadows such built-in weaknesses. The plots of both *Main Street* and *Babbitt* are built around the protagonists' search for freedom, but in both novels, the plot disappears behind the pervasive satirical image of universal mechanism and banality, just as Frank Shallard's quest in *Elmer Gantry* disappears behind the all-voracious image of Elmer Gantry himself, Lewis' ultimate caricature of mindless motion. (Gantry's own parody quest after Sharon Falconer is successful.) In the face of the boisterous satire of these novels, we are likely to forget the not infrequent intrusions of Lewis' hyperbanal version of romanticism, exemplified in this passage from *Main Street* in which Will Kennicott begins his clumsy courtship of Carol:

As their host left them, Kennicott awoke:

"Marbury tells me you're a high mogul in the public library. I was surprised. Didn't hardly think you were old enough. I thought you were a girl, still in college maybe."

"Oh, I'm dreadfully old. I expect to take to a lip-stick, and to find a gray hair any morning now."

"Huh! You must be frightfully old—prob'ly too old to be my granddaughter, I guess!"

Thus in the Vale of Arcady nymph and satyr beguiled the hours; precisely thus, and not in honeyed pentameters, discoursed Elaine and the worn Sir Lancelot in the pleached alley (13).

Does Lewis really believe that everybody—even purely imaginary characters—have always been as dull as the dullest members of the American middle class? Lewis' innate provincialism is obvious even in a novel whose main point was an attack on provincialism.

From one point of view, Maxwell Geismar notes, *Main Street* tells "the story of Gopher Prairie's revolt against Carol Kennicott." [10] *Babbitt* similarly could be read as the story of an erring rebel's reconciliation with the middle-class family. Neither reading would be accurate, but their very possibility, a quite genuine one, shows the ambivalence of the two novels. (There is no such ambivalence in *Gantry* because Lewis was ambivalent about the middle classes, but had his mind made up about, or rather against, religion.) From *Dodsworth* on, the satire largely disappears from Lewis' novels, and the ambivalences dominate. In *Dodsworth,* the central theme is the ambivalence of businessman *vs.* aesthete, America *vs.* Europe. The ambivalence is related to an ambiguity, an ambiguity that is perfectly captured by Perry Miller's description of Lewis, as Miller, admiring and bemused, observed him in Europe: " 'I love America,' he would shout into the unoffending European atmosphere; 'I love it, but I don't like it.' " [11] But Miller is not quite accurate in seeing ambiguity in Lewis' best novels. Lewis was stylistically incapable of expressing ambiguity; instead, his central quality is a nervous and confused ambivalence.

When Quentin Compson in *Absalom, Absalom!* feverishly maintains that he does not hate the South, Faulkner's meaning is that Quentin loves the South so much that he cannot forgive it or lie about it and that, if Quentin does hate the South, the hatred is definable only as an exasperated and hopeless love. Sinclair Lewis, like Faulkner, was an exasperated patriot, but he lacked the integrated sensibility necessary to fully express emotional ambiguity. Instead, Lewis presents a series of abstractions in support of an attitude, then a series of abstractions opposed to the attitude. Dodsworth defends America with one set of abstractions but can never quite dispute another set of negative abstractions. He is continually drawn between alternative ways of life, but—and this is the main weakness of the novel—neither alternative seems altogether real. The alternatives are unreal both because they are conceived in cliché terms and because the protagonist seems, in the final analysis, incapable of doing *anything* significant. In *Babbitt* and *Gantry*, Lewis played to his strength: the caricature of characters dominated by sociological mechanisms. But to make *Dodsworth* convincing, the hero needs to be really capable of meaningful choice—and Lewis himself was incapable of creating a free man. Ultimately, Lewis conceived of people not as integrated persons but in the sociological manner, as bundles of opinions and traits. There is truth in this viewpoint but only half-truth; it tells us much about humanity-in-the-mass but nothing about the free men in whom, if anywhere, our salvation lies.

In Lewis' later novels, his faults are magnified; the banalities that intrude into *Main Street, Babbitt,* and *Gantry* become the whole warp and woof of later novels. A sentence from Lewis' last novel, *World So Wide* (1951), is an example of Lewis' increasingly compulsive resort to mechanical stereotype: "And I agree with you that Lorry is a misguided and misguiding truck-driver. . . . But he is also a knight, a blithe and unconquerable knight." [12] The reader cannot help but be convinced by this sentence that Lorry, whoever he is, is *neither* a misguided and misguiding truck-driver *nor* a blithe and unconquerable knight. Described in such terms, Lorry does not exist at all. In fact, all of Lewis' later fiction is an exercise in nullification: people, places, and problems pop into nonbeing at the slightest touch of his pen. It is hard to imagine, for instance, how anyone but Lewis could have converted such intrinsically dramatic issues as American fascism and race prejudice into the trivial banalities of *It Can't Happen Here* (1935) or *Kingsblood Royal* (1947). In the latter novel, an average middle-class white man finds he has Negro blood and decides to assert a "Negro identity." But what ought to have been an existential problem becomes mere shoddy melodrama, for Lewis cannot give his character a genuine identity either before or after his conversion. The character has some prefabricated opinions before his conversion and a new set of prefabricated opinions after, this being his only change. In *It Can't Happen Here,* the Fascists are bully-boys, and their leaders are clods. There is some truth to this picture, but Lewis has not a ghost of a notion of the weird psychological complex of the will to power mixed with sexual sadism and perverted technology that constitutes modern fascism. Lewis understood the mental inertia that leads to stereotyping and self-complacency, but in *It Can't Happen Here* and *Kingsblood Royal,* he was dealing with malice, a more violent impulse, and one he did not understand.

It would be a pointless as well as a melancholy task to survey all of Lewis' later novels. *The Prodigal Parents* (1938) sufficiently indicates his new valorization of the middle classes. The hero of this novel is Fred Cornplow, a middle-aged member of the middle middle class. Cornplow is conventional and lowbrow; he even approvingly quotes a poem by Chum Frink, a newspaper versifier obviously based on Eddie Guest. Lewis tries to convince us that this banal boob is, correctly understood, the salt of the earth. The point is made partly by contrasting Cornplow with two strawman villains, a vicious radical who represents the lower classes and a supercilious aesthete who represents the upper classes. Cornplow, the owner of a car agency, is, Lewis assures us, the keystone to the universe: "He is the eternal bourgeois, the bourjoyce, the burgher, the Middle Class . . . who is most of the population worth considering in France and Germany and these United States. He is Fred Cornplow; and when he changes his mind, that crisis is weightier than Waterloo or Thermopylae." [13] But the plot of the novel contradicts Lewis. Cornplow's favorite quotation is some verses from Kipling which well-nigh obsessed Lewis during the rootless wanderings of his later life:

> For to Admire an' for to see,
> For to be'old this world so wide—
> It never done no good to me
> But I can't drop it if I tried.[14]

At the end of the novel, Cornplow, who has just returned from a European trip he did not enjoy, is about to set out for more traveling. Lewis is trying to have it both ways: Cornplow is the symbol of solid middle-class virtue, but he is also a driven and restless wanderer. Lewis may assert the value of a typical provincial bourgeois existence, but he cannot truly imagine it.

The main interest of the many bad novels Lewis wrote after *Dodsworth* is the light they cast on the few good novels he wrote in the twenties. It becomes evident that Lewis was entirely serious when he proclaimed, "I wrote *Babbitt* not out of hatred for him but out of love," [15] when he wrote, "I like the Babbitts, the Dr. Pickerbaughs [*Arrowsmith*], the Will Kennicotts, and even the Elmer Gantrys rather better than anyone else on earth. They are good fellows. They laugh— really laugh." [16] In this last statement, Lewis' ambivalence leads him into a patently false statement about his own created characters; none of the characters he mentions is capable of real laughter. In one mood, he created them and, in his creation, denied them the gifts of thought and laughter. In another mood, he retrospectively endows them with virtues that they are a very antitype of. It was in fact Lewis' own gift of laughter that was the major quality that enabled him to partially transcend his own bourgeois provincialism. Similarly, Willa Cather's gift for what she called "creative hate" gave her novels much of their intensity. But in Miss Cather's later fiction, her creative hate either becomes incoherent as in *My Mortal Enemy* (1926), a novel filled with a frustrated rage that neither characters nor plot adequately justify or explain, or it is altogether refined away into the somewhat dull tranquillity of *Death Comes for the Archbishop* (1927) and *Shadows on the Rock* (1931). These novels confirm the retreat begun in *The Professor's House*. Both are historical novels celebrating the establishment of order in pioneer communities. *Death Comes to the Archbishop* celebrates the two French clergymen who re-established an orderly Catholic church in the Southwest at the time that area became officially a part of the United States. *Shadows on the Rock* celebrates the orderly existence of a bourgeois Canadian family at the time of Frontenac's governorship. Both of these situations would seem to have in them the intrinsic drama of the conquest of disorder. Yet, both novels are curiously tensionless, graceful enough, but not really alive.

The absence of conflict was intentional; Miss Cather explained that in *Death Comes for the Archbishop* she was trying to create the effect of legend, a genre that she considered antithetical to drama.[17] Some legends are, to be sure, undramatic, but they make up for their lack of drama by the unintended charm of naïveté or by an aura of supernatural wondrousness. Miss Cather does not try for wondrousness, but she does aim at naïveté—with unfortunate results. The passages in *Death Comes for the Archbishop* about saints, miracles, and the holy family are painful in their false naïveté, their pretense of simple piety. For example, Miss Cather tells the story of two friars who set off on a trip through the

Southwestern desert without adequate provisions. They have nearly given up hope when they come upon a Mexican family living in a hacienda close to three cottonwood trees. When they eventually reach their destination, they are told there are no settlers in the area through which they had traveled. Returning they find only the three cottonwoods and no sign of habitation. "Then the two Fathers sank down upon their knees in that blessed spot and kissed the earth, for they perceived what Family it was that had entertained them there." [18]

Death Comes for the Archbishop reveals Cather's attraction to a sentimental idea of religion rather than to religion itself. It shows a desire to attain the consolations of a religious order, an order all too quaint and picturesque, without the necessary rigors of belief. The novel is pseudo-simplified and escapist, an irreligious use of religion. *Shadows on the Rock* is even more obviously escapist, and even more obviously, it celebrates not the stillness of religion but the religion of stasis. The novel is a paean of praise to the virtues of the *petit bourgeois,* a social group that, in Miss Cather's early fiction and in the writings of almost all other modern novelists, has been used as a symbol for whatever is most narrow, mean, petty, banal, and oppressive in life. The *petit bourgeois* in *Shadows* lack any such faults, and they have the immense virtue of orderliness. The reader is supposed to feel the heroism of their very routine, a routine asserted against the backdrop of dark, chaotic forests. In fact, the characters seem merely dull, and the novel itself is quite boring. The weakness in Miss Cather's idea of order has been, I think, precisely defined by Francis X. Connolly, who observes that a passion for order must be balanced by divine impatience to keep from lapsing into passivity. "For some types of the orderly mind everything is over before it is begun. . . . Such a mind is perilously satisfied with its own knowledge of past solutions." [19] In *Death Comes for the Archbishop* and *Shad-*

ows on the Rock, the effect is exactly that; everything is over before it is begun in both of Willa Cather's attempts to prop up her novels with other people's beliefs.

Van Wyck Brooks is yet one more of the village rebels whose course changed dramatically in the late twenties. *Emerson and Others* (1927) was as unlike Brooks' earlier books as could possibly be imagined. The sharp, sometimes unfair, cultural criticism gives way to a mellow evocation of a past in which conflict seems to have been happily absent. In the first volume of his autobiography, *Scenes and Portraits* (1954), Brooks admitted that in his early books he had seen America chiefly in terms of what it lacked.[20] In *Days of the Phoenix* (1957), Brooks noted that the twenties generation of writers had "criticized America in terms of Europe, which it never occurred to them to criticize at all." [21] But in *Emerson and Others,* Brooks decided, "One had to make much of one's own place, and it became in actuality all that one's fancy desired." [22] The American writers who, in the early books, seemed to offer so little in the way of a tradition of thought, a usable past, now also appeared to be "all that one's fancy desired." Even the graceless Middle West, the geographical villain of *The Ordeal,* took on grand and heroic qualities when seen through the eyes of Emerson: "He [Emerson] had always delighted in men who could 'do' things, men of the drastic class, and the Western farmers had drawn from their local necessities what stores of heroic energy! They lived on venison and quails like the children of Homer. He encountered again those men who were natural founders of cities, kings of Norway, sensible, steady, wise and prompt in action." [23] These observations on the "pioneers" are offered without the slightest hint of disagreement or ironic qualification on Brooks's part.

Emerson and Others is an adumbration of the "Makers and Finders" series that was begun with *The Flowering of New England* (1936) and continued through *The Confident*

Age (1952). These books, too, are characterized by an uncritical celebration and evocation of the American past. The two major flaws in *The Flowering of New England,* as noted by F. W. Dupee in his excellent article on Brooks, are (1) that Brooks overrates New England literature by considering it in a void rather than examining it against the standards of world literature and (2) that Brooks's New England has a false serenity, as a result of his having purged the actual culture of its intrinsic contradictions and conflicts.[24] Dupee's criticisms hold good for the entire "Makers and Finders" series. Brooks's new version of the past is too blandly lifeless to be genuinely usable.

This is not to say that Brooks had altogether lost his asperity; in *Opinions of Oliver Allston* (1941), the asperity appears in isolated and, as it were, pure form. Oliver Allston, the fictional diarist of this strange book, is an obvious mask for Brooks himself. *Opinions* is full of the self-contradictions so typical of Brooks's writings in the teens and twenties. Brooks is cranky and bleak but demands an optimistic belief in progress. Modern literature is terrible, Brooks believes, but he attacks the chapter of literary parodies in Joyce's *Ulysses* for its implication that literature has declined! In the usual Brooksian manner, striking insights are found side by side with incredible stupidities. As an example of the insights, there is the following definition of sophistication: "Sophistication, as the word is used, is a state of mind which consists in knowing too much and at the same time knowing too little,—too much of the periphery of life, too little of the core and centre. It expresses itself in a language of insinuation and is, for the rest, a sort of cosmetic equivalent of wisdom that is terrifying to the uninitiated."[25] A more precise definition could hardly be imagined.

Unfortunately, Brooks's blunders sometimes overshadow his insights. Brooks attacks not the worst but the best in modern literature and attacks it all too often without cogency or intelligence. The book is built around a comparison of "primary" writers with "coterie" writers. Brooks believes that writers ought to live in the primary life of their age. The Romantics, for instance, expressed the belief in humanitarianism and freedom that was, Brooks thinks, the prime note of their age. Brooks tells us that the major modern writers are out of touch with their age and express the values of only an isolated coterie, but Brooks never adequately defines the modern age that writers are supposedly out of touch with. Is it an age of humanitarianism and freedom? Or is it rather a period differentiated from all others by (1) a military technology capable of destroying all life on earth and (2) the experiments in totalitarian terror carried on by Hitler and Stalin? If the latter, is the darkness and pessimism of modern literature so out of touch with the spirit of the age? At one point, Brooks does mention the "union of mankind" as an instance of a proper modern ideal.[26] Modern writers, perhaps, have not propagandized for this ideal, but has modern society truly sought after it?

As Dwight Macdonald points out, Brooks, in his attack on modern writers, seems to assume that bourgeois culture is in flourishing condition. Brooks's central error, as Macdonald observes, is his failure to realize that "in an age of social decay, it is only by rejecting the *specific* and *immediate* values of society that the writer can preserve those general and eternal human values with which Brooks is concerned."[27] Brooks, it seems, was able to recognize values in literature only when they were grossly explicit and abstractly high minded. He intensely admired the Victorian critics, at one point contrasting his favorite critic, Ruskin, with modern writers, describing the latter as "sickly adolescents, self-centered and neurotic."[28] It is ironic that modern biographical research has established Ruskin as a major contender—along with Dostoevsky and Swinburne—for the post of the most neurotic literary personality of the nineteenth century, but Ruskin was addicted to an extremely idealistic rhetoric, and this is what Brooks responded to. As in *The Ordeal,* Brooks never faced up to the connection between violent mental and emotional contradictions and literary genius. Brooks sometimes recognized contradiction and conflict but never fully realized their necessity.

The key to the overstatements of *Opinions* is Oliver Allston's poignant notation that he felt he had to cling to America to preserve his personality from disintegration.[29] America is less contentiously appreciated in the two volumes of Brooks's autobiography, admirably fair-minded and thoroughly absorbing records of a rich and crowded cultural age, an age that Brooks himself helped to shape. In *The Confident Age,* the last volume of the "Makers and Finders" series, Brooks wrote again of many of the writers attacked in *Opinions,* treating them this time with mellow charm and only the mildest and most gentle touch of disapproval.

The major exception to this record of accommodation and decline was the later career of Sherwood Anderson. Anderson went through an extremely dark period in the middle and late twenties. *Horses and Men* (1923) was his last book of any value until *Perhaps Women* in 1931. One of Anderson's defenders, although conceding the dreariness of Anderson's twenties novels, notes that one of his best stories, "Death in the Woods," was originally published in 1926 and also claims *A Story Teller's Story* (1924) as a major work.[30] One or more stories, however worthy, is a rather slender production for seven years and the pseudo-autobiographical volume, *A Story Teller's Story,* is, as Irving Howe says, "false in its feeling, its thought, and its composition," "loyal neither to fact nor to imagination," a "grossly sentimentalized version of Anderson's life."[31] As for the novels, *Many Marriages* (1923) was effectively criticized by Rebecca West and William Faulkner. The novel is about a middle-aged man who suddenly receives mystical insights into life which he expresses by divesting himself of clothes and walking around a room muttering banal generalities that are supposed to be the groping first steps toward a new philosophy. Miss West's criticism was that Anderson's characters "never seemed to attain the dignity of complete nudity; their complexes clung to them like dark woolen socks." [32] Faulkner's criticism, befitting a novelist, was more technical. Noting that most people put their hands in their pockets when they are walking, Faulkner wondered aloud what Anderson's hero did with his hands. [33]

Anderson's novels are trying to sell doctrine and highly perishable doctrine to boot. What really goes wrong with them might be summed up by Kenneth Burke's notion of the "bureaucratization of ideals": even an intrinsically noble idea is corrupted or confused to the point of comedy when an attempt is made to literally realize it, institutionalize it, bureaucratize it. In his novels, Anderson tried to bureaucratize vague notions about universal love, free expression, etc., and succeeded only in reducing them to an ineffable banality. Thus, in *Many Marriages,* Anderson imagines a "bureaucratic" solution to the agonies of the buried life he had so much more symbolically rendered in *Winesburg.* The solution is utopian: "There was a question being asked. 'Are you for me? Am I for you?' People have developed a new sense, many new senses. . . . Now people could accept or dismiss one another with a gesture." [34] Anderson was beaten to this solution of the problem of communication by Momus, the Greek god of mockery, who complained that men should have been made with open chests so that each man could see what was in the other's heart. Eventually, Anderson recovered his perspective: "When I was younger, stronger, and perhaps more foolish, I used to think it would be well if everyone spoke their hidden thoughts aloud. Later I grew away from that notion. No one is good enough, strong enough, rich enough." [35]

Anderson's novels provoked a violent reaction from writers who had intensely admired him. Anderson's achievement in *Winesburg* and his best short stories had been the development of a style capable of expressing hitherto unreachable emotional nuances, but in his novels, he parodied himself in a way that seemed less a regrettable personal failure than a kind of deliberate insult to good writing, a desecration of his own fine talent. F. Scott Fitzgerald expressed the widespread feeling of disillusionment: "I agree with Ernest [Hemingway] that Anderson's last two books *have let everyone down who believed in him*—I think they're cheap, faked, obscurantic and awful." [36] As Fitzgerald's letter indicates, Anderson's contemporaries felt not only aggrieved but betrayed by his lapses. This, I think, accounts for the outright aggressive gestures aimed at Anderson: Faulkner's participation in the notorious parody *Sherwood Anderson and Other Famous Creoles* and Hemingway's parody novel, *The Torrents of Spring*. Thomas Wolfe's assault was even more direct: "According to what Wolfe told Miss Nowell later, he called Anderson out into the lobby and 'told old Sherwood off,' saying that *Winesburg, Ohio* had meant something important to him and his entire generation of writers, but that Anderson had 'failed them,' that he was 'washed up,' and that 'this business of sitting around and talking, naked, on parlor sofas was no good.' " [37] Anderson was, to a large extent, the victim of the large hopes he had aroused.

By the late twenties, Anderson himself had decided that the theme of sexual repression had lost its relevance: World War I had forced the young to face life and "Why talk of sex repressions now? Apparently there aren't any." [38] A writer without a subject, Anderson retreated to Marion, Virginia, a small town in the Virginia mountain country, where he bought two local newspapers. In his autobiographical reminiscences, Anderson had converted his early nervous breakdown into a deliberately symbolic retreat from business. In similar fashion, his Marion years (1927–29) were a symbolic attempt to convince himself that he was one of the boys, that he "belonged." As Anderson himself later admitted, "I had retreated from the city to the town, from the town to the farm."[39] Anderson's attempt at self-deception becomes painfully evident in *Hello Towns!* (1929), a collection of his pieces in his small-town papers. There are, it should be emphasized, some excellent things in this book, such as the haunting account of a strange impromptu dance engaged in by some mountaineers and the tongue-in-cheek query about Southern mulattoes: "The negro race in the south is so apparently getting lighter. How does that happen? What's going on? White blood constantly creeping in somewhere. Northern travellers can't do it all."[40]

The bulk of Anderson's writings, however, compares less than favorably with such contemporary analogues as Archer Fullingim's little newspaper in Kountze, Texas. When Anderson attempts folksiness, as he too often does, he becomes extremely painful. The mixture of spite and false naïveté in the following attack on Sinclair Lewis is detestable:

He [Sherwood Anderson] drives his car down to the town and parks it on Main Street. Since Sinclair Lewis wrote his book he has been hating the words, "Main Street." "I will call it something else," he says to himself. He hates all expressions that become, as it is said, "a part of the language." He is to hate later the name "Elmer Gantry" as representing preachers and "Babbitt" as representing the business man of the American small town.

"The names are lies in themselves," he is saying to himself. "They are too easy. There is too much malice in them."[41]

In his *Memoirs* (posthumously published in 1942), Anderson evokes a warm small-town world that is characterized by the gathering around a drinking keg in the woods after a baseball game; why did not "poor Lewis" have such experiences, Anderson wonders.[42] It might be well to recall that in

Winesburg, Ohio, Wing Biddlebaum sees a hay ride go past
—feeling his own exclusion; in "Unused," a short story in
Horses and Men, a local ballplayer gets drunk after a baseball game and attempts a brutal seduction. Anderson's early
stories show almost as little of the more genial aspects of
small-town life as do those of Lewis. In fact, it is evident that
Anderson was trying to use Lewis as a symbolic scapegoat; by
execrating Lewis, Anderson proved that he himself *belonged*
in the small town. These late writings about the small town
are a debased version of the participation mystique. (Anderson says, as it were, that Lewis does *not* "belong." What he
means is "But *I* do, *I* do, *I* do.") Anderson did to an extent
understand and share in the small-town outlook, as James
Boyd shows in his reminiscence of Anderson's visit to Southern Pines, North Carolina, but Boyd noted that Anderson's
freedom to fully express his thoughts differentiated him from
the prudent and conformist North Carolinians.[43] James K.
Feibleman observes that Anderson was quite deluded in his
belief that he blended perfectly into Marion, Virginia; in
fact, the locals thought of him as a likeable eccentric, never
as one of themselves.[44] In short, the evidence suggests that
Thomas Wolfe, who knew the impossibility of retreat, was
correct in his belief that "The Squire of Marion is, beneath
his guise of ambling folksiness, an embittered and defeated
man."[45]

Wolfe wrote this, however, at a time when Anderson had
made an admirable though not complete recovery. (It should
be noted that both this remark and Wolfe's confrontation
with Anderson recounted above came after a nasty quarrel
between the two men.) Anderson was never reliable when
he was playing the role of village spokesman; as late as the
forties, he was capable of a trite article on small towns.
("The small town has always been the backbone of the
living thing we call America.")[46] In 1930, Anderson began
to recover from the virtual collapse of talent which had

overtaken him in the twenties. The recovery can mainly be attributed to his relationship with Eleanor Copenhaver whom he married in 1933. Miss Copenhaver stimulated his interest in a new and fresh subject matter: Southern mill labor. The focus of Anderson's best writings from 1930 is on the South, the depression, and the mills.

Even the best of Anderson's thirties books—*Perhaps Women* (1931), *Death in The Woods* (1933), *Puzzled America* (1935), *Kit Brandon* (1936)—fall short of complete success, but not one of them is a bad book, and all have sections of considerable power and importance.[47] In the thirties, Anderson got back in touch with the times, contributing his own unique impressions to the major themes of the decade: the exploitation of labor, the need to cope with the as yet unassimilated machine, and the desperate quest for simple realities and concrete truths which was the reaction to the vicious and destructive abstractions of finance capitalism and undirected technology. Some of Anderson's innate qualities served him well in these new departures: his tentativeness, his distrust of dogmatizing, his unforced sympathy with poor laboring people. Confused himself, a half-acknowledged failure himself, he understood that the prevailing mood was not one of rebellion but of groping confusion, impotent despair, self-accusation, bewildered humiliation.

In the South, he found the same brutal transition from rural to industrial which, as a much younger man, he had witnessed in the Midwest. But there were differences between the South and Midwest, and these differences are reflected in Anderson's writings. *Poor White* (1920) is an early Anderson novel about industry's coming into a Midwestern town. Many recent critics consider *Poor White* his one novel of any value besides *Winesburg*. In fact, the novel is a relative failure (some passages do survive the wreckage), partly because of its style of false profundity and solemnly intoned triteness, but mainly because of its inventor hero, Hugh

McVey, who as characterized by Anderson appears to the reader as a muttering dolt hardly capable of inventing a complicated machine. In the South, perhaps because it was a region Anderson came to as an objective outsider, Anderson portrayed men and women of harder outline and firmer character, defeated but definite. The Southern qualities show up even in Andersons' Marion sketches whenever he is not confusing matters by trying to prove his hickyness. "These Mountaineers" (included in *Death in the Woods*) is an excellent and objective impression of mountain life, a "pure drawing," as Anderson noted,[48] centered on a tough, pregnant, unmarried mountain girl who rejects the narrator's sympathy and money, instructing him clearly just where to put it. Some of Anderson's Midwestern characters seem, by comparison, somewhat soft and squashy.

More analogous to *Poor White* is *Kit Brandon,* the story of an East Tennessee girl who goes from mill labor into the more profitable and dignified occupation of bootlegging. The novel is filled with sharp observation, such as the following passage on the humility of the poor:

The rich, the ones up above them, millowners, politicians, prominent men and women of all sorts in the milltowns were like the movie stars in Hollywood. "Their doing what they do is not like our doing it." The idea was in some indefinable way like that. "They must be smart. I'm not smart." There was a politician accused of stealing a million dollars from the state. He laughed. "Why you are mistaken. I didn't steal a million. I stole two million."

There were the poor, often scrupulously honest, curiously religious who gave him a kind of admiration. They went to the polls and voted for him. "After all, he's smart. He's a big man." [49]

Kit's lack of such humility is one of the qualities that marks her as an interesting and superior individual. Throughout the novel, Anderson notes that the almost conscious and deliberate program of industry is to debase and humiliate the laborers. The owners and managers seem to have some obscure compulsion, even beyond the greed for profits, to strip the laborers of self-respect, as is seen in the almost gratuitous insult of putting ingeniously constructed hoods on the machines to keep them clean by sucking the dust out, while the workers are left conspicuously unprotected from lung diseases developed from the lint dust they breathe.

Unfortunately, the bootlegging chapters in *Kit Brandon* are entirely lacking in the solidity, reality, and symbolic suggestiveness of the mill sections. The novel is, moreover, a structural mess. Its heroine, though believable and likeable, is thinly characterized, seen principally from the outside and at such a narrative distance that she is almost invisible at times. This is all the more regrettable because we see just enough of Kit to find her a valuable character, tough but not mean, intelligent, independent, somewhat cynical but wondering, and questioning. In short, the most upsetting thing in *Kit Brandon* is our realization of how good it might have been. Nevertheless, *Kit Brandon* is a better novel than *Poor White,* more subtle in its treatment of industrialization and firmer in style; the rhythms are short and repetitive in the usual Anderson manner but with a refreshing lack of either the pretentiousness or silliness that Anderson's novels generally fall into.

Perhaps Women and *Puzzled America,* Anderson's two semidocumentaries, are uneven in quality, but both are among the most effective volumes of reportage of an era distinguished for the high literary quality of its documentary explorations. "Loom Dance," in *Perhaps Women,* is a memorable account of a spontaneous rebellion in a Southern mill which broke out when the ubiquitous minuteman (i.e., efficiency expert) perpetrated the ultimate indignity: following a woman to the toilet with his stop watch. *Puzzled America* is the portrait of the "rat king," who has cornered the Louisiana muskrat market and is convinced that the Northern muskrat is an inferior breed: " 'You'll see,' he declared, 'the time will yet come when the Southern rat will come into his own.' " [50]

11. Conclusion: The Village Rebels and the Kicking Season

The critical reputation of most of the village rebels went down in the thirties and is still quite low. In the conclusion to this study, I would like to suggest some reasons for this prolonged "kicking season"—to borrow Pamela Hansford Johnson's term for that period in which a common impulse seizes a number of critics to revalue downwards a particular author or school of literature [1]—and propose that a revaluation upwards of these writers might be reasonable.

Business was as much an object of literary attack in the thirties as it had been in the teens and twenties, but the attack was conducted from quite different intellectual bases. In the teens and twenties, the central opposition had been the aesthetic *vs.* the acquisitive. Insensitivity and bad taste were the main indictments against a business culture. Presumably, despite the vaguely liberal or even socialist viewpoint of the rebels, most of them would have had no real ground of attack on a paragon of the businessman who happened to be intellectually honest and emotionally aware, neither a Philistine nor a puritan (Dodsworth, for instance). A literary radical of the thirties would be able to grant all this and still maintain that, by his very position of power in an exploitative society, this ideal businessman was objectively vicious, whatever his subjective nature might be. It is easy to understand why thirties radicals saw the village rebels in retrospect

244

as not exactly wrong, not exactly useless, but at least off center, irrelevant. The plight of an aesthetic individual in an acquisitive society seemed to such radicals to be a somewhat *precious* subject as opposed to the conflict between the oppressed proletarian working man and the exploiting Fascistic capitalist. The stock hero of the village rebel, when he had a hero at all, was a bourgeois infected with a germ of revolt against the dominant pieties: Carol Kennicott, Babbitt. A stock hero of the thirties radical fiction was the rebellious working man whose rebellion is both more generalized and specific, as it was against the entire capitalistic system. The more priggish radicals of the thirties were capable of dismissing the aesthetic revolt of the village rebels as mere dilettantism.

But radical "proletarian" fiction was less widespread in the thirties and early forties than another literary phenomenon that was even more opposed to the central notions of the village rebels: the return to the soil motif. There are a remarkable number of thirties and forties works that have "land," "soil," or "earth" as part of their titles (e.g., "The Landscape as Nude"; "The Web of Earth"; "Build Soil"; *Study out the Land*) and that develop a mystique based on contact with the elemental qualities of the land (whatever these might be). It would be difficult to exaggerate the importance of the soil motif in thirties literature,[2] for it crosscut many of the seemingly unrelatable positions, finding expression both in radical novels about the sharecroppers and in reactionary Southern agrarian tracts. The motivation behind this impulse toward a new valorization of a somewhat mystically conceived "land" may be summed up in Archibald MacLeish's opposition to the evil financial forces of Mr. Rockefeller's city, which is found in "The Landscape as Nude." The primitivistic myth of the superior reality of the man who is close to the earth and to nature becomes operative again in these thirties writings. James Agee's *Let Us*

Now Praise Famous Men paradoxically combines anguish at the miserable condition of the Alabama tenant farmers with a celebration of the beauty and dignity of lives led in a natural setting. Robert Penn Warren's Southern agrarian novel, *At Heaven's Gate,* is a version of pastoral in which the villain is a financier and the normative values are those of the poor farmers. It is no wonder that the neoprimitivist writers found little value in the village rebels, for one of the major assaults by the rebels had been on the primitivists' valorization of the rural, though a much less-sophisticated form of it than was prevalent in the thirties.[3] Carol Kennicott was disillusioned by the discovery that farmers were no less banal than townspeople, and H. L. Mencken's "The Husbandman" is simply another item in the Mencken bestiary.

From the hindsight of the thirties, many of the twenties writers, the village rebels among them, seemed excessively individualistic in their values. The village rebels now appeared superficial and heartless in their scorn for rural folk and folkways and in their self-images as natural aristocrats who were set off from the mediocre herd. In this reaction, many writers of the thirties showed a tendency to grasp at various forms of collective experience. The proletarian hero of the radical novel was not so much a self-conscious individual as a class-conscious representative of the workers or tenant farmers. American folklore (much of it more accurately denominated by Richard Dorson's term "fakelore") began to pour out of the presses, providing comforting if factitious evidence that America had a rich tradition of folk wisdom to draw on in its time of trouble. Lewis and Mencken had been interested in the folk mind, too, but from a different perspective, their term for it being the "herd mind." An index of change can be seen in Thomas Wolfe. His last manuscript still centers around the inevitable artist-hero, but there is an attempt to capture the generic experience of "man alive" (*You Can't Go Home Again*), a character who has a certain resemblance to John Steinbeck's "manself" (*The Grapes of Wrath*). The village rebels, on the other hand, were usually hostile to any manifestation of the participation mystique. With the advent of World War II, the new emphasis on positive collective experience became even more pronounced as the country began to require myths of its own with which to counter the Fascist myths. The account of American character and conditions given by the village rebels and other negativistic twenties writers seemed a mere "literary fallacy" to critics seeking to accentuate the positive. Bernard De Voto's *Mark Twain's America* (1932) (see Chapter 3) illustrates a number of these thirties motifs, particularly in its emphasis on folklore and its defense of Midwestern civilization.

Almost inevitably, even the collective experience and traditional wisdom to be found in fundamentalism would find a sophisticated defender as it did in John Crowe Ransom's *God Without Thunder* (1930), although the tradition-loving intellectual "fundamentalist" whom Ransom praises could hardly have been found at any Southern camp meeting. With a defense of fundamentalism, we need only one thing more to carry us full circle and that is a full-scale revival of the myth of the small town, found in some of Sherwood Anderson's later writings and in Thornton Wilder's *Our Town* (1938).

In sum, the thirties had come to admire certain qualities of American life that could on a hazy day be mistaken for just those qualities the village rebels had attacked. But the revaluation, or rather devaluation, of the village rebels which was the natural result of new cultural needs and tastes was by no means uniform. Willa Cather's fiction has more than a touch of the land mystique in it, and Thomas Wolfe's later fiction presents a self-image of the author as a culture-hero binding America's divisions with a grandiosely general rhetoric. As for Van Wyck Brooks, as seen in the previous chapter, he had moved over to most of the positions just described as characteristic of the thirties. Lewis and Mencken, the most blatant village rebels, suffered sharp declines in reputation.

The reputations of a good many twenties' writers, not just the village rebels, declined in the thirties, and many twenties' writers, Scott Fitzgerald in particular, were spectacularly revived in the fifties. But not the village rebels. Indeed, after the kicking season of the fifties, the literary lives of Lewis, Masters, and Wolfe were fairly well snuffed out. Anderson survived but not without some buffets. Needless to say, the rejection by the fifties' critics of these writers proceeded on quite different grounds than it had in the thirties, since the intellectual drifts of the fifties are definable mainly in terms of an extreme reaction from the collectivist "progressive" values of the thirties. If thirties intellectuals defined themselves generally in social, economic, and political terms, those of the fifties had a more strictly literary sensibility. Defining itself through intense self-consciousness, subtle irony, and pleasure in complexity, this sensibility found little delight in the village rebels. The relatively crude ironies of Lewis and Masters did not impress critics who used Joyce as a touchstone, nor did Wolfe's jejune self-explorations compete very effectively with Marcel Proust's recovery of the past. Such comparisons were made since it seemed to be a dictum of fifties' criticism that only the very best books should be read —though, in practice, exceptions were made for lesser writers if they seemed properly Jamesian, Joycean, or at least spirits grown Eliotic. The village rebels could not provide the fifties critics with the psychological complications, the subtle problems of identity, or the dense symbolic texture that an austere formalistic criticism had been developed to explicate. Naturally enough, the critics decided that something must be very wrong with writers who so completely failed to match the tools that the critics had so painstakingly acquired. Wolfe and Lewis failed to meet the demands of a prose aesthetic based on Percy Lubbock's systematized version of what he conceived to be the critical principles of Henry James's prefaces. Masters lacked the rich complexity of verbal texture that Cleanth Brooks and Robert Penn Warren demanded in poetry. All of these are, of course, legitimate critical criteria if not, perhaps, the only meaningful ones. Possibly somewhat less legitimate was the rejection of these writers for having failed to meet the cultural criteria of the fifties: the requisite belief in "original sin" and in the "tragic sense of life." A number of fifties' critics followed distantly in the path of T. S. Eliot, becoming somewhat pale converts to the Anglican or Roman Catholic faith and making heavy use in their criticism of such terms as "heresy," "sacramental," "Communion," etc. To such sensibilities, the writings of Lewis, Mencken, Masters, Stribling, Anderson, and Wolfe failed to appeal.

The above sketch of the stock sensibility of the fifties is not intended as a denial of the immense critical achievement of the era. Although Allen Tate, for instance, shows many of the characteristics of the fifties which I have outlined, his critical and creative genius can hardly be circumscribed in such narrow categories. Nor does my stereotype include such central figures as Kenneth Burke and Lionel Trilling. Nevertheless, it does characterize, or at least caricaturize, some of the major critical tendencies of the fifties, particularly those tendencies that most contributed to the denigration of the village rebels. One critic, for instance, contrasted Lewis with Faulkner, correctly noting Faulkner's superiority (to be fair this was just *before* Faulkner's reputation skyrocketed), then complaining that Carol Kennicott was not a tragic heroine, a true if somewhat mysterious grievance. What evidently bothered this critic was Lewis' lack of the Tragic Sense of Life. Even Trilling's brilliant article on Sherwood Anderson's works misleadingly attributed the worst faults of

Anderson's worst writings to his total corpus. The precise reverse of this procedure was applied to the writers held in critical favor during the era; many of the academic camp followers of the new criticism seemed incapable of discovering flaws in such works as *Mosquitoes* or *The Town*. The best work of the village rebels was not to be mentioned in the same breath with the least of Faulkner, Fitzgerald, or James.

The fifties can now be seen as an historical era with its outlines, as time goes on, becoming ever more distinct. Sixties critics like F. C. Crews are conducting the sort of destructive review of dominant notions of the fifties with which the fifties critics had demolished the thirties. Indeed, the pendulum swing that is beginning to devalue the fifties is concomitantly revaluing the thirties. The critical tendency of the sixties seems to be toward a new interest in the sociology and politics of literature. Also, recent criticism shows a diminished concern with the Tragic Sense of Life and an increasing taste for satire and comedy. Even much-maligned historical criticism seems to be coming back into its own now that the new criticism is no longer so new. The reception accorded to books like Larzer Ziff's *The American 1890's,* Jay Martin's *Harvests of Change,* and Chester Eisinger's *Fiction of the Forties* shows a revived interest in the minor as well as major works of the national literature. This shows, too, a revived interest in a connected historical account of our writers which relates their sensibility to their milieu. Some of these tendencies of the sixties are, I think, propitious to a revaluation of the village rebels.

This is not to indicate that the village rebels were really very politically or socially radical, particularly when seen from a contemporary perspective. Many of the village rebels, as I have shown, became quite conservative when, in the thirties, they were faced with what seemed possible radical alternatives to the dominant social structure. Even earlier, their revolt had been primarily social rather than political, its main targets being puritanism and conformity. Puritanism and conformity may seem irrelevant issues in the context of the political conflicts of the sixties, but it is possible that they are quite relevant. A possible thesis is that the sources of the aggression and anger, the anti-intellectualism and emotional sterility that characterize some aspects of American life, were at least partially explored by the village rebels and cannot be thoroughly understood without reference to them.

The analysis by Lewis and Mencken of the herd mind anticipates such recent studies of contemporary intolerance and the right wing mind as T. W. Adorno's *The Authoritarian Personality* and Daniel Bell's essays in *The Radical Right*. One of the social sources of right wing politics, Bell says, is "The 'old' middle class—the independent physician, farm owner, small-town lawyer, real-estate promoter, home builder, automobile dealer, gasoline station owner, small businessman and the like . . ."—the contemporary avatars, it would seem, of Doc Kennicott and of Babbitt's friends. Bell goes on to say, "A much more tell tale indicator of the group . . . is the strain of the Protestant fundamentalism, of nativist nationalism, of good-and-evil moralism which is the organizing basis for the 'world-view' of such people. For this is the group whose values predominated in the nineteenth century, and which for the past forty years has been fighting a rear-guard action." [4] Part of this rear-guard action I have discussed as the twenties Reaction; as Bell makes clear, the Reaction is by no means over. Any reader of Adorno's study of the "authoritarian personality" will note that the traits Adorno describes are precisely those that Mencken, Lewis, Cather, and Stribling attacked in their bourgeois villains.

The themes of the buried life and of the herd mind may have some relevance to our own times. The village rebels, at their best, made a considerable contribution to cultural articulation in America, and their best has been too easily and smugly dismissed. What they revealed of the conformity and emotional suffocation of American life may seem simple and obvious now, but that is true of most *gained* insights. If Lewis and Mencken were limited by and to the herd mind they attacked, they, nevertheless, clarified the enemy more clearly than anyone had before, or since, for that matter. No book has superseded *Babbitt* in the completeness of its analysis of the stock of banalities many Americans live by. The conformity, banality, emotional sterility, and fear that Lewis, Cather, Anderson, and the rest wrote of has hardly disappeared, and these writers aid us in understanding these qualities. It is unnecessary to write another *Babbitt,* not because Babbitt no longer exists, but because he has not changed that much. Lewis' contemporaries might have thought *Babbitt* was the book to destroy Babbitts, but they had too much confidence in literature. Moreover, some current social fiction reveals a world not so greatly different from that of the village rebels. Jesse Hill Ford's modern South (see *The Liberation of Lord Byron Jones*) has structural affinities with the hypocritical and bigoted South that was analyzed by T. S. Stribling. The suburbia and missile-center sites of John Cheever's fiction have affinities with the madly mechanical world of *Babbitt* but are subverted by freaky irruptions of the buried life. Both Cheever and Ford are more clearly understood in relation to the body of writing central to this study.

It may be that predominantly realistic, predominantly social fiction is innately inferior to predominantly symbolic and psychological literature. Even granting this, realistic social fiction performs some functions that symbolic and psychological literature does not, and these are, I think, necessary functions. One could read through all of Faulkner's fiction without learning as much about the concrete process by which a white Southerner is able to nullify the reality of a Negro as is revealed in one chapter of a Ford or Stribling novel. This is not to diminish Faulkner's admittedly far greater value but to assert the presence of *a* value in Stribling that a purely formalistic criticism will not find because it will not seek. The presence of similar articulations in Masters, Lewis, and the rest is part of the case for them and part of the case for such literature. If their characters were largely stereotypes, one might keep in mind T. W. Adorno's warning that modern civilization produces stereotypes and that only by identifying stereotypical traits can this trend be resisted.[5]

I said earlier that the village rebels at their best made a considerable contribution to cultural articulation. It might be added that, from the point of view of literary history, they made such a contribution even at their worst. This seems to be what Mark Schorer had in mind when he subtitled his lengthy biographical polemic *Sinclair Lewis: An American Life. An* American life—surely a moderate enough statement of Lewis' representativeness. I believe a similarly qualified statement could be made of all the village rebels: Lewis, Mencken, Stribling, Wolfe, Masters, Anderson. Their provincialism was no less their limitation than their subject. All of the village rebels had moments in which they announced with an air of great discovery some evident and obvious fact of human existence which had been the common stock of cultured people for some centuries. Like the archetypal provincial crank, they wasted much of their energy in laboriously discovering for themselves what in another cultural sphere was merely common knowledge. Mark Twain could think of his "What is Man?" as a subversive document only because, in his imaginative vision of the American public, he saw only the most conventional of the Hannibal-Hadleyburg pew holders. It was inconceivable to him that the mutterings of the village atheist might be old stuff to the city folk. The historical value of the village rebels is that they expose just this thinness of American provincial culture by their *example* as well as their polemic. They wrote out of their own buried lives and never quite broke their own dependence on the banal categories of American thought to which they submitted themselves in the very process of attacking. As I have shown in my chapter on Masters, this very thinness of culture could at times become almost luminously expressive, providing some real and true insights into the quality of American life. Could, indeed, this destructive element have been so clearly recorded except by those who were immersed in it? Without appealing to the naïvely primitivistic notion of the untutored genius, I think it possible that the village rebels might have been really less interesting had they been more sophisticated. The archetypal village atheist is a man who has become dogmatic and soured by his insistence on a few quite limited truths in the face of the totally unthinking herd mind of the village. He has become hardened and inflexible because he lacks the challenge of sophisticated opposition, the challenge of minds as, or more free, than his own which take quite different intellectual stances. Nevertheless, there is a charm in his intense and dogmatic integrity, in his refusal to be sold. Sometimes even his simplification of issues may cut embarrassingly through to some important flaw that the most sophisticated of the orthodox have conveniently ignored or papered over with a rich and irrelevant rhetoric. Above all, he has the charm of being the honest man in a village of hypocrites.

Notes

Chapter 1

1. Carl Van Doren, "The Revolt from the Village: 1920," *The Nation*, CXIII (October 12, 1921), 407–12.

2. See Frederick J. Hoffman, *The Twenties* (New York, 1955), p. 328.

3. Max Lerner, *America as a Civilization* (New York, 1957), p. 150.

4. *Ibid.*, p. 150.

5. Lewis Atherton, *Main Street on the Middle Border* (Bloomington, Ind., 1954), p. 66.

6. *Ibid.*, p. 49.

7. *Ibid.*, pp. 232–33.

8. *Ibid.*, p. 64.

9. See Richard Poirier, *A World Elsewhere* (New York, 1966) and A. N. Kaul, *The American Vision* (New Haven, 1963).

10. Meredith Nicholson, *The Valley of Democracy* (New York, 1919), p. 88.

11. Ima Honaker Herron, *The Small Town in American Literature* (Durham, N.C., 1939), pp. 34, 37–38.

12. Sarah Orne Jewett, *The Country of the Pointed Firs and Other Stories* (New York, n.d.), p. 13.

13. Herron, *Small Town*, p. 85.

14. Thornton Wilder, *Our Town* (New York, 1938), p. 29.

15. *Abstract of the Census, Thirteenth Census of the U.S.* (Washington, 1913), p. 57 and *passim*.

16. Nicholson, *Valley of Democracy*, p. 2.

17. *Ibid.*, p. 60.

18. *Ibid.*, p. 56.

19. Hamlin Garland, *Main-Travelled Roads* (New York, 1899), p. 308.

20. Booth Tarkington, *The Gentleman from Indiana* (New York, 1902), p. 105.

21. *Ibid.,* p. 384.

22. Zona Gale, *Friendship Village Love Stories* (New York, 1909), p. 6.

23. *Ibid.,* p. 321.

24. *Ibid.,* p. 256.

25. *Ibid.,* p. 93.

26. Wilder, *Our Town,* p. 58.

27. Harold P. Simonson, *Zona Gale* (New York, 1962), p. 20.

28. James Woodress, *Booth Tarkington* (Philadelphia, 1955), pp. 34–35.

29. Theodore Dreiser, *A Hoosier Holiday* (New York, 1916), p. 265.

30. *Ibid.,* p. 335.

31. *Ibid.,* p. 336.

32. *Ibid.,* p. 290.

33. Theodore Dreiser, *Dawn* (New York, 1931), p. 125.

34. Dreiser, *Holiday,* p. 192.

35. *Ibid.,* p. 296.

36. *Ibid.,* p. 113.

37. *Ibid.,* p. 120.

38. *Ibid.,* p. 119.

39. Theodore Dreiser, *Newspaper Days* (New York, 1931), p. 426.

40. Great tragedy, however, always assumes more responsibility in the protagonists than Dreiser allowed his hapless heroes and heroines.

41. Matthew Arnold, "The Buried Life," *Poems of Matthew Arnold* (London, 1920), p. 159. See W. P. Albrecht, "Time as Unity in Thomas Wolfe," in *The Enigma of Thomas Wolfe,* ed. Richard Walser (Cambridge, Mass., 1953), p. 244.

42. H. L. Mencken, *Prejudices: Fourth Series* (New York, 1924), p. 287.

43. See Henry F. May, "Shifting Perspectives on the 1920's," *Mississippi Valley Historical Review,* XLIII (December, 1956), 24.

44. Alexis de Tocqueville, *Democracy in America,* ed. Phillips Bradley (New York, 1958), II, 11.

45. *Ibid.,* p. 81.

46. See Richard Chase, *The American Novel and Its Tradition* (Garden City, N.Y., 1957).

47. James Fenimore Cooper, *The American Democrat* (New York, 1956), p. 147.

48. Sinclair Lewis read and admired Garland and Frederic. See Sinclair Lewis, "The American Fear of Literature," in *A Sinclair Lewis Reader: The Man from Main Street,* ed. Harry E. Maule and Melville H. Cane (New York, 1962), pp. 15–16, and Sinclair Lewis, *Main Street* (New York, 1920), p. 66.

Chapter 2

1. Edward Eggleston, *The Hoosier School-Master* (New York, 1913), p. 29.
2. E. W. Howe, *The Story of a Country Town,* ed. Claude M. Simpson (Cambridge, Mass., 1961), pp. 196–97.
3. *Ibid.,* p. xviii.
4. E. W. Howe, *Plain People* (New York, 1929), p. 185.
5. Quoted in E. W. Howe, *The Story of a Country Town,* ed. John William Ward (New York, 1964), p. 314.
6. E. W. Howe, *The Story of a Country Town,* ed. Brom Weber (New York, 1964) pp. xiv–xv.
7. Quoted in Henry Nash Smith, *Virgin Land* (New York, 1959), p. 286.
8. Joseph Kirkland, *Zury: The Meanest Man in Spring County,* ed. John T. Flanagan (Urbana, Ill., 1956), pp. xiv–xv.
9. *Ibid.,* p. 86.
10. Hamlin Garland, *A Son of the Middle Border* (New York, 1928), p. 377.
11. Hamlin Garland, *Main-Travelled Roads* (New York, 1899), p. 259.
12. Also known under her married name, Mary E. Wilkins Freeman.
13. Mary E. Wilkins, *A New England Nun* (New York, 1920), p. 162.
14. Sinclair Lewis, "The American Fear of Literature," in *A Sinclair Lewis Reader: The Man from Main Street,* ed. Harry E. Maule and Melville H. Cane (New York, 1962), p. 15.
15. William Dean Howells, *A Modern Instance* (Boston, 1882), p. 27.
16. Harold Frederic, *Seth's Brother's Wife* (New York, 1887), p. 34.
17. Harold Frederic, *The Damnation of Theron Ware,* ed. Everett Carter (Cambridge, Mass., 1960), p. 14.
18. John Henry Raleigh, "The Damnation of Theron Ware," *American Literature,* XXX (May, 1958), 215.
19. Raleigh points out that the British title of Frederic's book was *Illumination* in *ibid.,* p. 211.
20. Stephen Crane, *Whilomville Stories* (New York, 1900), p. 198.
21. Stephen Crane, *The Monster and Other Stories* (New York, 1899), p. 3.

Chapter 3

1. Mark Twain, *The Autobiography of Mark Twain,* ed. Charles Neider (New York, 1961), p. ix. For a definitive attack on Mr.

Neider's introduction and editorial selections, see Dwight Macdonald, *Against the American Grain* (New York, 1965), pp. 82–83.

2. Cited in Walter Blair, *Mark Twain and Huck Finn* (Berkeley, 1960), p. 57.

3. See Bernard De Voto, *Mark Twain at Work* (Cambridge, Mass., 1942).

4. Bernard De Voto, *Mark Twain's America* (Boston, 1932), p. 223.

5. Randolph Bourne, "The Puritan's Will to Power," in *History of a Literary Radical,* ed. Van Wyck Brooks (New York, 1920), p. 176. See Frederick J. Hoffman, *The Twenties* (New York, 1955), p. 319.

6. De Voto, *Mark Twain's America,* p. 43.

7. Dixon Wecter, *Sam Clemens of Hannibal* (Boston, 1952), pp. 175–76.

8. Mark Twain, *The Portable Mark Twain,* ed. Bernard De Voto (New York, 1946), p. 18. Gladys Bellamy notes that Brooks partially revised his estimate of Twain and the frontier while De Voto came very near Brooks in his later view of sex in Twain's writings. Miss Bellamy also notes that both Brooks and De Voto blamed the frontier for literary defects that might more logically be blamed on Twain himself. Gladys Bellamy, *Mark Twain as a Literary Artist* (Norman, Okla., 1950), pp. 30–31.

9. Quoted in C. E. Schorer, "Mark Twain's Criticism of *The Story of a Country Town,*" *American Literature,* XXVII (March, 1955), 110.

10. Mark Twain, *Mark Twain's Autobiography,* ed. Albert Bigelow Paine (New York, 1924), II, 28.

11. Wecter, *Sam Clemens,* p. 199.

12. See *A Case Book on Mark Twain's Wound,* ed. Lewis Leary (New York, 1962). Leslie Fiedler is a contemporary Brooksian.

13. Justin Kaplan, *Mr. Clemens and Mark Twain* (New York, 1966).

14. Kenneth Lynn, *Mark Twain and Southwestern Humor* (Boston, 1959), pp. 64–65.

15. *Humor of the Old Southwest,* ed. Hennig Cohen and William B. Dillingham (Boston, 1964), p. 157.

16. Edmund Wilson, *Patriotic Gore* (New York, 1962), p. 510.

17. *Ibid.,* p. 509.

18. Faulkner admired both Harris and his character. See Jean Stein, "William Faulkner: An Interview," in *William Faulkner: Three Decades of Criticism,* ed. Frederick J. Hoffman and Olga W. Vickery (East Lansing, Mich., 1960), p. 79.

19. See Lynn, *Mark Twain,* p. 134.

20. Mark Twain, *The Adventures of Tom Sawyer* (New York, 1920), pp. 7, 12.

21. Van Wyck Brooks, *The Ordeal of Mark Twain* (New York, 1920), p. 240.

22. Macdonald, *Against the American Grain,* p. 89, and Leslie

Fiedler, *Love and Death in the American Novel* (Cleveland, Ohio, 1962), pp. 267–72. For a more sympathetic view, see James M. Cox's brilliantly argued interpretation in *Mark Twain: The Fate of Humor* (Princeton, N. J., 1966).

23. Mark Twain, *Letters from the Earth*, ed. Bernard De Voto (New York, 1962), p. 156.

24. Mark Twain, *The Adventures of Huckleberry Finn* (New York, 1885), p. 149.

25. Mark Twain, *Life on the Mississippi* (New York, 1944), p. 392. This passage was among those suppressed in the original publication of the book.

26. Louis J. Budd, *Mark Twain: Social Philosopher* (Bloomington, Ind., 1962), pp. 86–103.

27. Twain, *Autobiography*, ed. Paine, II, 123.

28. Quoted in Mark Twain, *The Adventures of Huckleberry Finn*, ed. Henry Nash Smith (Boston, 1958), p. xvi.

29. *Ibid.*, p. xv.

30. James M. Cox, *Mark Twain: The Fate of Humor* is a provocative critique of Twain's shift from the romance and humor of his earlier writings to the bitter satire of his late. Henry Nash Smith shows much the same development in Twain's treatment of the Southwestern town. See Smith, "Mark Twain's Images of Hannibal," *Texas Studies in English* (1958), 3–23.

31. Twain, *Pudd'nhead Wilson* (New York, 1899), pp. 11–13.

32. See Robert A. Wiggins, *Mark Twain: Jackleg Novelist* (Seattle, 1964), pp. 107–12 for an account of the structural defects of Twain's attempts at humor (as opposed to satire) in *Pudd'nhead Wilson*.

Chapter 4

1. Carl Van Doren, *Contemporary American Novelists, 1900–1920* (New York, 1922), p. 117.

2. Edward Wagenknecht, "Willa Cather," *Sewanee Review* XXXVII (April–June, 1929), 224.

3. T. K. Whipple, *Spokesmen* (New York, 1928), p. 155.

4. Willa Cather, *Early Stories of Willa Cather*, ed. Mildred R. Bennett (New York, 1961), pp. 62–63.

5. Willa Cather, *The Troll Garden* (New York, 1905), p. 197.

6. *Ibid.*, opposite title page. On the title page Miss Cather quotes Charles Kingsley on the trolls, her symbol of the artistic life as opposed to the sterility of the goblin men.

7. E. K. Brown notes that Willa Cather's conception of artists changed as she got to know them better. She came to realize that true artists were too tough to be ruined by the petty. E. K. Brown and Leon Edel, *Willa Cather* (New York, 1953), pp. 211–12.

8. John H. Randall III, *The Landscape and the Looking Glass* (Cambridge, Mass., 1960), pp. 29–31.

9. Willa Cather, *O Pioneers!* (Boston, 1929), p. 3.

10. Willa Cather, *The Song of the Lark* (Boston, 1915), pp. 34–35.

11. Philip L. Gerber, "Willa Cather and the Big Red Rock," *College English*, XIX (January, 1958), 152–57.

12. Robert Frost, *Complete Poems* (New York, 1949), pp. 520–21.

13. Randall, *Landscape*, p. 64.

14. I am following the definitions in Northrop Frye, *Anatomy of Criticism* (Princeton, N.J., 1957).

15. Brown and Edel, *Willa Cather*, p. 204.

16. Willa Cather, *My Ántonia* (Boston, 1918), p. 165.

17. Quoted in Mildred R. Bennett, *The World of Willa Cather* (Lincoln, Neb., 1961), p. 234.

18. Willa Cather, *One of Ours* (New York, 1922), p. 101.

19. See Miss Cather's lament on the decline of good carpentry and good weaving in Bennett, *The World of Willa Cather*, p. 159.

20. Mark Twain, *The Adventures of Huckleberry Finn* (New York, 1885), p. 137.

21. Elizabeth Shepley Sergeant, *Willa Cather: A Memoir* (Philadelphia, 1953), pp. 180–81.

22. Cather, *My Ántonia*, p. 419.

23. Willa Cather, *A Lost Lady* (New York, 1958), pp. 9–10.

24. Lena Lingard in *My Ántonia* is an exception.

25. Sergeant, *Willa Cather*, p. 186.

26. Maxwell Geismar expresses doubt about Miss Cather's idealization of the railroad aristocracy. Maxwell Geismar, *The Last of the Provincials* (New York, 1959), pp. 182–83.

27. Randall, *Landscape*, pp. 214–15.

28. Frost, *Complete Poems*, pp. 520–21. My italics.

29. *Ibid.*, p. 449.

30. David Daiches, *Willa Cather* (Ithaca, New York, 1951), p. 94.

31. Robert L. Gale, "Willa Cather and the Past," *Studi Americani*, IV (1958), 209–22. John H. Randall III is an exception; his moderate evaluation of Miss Cather is intelligent and well-considered.

32. Whipple, *Spokesman*, p. 148.

33. R. K. Gordon, trans., "The Seafarer" in *Anglo-Saxon Poetry* (London, n.d.), p. 85.

Chapter 5

1. Henry F. May, *The End of American Innocence* (Chicago, 1964), p. ix.

2. Bernard Duffey, *The Chicago Renaissance in American Letters* (East Lansing, Mich., 1954), p. 141.

3. The terms "creative impulse" and "acquisitive impulse" are drawn

from T. K. Whipple, who articulated, synthesized, and applied Brooks's cultural critique in his excellent critical study, *Spokesmen* (New York, 1928). As for the accuracy of the creative-acquisitive dichotomy, Max Weber argues convincingly that the modern capitalistic era is no more acquisitive than earlier periods but is characterized by the immense emphasis on rationalism. Mere greed is as strong or stronger in the noncapitalistic cultures as it is in the capitalistic ones. Max Weber, *The Protestant Ethic and the Spirit of Capitalism,* trans. Talcott Parsons (New York, 1958), pp. I(d)-I(e), 56–57. Similarly, late nineteenth- and early twentieth-century America differed from Europe probably not in any greater degree of acquisitiveness but in a more highly rationalized culture.

4. Quoted in Van Wyck Brooks, *Days of the Phoenix* (New York, 1957), p. 109.

5. George Santayana, *Winds of Doctrine* (London, 1926), p. 188.

6. *Ibid.,* p. 211.

7. *Ibid.,* p. 205.

8. The theory goes back to an earlier book, Van Wyck Brooks, *The Wine of the Puritans* (New York, 1909).

9. Van Wyck Brooks, *America's Coming of Age* (Garden City, N.Y., 1958), p. 105.

10. *Ibid.,* p. 84.

11. *Ibid.,* p. 18. Brooks never adequately defines what he means by an organic culture. He is obviously influenced by Ruskin and Morris, but they believed that Europe had lost its organic culture, which would make Brooks's apparent comparison of an organic European culture with an inorganic American culture somewhat anomalous. But it is not certain that Brooks means "organic" in this sense.

12. *Ibid.,* p. 95.

13. *Ibid.,* p. 78.

14. *Ibid.,* pp. 181–82.

15. Edmund Wilson, *Discordant Encounters* (New York, 1926), pp. 50–51.

16. F. W. Dupee perceptively reveals some of Brooks's major contradictions in "The Americanism of Van Wyck Brooks," *Critiques and Essays in Modern Criticism,* ed. R. W. Stallman (New York, 1949), pp. 460–71.

17. Brooks, *America's Coming of Age,* p. 27.

18. *Ibid.,* p. 36.

19. *Ibid.,* p. 32.

20. Dupee, "Van Wyck Brooks," in *Critiques and Essays,* ed. Stallman, p. 469.

21. Van Wyck Brooks, *The Malady of the Ideal* (Philadelphia, 1947), pp. 86–87.

22. Dupee, in *Critiques,* ed. Stallman, p. 461.

23. Randolph Bourne, "The Puritan's Will to Power," in *History of*

a Literary Radical, ed. Van Wyck Brooks (New York, 1920), p. 187.

24. Van Wyck Brooks, *The Ordeal of Mark Twain* (New York, 1920), p. 30.

25. Brooks, *The Ordeal,* p. 37. Brooks invokes E. W. Howe and Edgar Lee Masters as witnesses to the horrors of the Middlewest.

26. *Ibid.,* p. 64.

27. *Ibid.,* p. 136.

28. *Ibid.,* pp. 213–14.

29. Paul Rosenfeld, *Port of New York* (Urbana, Ill., 1961), p. 56.

30. Brooks, *America's Coming of Age,* p. 128.

31. *Ibid.,* p. 169.

32. Rosenfeld, *Port of New York,* p. 59.

33. *Ibid.,* p. 49.

34. *Ibid.,* pp. 59–60.

35. Wilson, *Discordant Encounters,* p. 41.

36. Duffey, *Chicago Renaissance,* pp. 176–77.

37. H. L. Mencken, *Letters of H. L. Mencken,* ed. Guy Forgue (New York, 1961), p. 458.

38. See H. L. Mencken, *Prejudices, Second Series* (New York, 1920), p. 12.

39. H. L. Mencken, *A Book of Prefaces* (New York, 1927), pp. 202–3.

40. E. A. Martin, "The Ordeal of H. L. Mencken," *South Atlantic Quarterly,* LXI (Summer, 1962), 329–30.

41. H. L. Mencken, *Prejudices, Sixth Series* (New York, 1927), pp. 69–70.

42. Santayana, *Winds of Doctrine,* p. 201. Literary scholars had not yet pointed out the Whig ideology of much Southwestern humor. Even so, Santayana's insight can be applied to Longstreet.

43. Frederick J. Hoffman, *The Twenties* (New York, 1955), p. 305.

44. Mencken, *Prejudices, Second Series,* p. 103.

45. William Graham Sumner, *Folkways* (Boston, 1913), p. 14.

46. *Ibid.,* p. 23.

47. *Ibid.,* p. 47.

48. H. L. Mencken, *Prejudices, First Series* (New York, 1919), pp. 155–56. Mencken praises Elsie Clews Parson's *Fear and Conventionality,* a study of conformity, and disparages the Freudians as "circus clowns."

49. George Jean Nathan and H. L. Mencken, *The American Credo* (New York, 1921), p. 68.

50. H. L. Mencken, *Americana, 1925* (New York, 1925), p. vi.

51. Nathan and Mencken, *American Credo,* p. 63.

52. Philip Rahv, *Image and Idea* (Norfolk, Conn., 1957), p. 4.

53. *Ibid.*

54. Richard Hofstadter, *Anti-Intellectualism in American Life* (New York, 1963), p. 118.

55. Mencken, *A Book of Prefaces,* p. 198.

56. Quoted in Heywood Broun and Margaret Leech, *Anthony Comstock, Roundsman of the Lord* (New York, 1927), p. 89.

57. Quoted in William E. McLoughlin, Jr., *Billy Sunday Was His Real Name* (Chicago, 1955), p. 6.

58. Mencken, *A Book of Prefaces,* p. 248.

59. See Hofstadter, *Anti-Intellectualism,* and *The Radical Right,* ed. Daniel Bell (Garden City, N.Y., 1964). Cf. David M. Chalmers, *Hooded Americanism, The First Century of the Ku Klux Klan: 1865 to the Present* (Garden City, N.Y., 1965).

60. H. L. Mencken, *The Vintage Mencken,* ed. Alistair Cooke (New York, 1956), pp. 130–31. Originally published in the Baltimore *Evening Sun,* 1923.

61. *Ibid.,* pp. 136–37.

62. James T. Farrell's Introduction to H. L. Mencken, *Prejudices: A Selection* (New York, 1959), pp. ix–x.

63. Andrew Sinclair, *Era of Excess* (New York, 1964), p. 5.

64. *Ibid.,* p. 18.

65. *Ibid.,* pp. 64–65.

66. *Ibid.,* pp. 18–20.

67. H. L. Mencken, *Prejudices: Fourth Series* (New York, 1924), p. 45.

68. *Ibid.,* p. 54. Sinclair notes, "The prohibitionists were always conscious that their support lay in the country. They carefully attacked alcohol in its urban and foreign forms—beer and rum. They did not crusade with any vigor against country liquor—hard cider and corn whisky." Sinclair, *Era of Excess,* p. 18. A graphic illustration is provided by Burton Rascoe's account of his experience in a return to the Oklahoma town he hailed from. Rascoe was given a drink of a popular local concoction called "jake." A second later he found himself flat on his back. "Jake" consisted of Jamaica ginger added to straight alcohol. Burton Rascoe, *We Were Interrupted* (Garden City, N.Y., 1947), p. 45.

69. Mencken, *Prejudices: Fourth Series,* p. 55.

70. *Ibid.,* p. 56.

71. *Ibid.,* p. 60.

72. Edmund Wilson, *A Literary Chronicle, 1920–1950* (Garden City, N.Y., 1952), pp. 95–96.

73. Louis Kronenberger, "H. L. Mencken," in *After the Genteel Tradition,* ed. Malcolm Cowley (Gloucester, Mass., 1959), pp. 110–11.

74. Ernest Boyd, *H. L. Mencken* (New York, 1925), p. 44.

75. H. L. Mencken, *Happy Days* (New York, 1940), p. 163.

76. H. L. Mencken, "Credo," in *Literature in America,* ed. Philip Rahv (New York, 1957), pp. 300–1. See also Raymond L. Francis, "Mark Twain and H. L. Mencken," *Prairie Schooner,* XXIV (1950), 31–39.

77. Wilson, *Literary Chronicle*, p. 93.
78. Henry Steele Commager, *The American Mind* (New Haven, 1950), pp. 116–19.
79. Mencken, *Prejudices, Fourth Series*, p. 289.
80. Mencken, *Prejudices, Fifth Series* (New York, 1926), pp. 19–20.
81. Cited in Boyd, *H. L. Mencken*, p. 80.
82. Zona Gale, *Birth* (New York, 1937), p. 20.
83. Zona Gale, *Miss Lulu Bett* (New York, 1921), p. 4.

Chapter 6

1. Van Wyck Brooks, *America's Coming of Age* (Garden City, N.Y., 1958), p. 99.
2. Waldo Frank, *Our America* (New York, 1919), p. 128.
3. *Ibid.*, p. 128.
4. Edgar Lee Masters, "The Genesis of Spoon River," *American Mercury*, XXVIII (January, 1933), 39–41.
5. Edgar Lee Masters, *Across Spoon River* (New York, 1936), p. 83.
6. Masters, "Genesis of Spoon River," p. 41.
7. Masters, *Spoon River Anthology* (New York, 1948), p. 240.
8. Masters compared his book to *The Divine Comedy*, "Genesis of Spoon River," p. 50.
9. Masters, *Across Spoon River*, p. 10.
10. Dylan Thomas, "Dylan Thomas on Edgar Lee Masters," *Harper's Bazaar* (June, 1963), 115. Thomas also values Masters' understanding of the fact that "man moves in a mysterious way his blunders to perform." *Under Milk Wood* is a Welsh Spoon River—portrayed through a comic imagination immeasurably richer than that of Masters.
11. William L. Phillips, "How Sherwood Anderson Wrote Winesburg, Ohio," *American Literature*, XXIII (March, 1951), 16–17.
12. Sherwood Anderson, *Letters of Sherwood Anderson*, ed. Howard Mumford Jones and Walter B. Rideout (Boston, 1953), p. 39.
13. Sherwood Anderson, *Windy McPherson's Son* (New York, 1916), p. 32.
14. Northrop Frye, *Anatomy of Criticism* (Princeton, N.J., 1957), pp. 38–40.
15. Sherwood Anderson, *Sherwood Anderson's Memoirs* (New York, 1942), p. 289.
16. Jarvis Thurston, "Anderson and 'Winesburg': Mysticism and Craft," *Accent*, XVI (Spring, 1956), 116–17.
17. Sherwood Anderson, "Letters to Van Wyck Brooks," in *The Shock of Recognition*, ed. Edmund Wilson (New York, 1955), pp. 1270–71. Mumford and Jones do not, unfortunately, print all of

Anderson's letters to Brooks, whereas the letters printed in *Story* in 1941 and edited by Brooks which Wilson reprints leave out some passages related to people still living in 1941.

18. Anderson, *Letters,* ed. Jones and Rideout, p. 84.

19. Waldo Frank, "Winesburg, Ohio," *Story,* XIX (September–October, 1941), 31.

20. *Ibid.,* p. 32.

21. Paul Rosenfeld, *Port of New York* (Urbana, Ill., 1961), p. 187. Walcutt, in an excellent article, also notes the lack of a tradition of manners as the explanation of Winesburg. Charles Child Walcutt, "Sherwood Anderson: Impressionism and the Buried Life," *Sewanee Review,* LX (January–March, 1952), 35.

22. Sherwood Anderson, *The Sherwood Anderson Reader,* ed. Paul Rosenfeld (Boston, 1947), pp. xxi–xxii.

23. Irving Howe, *Sherwood Anderson* (New York, 1951), p. 100.

24. Sherwood Anderson, *Winesburg, Ohio* (New York, 1919), pp. 21–22.

25. Howe, *Sherwood Anderson,* p. 97.

26. Cited in Edward Wagenknecht, *Cavalcade of the American Novel* (New York, 1952), p. 312.

27. See Anderson, *Reader,* ed. Rosenfeld, p. xxi. Rideout, in another fine article, notes the abstractness of *Winesburg* and also the striking similarities between Winesburg and Anderson's home town of Clyde, Ohio. Walter B. Rideout, "The Simplicity of *Winesburg, Ohio,*" *Shenandoah,* XIII (1962), 20–22.

28. Howe, *Sherwood Anderson,* pp. 105–6.

29. Walcutt and Rideout excellently interpret "Sophistication," pointing out a number of the qualities I have described.

30. Anderson, *Letters,* ed. Jones and Rideout, p. 34.

31. *Ibid.,* p. 31. My italics.

32. Anderson, "Letters," in *The Shock of Recognition,* ed. Wilson, p. 1261.

33. *Ibid.,* p. 1285. What Anderson perceived was the Arnoldian side to Brooks.

34. Anderson, *Letters,* ed. Jones and Rideout, pp. 77–78.

35. Anderson, "Letters," in *The Shock of Recognition,* ed. Wilson, p. 1255.

Chapter 7

1. Mark Schorer, "Sinclair Lewis and the Method of Half-Truths," in *Sinclair Lewis,* ed. Mark Schorer (Englewood Cliffs, N.J., 1962), p. 49.

2. Ernst Kris, *Psychoanalytic Explorations in Art* (New York, 1964), p. 175. The following remarks on caricature are much indebted to Mr. Kris's study.

3. Arnold Hauser, *The Social History of Art,* IV, tr. Stanley Goodman (New York, n.d.), pp. 216–19.

4. Mark Schorer, *Sinclair Lewis* (New York, 1961), p. 102.

5. Sinclair Lewis, *Main Street* (New York, 1948), pp. 117, 263.

6. Daniel Aaron, "Sinclair Lewis' *Main Street,*" in *The American Novel,* ed. Wallace Stegner (New York, 1965), p. 170.

7. Percy H. Boynton, *America in Contemporary Fiction* (Chicago, 1940), pp. 168–73.

8. William E. Leuchtenburg, *The Perils of Prosperity* (Chicago, 1958), p. 108.

9. *Ibid.,* pp. 8–9.

10. *Ibid.,* p. 225.

11. Chalmers notes that the Ku Klux Klan was strong in American cities despite its small-town values: "The explanation for the Klan's urban strength is probably to be found in the degree to which the rapidly expanding cities were being fed by the native American stock from the country's small towns and rural areas. The average city dweller in the 1920's was far from cosmopolitan, and the chances were that he was no more than one generation away from either the farm or the immigrant ship. The internal migrant brought his heartland values and his defensiveness with him to the metropolis." David M. Chalmers, *Hooded Americanism* (Garden City, N.Y.), p. 114.

12. Lewis Atherton, *Main Street on the Middle Border* (Bloomington, Ind., 1954), pp. 217–42.

13. Leuchtenburg, *Perils of Prosperity,* p. 194.

14. *Ibid., passim.*

15. *Ibid.,* p. 238.

16. See the analysis of an RCA advertisement in Marshall McLuhan, *The Mechanical Bride* (Boston, 1967), pp. 20–22.

17. "By the end of the Harding administration, the Republican party was firmly committed to a single-interest government. By allying the government with business, the Republicans believed they were benefiting the entire nation." Leuchtenburg, *Perils of Prosperity,* p. 103.

18. *Ibid.,* pp. 227–28 and *passim.*

19. *Ibid.,* p. 272 and *passim.*

20. Cited in Schorer, *Sinclair Lewis,* p. 286.

21. Sinclair Lewis, *A Sinclair Lewis Reader: The Man from Main Street,* ed. Harry E. Maule and Melville H. Cane (New York, 1962), pp. 26–27.

22. *Ibid.,* p. 24.

23. Sinclair Lewis, *Babbitt* (New York, 1950), p. 2.

24. Aaron, "Sinclair Lewis," in *The American Novel,* ed. Stegner, p. 171, notes Thoreau's influence on Lewis. See also Lewis' article, "One-Man Revolution," in *Lewis Reader,* ed. Maule and Cane, pp. 242–44.

25. See Schorer, *Sinclair Lewis,* p. 277.

Chapter 8

1. *The American Puritans,* ed. Perry Miller (Garden City, N.Y., 1956), p. 216.
2. Cotton Mather, "Bonifacius," in *ibid.,* p. 218.
3. William G. McLoughlin, *Billy Sunday Was His Real Name* (Chicago, 1955), pp. 192, 225–26.
4. *Ibid.,* pp. 2, 14, 28, 132, 136–37, 141–42, 179 and *passim.*
5. H. L. Mencken, *Prejudices: Third Series* (New York, 1922), p. 32.
6. David M. Chalmers, *Hooded Americanism* (Garden City, N.Y., 1965), p. 293.
7. *Ibid.,* 76.
8. *Ibid.,* p. 111. Leuchtenburg observes that the ugly side of the Klan "lay in the fact that it appealed to many who were frustrated by the rigid moral code of the small town. Klansmen often felt tempted by that which they were condemning—the city, sexual freedom, modern life—and their frustration often took a sadistic turn." William E. Leuchtenburg, *The Perils of Prosperity* (Chicago, 1958), p. 213.
9. Chalmers, *Hooded Americanism,* pp. 113–14.
10. Leuchtenburg, *Perils of Prosperity,* p. 209.
11. See Andrew Sinclair, *Era of Excess* (New York, 1964), *passim;* Chalmers, *Hooded Americanism, passim.*
12. See Ray Ginger, *Six Days or Forever?* (New York, 1958), pp. 7–24 *passim.*
13. H. L. Mencken, *Americana, 1925* (New York, 1925), p. 303.
14. William Manchester, *H. L. Mencken: Disturber of the Peace* (New York, 1951), p. 84.
15. Mencken, *Prejudices: Third Series,* p. 270.
16. Manchester, *H. L. Mencken,* p. 82.
17. H. L. Mencken, *Prejudices: Fifth Series* (New York, 1926), p. 76.
18. Sinclair Lewis, *Arrowsmith* (New York, 1952), p. 202.
19. Sinclair Lewis, *Elmer Gantry* (New York, 1927), p. 17.
20. One of Billy Sunday's sermons was traced to its source in Ingersoll. See McLoughlin, *Billy Sunday,* p. 166.
21. See Mark Schorer's analysis in *Sinclair Lewis* (New York, 1961), p. 477.

Chapter 9

1. H. L. Mencken, *Prejudices: Second Series* (New York, 1920), p. 136.
2. H. L. Mencken, "The Library," *American Mercury,* VIII (1926), 510.

3. H. L. Mencken, *Letters of H. L. Mencken,* ed. Guy J. Forgue (New York, 1961), p. 332.

4. T. S. Stribling, *The Forge* (Garden City, N.Y., 1933), p. 83.

5. T. S. Stribling, *Bright Metal* (Garden City, N.Y., 1928), pp. 80–81.

6. T. S. Stribling, *Teeftallow* (Garden City, N.Y., 1926), p. 221.

7. Stribling, *The Forge,* p. 162.

8. T. S. Stribling, *The Store* (Garden City, N.Y., 1932), p. 377.

9. T. S. Stribling, *The Unfinished Cathedral* (Garden City, N.Y., 1934), p. 258.

10. The relevant sociological work is T. W. Adorno, *The Authoritarian Personality* (New York, 1950).

11. Robert Penn Warren, "T. S. Stribling: A Paragraph in the History of Critical Realism," *The American Review,* II (February, 1934), 480.

12. Ray Ginger, *Six Days or Forever?* (New York, 1958), p. 8.

13. *Ibid.,* p. 17.

14. *Ibid.,* p. 127.

15. Thomas Wolfe, *Thomas Wolfe's Letters to His Mother,* ed. C. Hugh Holman and Sue Fields Ross (Chapel Hill, 1968), pp. 42–43.

16. *Ibid.,* p. 64.

17. Thomas Wolfe, "Welcome to Our City," *Esquire Magazine,* XLVIII (October, 1957), 69.

18. Louis J. Budd, "The Grotesques of Anderson and Wolfe," *Modern Fiction Studies,* V (Winter, 1959–60), 306.

19. Thomas Wolfe, *Look Homeward, Angel* (New York, 1929), p. 119.

20. George Santayana, *The Works of George Santayana* (New York, 1937), p. 139.

21. Thomas Wolfe, *You Can't Go Home Again* (New York, 1942), pp. 84–85.

22. Wolfe, *Look Homeward, Angel,* p. 2.

Chapter 10

1. See Ruth McKenney, *Industrial Valley* (New York, 1939).

2. See M. K. Singleton, *H. L. Mencken and the American Mercury Adventure* (Durham, N.C., 1962), p. 237.

3. Ernest Boyd, *H. L. Mencken* (New York, 1925), pp. 3–4, 12.

4. H. L. Mencken, *Happy Days* (New York, 1940), p. viii.

5. H. L. Mencken, *Letters of H. L. Mencken,* ed. Guy G. Forgue (New York, 1961), p. 342.

6. Mark Schorer, *Sinclair Lewis* (New York, 1961), p. 517.

7. *Ibid.,* 515.

8. See *ibid., passim,* and Martin Light, "Lewis's Finicky Girls and Faithful Workers," *University Review,* XXX (Winter, 1963), 151–59.

9. Sinclair Lewis, *The Trail of the Hawk* (New York, 1915), p. 169.

10. Maxwell Geismar, *The Last of the Provincials* (New York, 1959), p. 85.

11. Perry Miller, "The Incorruptible Sinclair Lewis," *The Atlantic,* CLXXXVII (April, 1951), 34.

12. Sinclair Lewis, *World So Wide* (New York, 1951), p. 197.

13. Sinclair Lewis, *The Prodigal Parents* (Garden City, N.Y., 1938), p. 100.

14. *Ibid.,* p. 250.

15. Quoted in Miller, "The Incorruptible Sinclair Lewis," p. 34.

16. Schorer, *Sinclair Lewis,* p. 501.

17. Willa Cather, *On Writing* (New York, 1949), p. 9.

18. Willa Cather, *Death Comes to the Archbishop* (New York, 1927), p. 283.

19. Francis X. Connolly, "Willa Cather: Memory as Muse," in *Fifty Years of the American Novel,* ed. Harold C. Gardiner, S.J. (New York, 1952), p. 86.

20. Van Wyck Brooks, *Scenes and Portraits* (New York, 1954), p. 149.

21. Van Wyck Brooks, *Days of the Phoenix* (New York, 1957), p. 168.

22. Van Wyck Brooks, *Emerson and Others* (New York, 1927), p. 44.

23. *Ibid.,* p. 95.

24. F. W. Dupee, "The Americanism of Van Wyck Brooks," in *Critiques and Essays in Modern Criticism,* ed. R. W. Stallman (New York, 1949), pp. 470–71.

25. Van Wyck Brooks, *Opinions of Oliver Allston* (New York, 1941), pp. 276–77.

26. *Ibid.,* p. 233.

27. Dwight Macdonald, *Memoirs of a Revolutionist* (New York, 1957), p. 211. The title of Mr. Macdonald's article, "Kulturboshewismus and Mr. Van Wyck Brooks," reflects his belief that Brooks is demanding the same kind of cultural conformity of writers that produced the tasteless pablum typical of "critical realism" in Russia.

28. Brooks, *Opinions,* p. 248.

29. *Ibid.,* p. 259.

30. See Brom Weber, *Sherwood Anderson* (Minneapolis, Minn., 1964) and Brom Weber, "Anderson and the Essence of Things," *Sewanee Review,* LIX (1951), 678–92.

31. Irving Howe, *Sherwood Anderson* (New York, 1951), pp. 143–44.

32. Rebecca West, *The Strange Necessity* (New York, 1928), pp. 310–11.

33. William Faulkner, "Sherwood Anderson," *Princeton University*

Library Chronicle, XVIII (Spring, 1957), 91. The article was originally printed in the Dallas *Morning News,* April 26, 1925.

34. Sherwood Anderson, *Many Marriages* (New York, 1923), p. 170.

35. Sherwood Anderson, *Sherwood Anderson's Notebook* (New York, 1926), p. 185.

36. F. Scott Fitzgerald, *The Letters of F. Scott Fitzgerald,* ed. Andrew Turnbull (New York, 1963), p. 195.

37. Thomas Wolfe, *The Letters of Thomas Wolfe,* ed. Elizabeth Nowell (New York, 1956), p. 688.

38. Sherwood Anderson, *Letters of Sherwood Anderson,* ed. Howard Mumford Jones and Walter B. Rideout (Boston, 1953), p. 198.

39. Sherwood Anderson, *Perhaps Women* (New York, 1931), p. 113.

40. Sherwood Anderson, *Hello Towns!* (New York, 1929), p. 57.

41. *Ibid.,* p. 19.

42. Sherwood Anderson, *Sherwood Anderson's Memoirs* (New York, 1942), p. 14.

43. James Boyd, "A Man in Town," *Story,* XIX (September–October, 1941), 88–91.

44. James K. Feibleman, "Memories of Sherwood Anderson," *Shenandoah,* XIII (Spring, 1962), 41.

45. Quoted in Elizabeth Nowell, *Thomas Wolfe* (Garden City, N.Y., 1960), p. 412.

46. Sherwood Anderson, *The Sherwood Anderson Reader,* ed. Paul Rosenfeld (Boston, 1947), p. 743.

47. A collection of Anderson's best writings of the thirties is badly needed. *The Sherwood Anderson Reader,* published in 1947, contains some of the best pieces but really does not fill the need.

48. Anderson, *Letters,* ed. Jones and Rideout, p. 195.

49. Sherwood Anderson, *Kit Brandon* (New York, 1936), pp. 254–55.

50. Sherwood Anderson, *Puzzled America* (New York, 1935), p. 174.

Chapter 11

1. Pamela Hansford Johnson, "Thomas Wolfe and the Kicking Season," *Encounter,* XII (April, 1959), 77–80.

2. Some of the masterpieces of what is generally thought of as "thirties literature" were actually written in the early forties. The "progressive" and radical strains characteristic of the thirties as well as the land motif seem to carry over until about 1945. From this time on, the tendency is toward the political withdrawal and the concern with inner "sin" that are generally thought of as characteristics of the "fifties." See Chester Eisinger, *Fiction of the Forties* (Chicago, 1963)

for a much more precise chronology of this transition. I use the imprecise term "thirties" to avoid the awkwardness of having repeatedly to say "thirties and early forties."

3. The tendency of the thirties was not to prettify rural life but rather to emphasize its grittiness. Grittiness becomes romanticized.

4. Daniel Bell, "The Dispossessed," in *The Radical Right*, ed. Daniel Bell (Garden City, N.Y., 1964), p. 24.

5. T. W. Adorno, *The Authoritarian Personality* (New York, 1950), p. 747.

Index

273